Longman Exam Guides
Secretarial Skills

Longman Exam Guides

Series Editors: Stuart Wall and David Weigall

Titles available

Bookkeeping and
    Accounting
Business Law
Economics
English as a Foreign
    Language: Intermediate
English Literature
Monetary Economics
Office Practice and
    Secretarial Administration
Pure Mathematics
Secretarial Skills

Forthcoming:

Biology
Business Communication
Business Studies
Chemistry
Commerce
Computer Science
Electronics
English as a Foreign
    Language: Advanced
English as a Foreign
    Language: Preliminary
French
General Principles of Law
General Studies
Geography
Mechanics
Modern British History
Physics
Politics
Principles of Law
Quantitative Methods
Sociology
Taxation

Longman Exam Guides

SECRETARIAL SKILLS

Andrea Freeman
Ruth Martindale
Judith Mancktelow

LONGMAN
London and New York

Longman Group Limited
Longman House, Burnt Mill, Harlow
Essex CM20 2JE, England
Associated companies throughout the world

*Published in the United States of America
by Longman Inc., New York*

© Longman Group Limited 1986

First published 1986

British Library Cataloguing in Publication Data

Freeman, Andrea
 An examinees guide to secretarial skills. –
 (Longman exam guides)
 1. Secretaries   2. Office practice
 I. Title   II. Mancktelow, Judith
 III. Martindale, Ruth
 651.3'741   HF5547.5

ISBN 0-582-29706-0

Set in 9 pt Times
Printed in Great Britain at Bath Press, Avon.

Contents

Editors' Preface		vii
Acknowledgements		viii
Chapter 1	The Examinations	1
Chapter 2	Examination Techniques	4
Chapter 3	Typewriting	17
Chapter 4	Shorthand	66
Chapter 5	Shorthand-Typewriting	121
Chapter 6	Audio-Typewriting	150
Chapter 7	Word Processing – Theory	192
Chapter 8	Word Processing – Practical	213
Index		245

Editors' Preface

Much has been said in recent years about declining standards and disappointing examination results. While this may be somewhat exaggerated, examiners are well aware that the performance of many candidates falls well short of their potential. Longman Exam Guides are written by experienced examiners and teachers, and aim to give you the best possible foundation for examination success. There is no attempt to cut corners. The books encourage thorough study and a full understanding of the concepts involved and should be seen as course companions and study guides to be used throughout the year. Examiners are in no doubt that a structured approach in preparing for and taking examinations can, together with hard work and diligent application, substantially improve performance.

The largely self-contained nature of each chapter gives the book a useful degree of flexibility. After starting with Chapters 1 and 2, all other chapters can be read selectively, in any order appropriate to the stage you have reached in your course. We believe that this book, and the series as a whole, will help you establish a solid platform of basic knowledge and examination technique on which to build.

Stuart Wall and David Weigall

Acknowledgements

The authors would like to thank everyone who has assisted them in the preparation of this book, in particular Mrs Jean Wilson for her help with the Gregg shorthand.

We are grateful to the following Examination Boards for permission to reproduce past examination questions:

The London Chamber of Commerce and Industry; Pitman Examinations Institute; The Royal Society of Arts Examinations Board; Scottish Examination Board; Scottish Vocational Education Council.

The authors accept sole responsibility for the answers provided.

Chapter 1

The Examinations

The chapters of this book are concerned with helping you as you work towards an examination in the secretarial skills of shorthand, typewriting and word processing. The information given should be valuable for a single subject examination as well as for a group certificate or diploma. If your studies involve using these skills in a specialist field, such as in a foreign language or with a medical content, you should also find this book valuable.

Tables presented within each chapter show the various types of **single** subject examination at present offered by the various boards, but they are intended only as guides as new examinations are frequently being added and existing ones revised or withdrawn.

Table 1.1 shows the various **group** certificates and diplomas for which these skills are required. Table 2.1 gives more detailed information on the content of these examinations.

If you are taking a full- or part-time school or college course you should be guided by your Course Tutor as to which examinations to enter. If you are considering taking shorthand in a foreign language it is recommended that you should have completed an "A" level course of study. It is also beneficial to continue your study of the language in a business context during your secretarial training.

The following boards offer single subject examinations and/or group certificates and diplomas.

- Association of Medical Secretaries, Practical Administrators and Receptionists, Tavistock House South, Tavistock Square, London WC1. Tel: 01-387 6005
- Business and Technician Education Council, Central House, Upper Woburn Place, London WC1H 0HH. Tel: 01-388 3288
- London Chamber of Commerce and Industry, Marlowe House, Station Road, Sidcup, Kent DA15 7BJ. Tel: 01-309 0440
- Pitman Examinations Institute, Godalming, Surrey. Tel: 048 68 5311

- Royal Society of Arts Examinations Board, Murray Road, Orpington, Kent BR5 3RD. Tel: 0689 32421
- Scottish Business Education Council (now Scottish Vocational Education Council), 22 Great King Street, Edinburgh EH3 6QH. Tel: 031-557 4555
- Scottish Examination Board, 15 Ironmills Road, Dalkeith, Edinburgh. Tel: 031-225 5486
- Teeline Education Limited, 128 Kent Road, Mapperley, Nottingham NG3 6BS. Tel: 0602 205936
- Welsh Joint Education Committee, 245 Western Avenue, Cardiff, Wales. Tel: 0222 561231

Table 1.1 Examinations — Certificates and Diplomas

Board	Elementary	Intermediate	Advanced
Association of Medical Secretaries, Practical Administrators and Receptionists		Certificate for Medical Secretaries	Diploma for Medical Secretaries
BTEC		National Award — Secretarial Studies Option Modules	
London Chamber of Commerce and Industry	Secretarial Studies Certificate	Private Secretary's Certificate	Private and Executive Secretary's Diploma
	Secretarial Language Certificate (French/German/Spanish)	Advanced Secretarial Language Certificate (French/German/Spanish)	Secretarial Language Diploma (French/German/Spanish)
Pitman's Examination Institute	Basic Secretarial Group Certificate	Secretarial Group Certificate	Higher Secretarial Group Certificate

Table 1.1 continued

Board	Elementary	Intermediate	Advanced
Royal Society of Arts	Diploma in Office Studies	Diploma in Secretarial Studies	Diploma for Personal Assistants
	Diploma in Office Studies (Pilot scheme)		
	Diploma in General Reception	Diploma in Business Studies	
	Certificate in Language for the Office	Certificate for Secretarial Linguists	Diploma for Bi-Lingual Secretaries
	Diploma in Distribution (Pilot scheme)		
Scottish Business Education Council (now SCOTVEC)	Certificate in Office Skills	Secretarial Certificate	Scottish Higher Certificate in Secretarial Studies
		Scottish National Certificate in Secretarial Studies	Scottish Higher National Diploma in Secretarial Studies
		Scottish National Diploma for Agricultural Secretaries	Scottish Higher National Diploma in Secretarial Studies (with Languages)
		Diploma for Medical Secretaries	Diploma for Graduate Secretaries

Chapter 2

Examination Techniques

METHODS OF TESTING

Secretarial skills are generally tested by presenting practical tasks of varying complexity, designed to show the ability of the candidate in the skill concerned. In their syllabus booklets, the examination boards indicate the level of ability and content of each examination, and you will find these summarised in Table 2.1 (p. 6) for group certificates and in the relevant chapters for single subjects.

In **practical typewriting** examinations all questions must be attempted and you should have the minimum typewriting speed recommended by the board. Some papers present copy in clear and simple form, requiring you to prove that you are competent at manipulating the typewriter accurately and can produce "mailable" copy. In almost every paper you will find a letter and a variety of other documents, one of which will require a carbon copy. In other papers, candidates are expected to be more aware of typewriting conventions and tasks may not be presented in a consistent form. They may also involve altering the layout from the copy shown. It may be necessary to extract information from one document to include in the finished task, perhaps in an amended form. Specialised documents may be included and some papers may include questions which require you to identify and correct errors in spelling, typewriting or English grammar.

Some boards include an optional or compulsory speed test of either 5 or 10 minutes, where correcting is not allowed. It is necessary to pass the practical examination to gain the endorsement for your speed test. Some boards prefer to set a speed test which is completely separate from the production examination, when a separate certificate is, of course, awarded.

Shorthand examinations usually consist of a preliminary warm-up passage (which is not transcribed) followed by one, two or three passages for transcription with a short interval between each. The passages are longer at higher speeds but rarely last for more than 4 minutes. One passage is normally of commercial interest, the others being on general topics. Any system of shorthand or speedwriting may be used, except where stated by examining boards.

Candidates may have the opportunity to attempt one of two speeds and there may be a choice of transcribing by hand or on the typewriter. The examiners are, however, primarily testing a candidate's ability to transcribe accurately, although a well-typed transcript will be awarded an endorsement on the certificate.

Specialist examinations are available for shorthand in several foreign languages, for journalists, and in medical and legal terminology. These follow a similar format but many of them must be transcribed by typewriter. Some boards set theory papers to examine the ability to write a certain system of shorthand with accuracy.

Examinations in **shorthand-typewriting** require the accurate transcription of dictated material within the time allowed. Some include typing from printed matter and the composition of a letter from dictated notes. In many of these examinations, dictation will *not* be read at a consistent speed, to give a more realistic office style approach. Others have a timed reading but may require corrections to be made to spelling or English grammar. Examinations may also be taken in medical shorthand-typewriting.

Practical examinations in **audio-typewriting** vary considerably in length and content, as can be seen from Table 6.1 (p. 151). It is possible to take a test lasting approximately 30 minutes, consisting of the transcription of two business documents. Most examinations, however, include a much wider variety of documents, last for two or three hours and include a manuscript and composition. Some boards offer audio-typewriting examinations in foreign languages or with medical content.

Word processing is still a relatively new area for examiners. Table 7.1 (p. 193) shows that these examinations may be theoretical or practical or a combination of both. Word processing may be taken as a single subject examination and is also now included as an option in some group certificates and diplomas. The aim of the practical examinations is to test your ability to follow explicit instructions and perform a variety of functions on a word processor. The examining boards usually recommend a minimum number of hours of "hands on" experience for their candidates. All the practical examinations set tasks involving text creation, revision and insertion, proof-reading and printing out. The theoretical examinations test your knowledge of terminology and your ability to demonstrate an understanding of word-processing functions, capabilities and role in an office. The questions fall into three categories – multiple choice, objective and case studies.

Table 2.1 Format of examinations – Certificates and Diplomas

Examining board: Business and Technician Education Council (BTEC)

Students choosing a secretarial module for a BTEC qualification will find that examinations vary from college to college. Examinations are set and assessed internally and it is difficult therefore to give precise details of format and regulations. Nevertheless the content of this book is directly relevant to such examinations.

Examining Board: London Chamber of Commerce and Industry (LCCI)

Title	Length of Examination		Format and Regulations
Secretarial Studies Certificate	4 parts –	2 hrs 2.5 hrs	1 Communications – use of English. 2 Secretarial skills – shorthand/typewriting (80 wpm shorthand, 35 wpm typing); Audio/typewriting.
	and/or Optional	2.25 hrs 2 hrs 2 hrs	3 Office procedures. 4 Background to business.
	Optional	2 hrs	5 Word processing.
			Pass level 50%, 75% for distinction. Dictionaries allowed. Referrals may be granted where 1 compulsory component failed. Passes in 1, 2, and 5 above – Word Processing Group Certificate awarded. Passes in 1 and 2 above – Shorthand-Typist or Audio-Typist Certificate awarded.
Private Secretary's Certificate	5 compulsory parts – and/or	2.5 hrs 2.5 hrs 2.25 hrs 2.5 hrs 2.5 hrs	1 Communications – use of English 2 Secretarial skills – shorthand/typewriting; Audio/typewriting 3 Office organisation and secretarial procedures. 4 Structure of business. 5 Interview.
	Optional	2 hrs	6 Information processing.
			Pass level 50%, 75% for distinction. Dictionaries allowed. Referrals may be granted where 1 compulsory component failed. Passes in 1, 2, and 6 above – Information Processing Group Certificate awarded Passes in 1 and 2 above – Shorthand-Typist or Audio-Typist Certificate awarded

Table 2.1 continued

Title	Length of Examination		Format and Regulations
Private and Executive Secretary's Diploma	6 compulsory parts –	2.5 hrs 2.25 hrs 2 hrs	1 Communications – use of English. 2 Meetings. 3 Secretarial skills – shorthand/typewriting duties; Audio/typewriting duties.
	and/or	1.75 hrs 2.5 hrs 3 hrs	4 Secretarial administration. 5 Management appreciation. 6 Interview.
	Optional	2 hrs	7 Information processing. Pass level 50%, 75% for distinction. Dictionaries allowed. Referrals may be granted where 1 compulsory component failed.
Secretarial Language Certificate	3 parts –	2.5 hrs	1 Translation and summary – 2 texts from foreign language into English. Passage in foreign language to be summarised in English.
(French, German, Spanish)		2 hrs + 10 mins for practice passage 3 × 5 min	2 Audio and copy typing – tape in foreign language giving instructions for various tasks. Manuscript in foreign language. 3 Oral test – 3 sections all to be passed.
Advanced *Secretarial Language*	3 parts –	3 hrs	1 Translation and summary – 2 passages from foreign language into English. Passage in foreign language to be summarised in English.
Certificate (French, German, Spanish)		2.5 hrs + 10 mins for practice passage 25 mins	2 Secretarial skills – tape in foreign language giving instructions for various tasks including composition from notes. 3 Oral test – 5 sections all to be passed. Foreign language dictionaries allowed.

Table 2.1 continued

Title	Length of Examination	Format and Regulations
Secretarial Language Diploma	3 parts — 3 hrs	All work to be typewritten. 1 Translation and summary — passage from foreign language into English. Passage in foreign language to be summarised in English. Report in foreign language. Marks 30, 35, 35.
	3 hrs	2 Translation of English into foreign language + composition in foreign language from notes. Typed transcription of handwritten matter in foreign language.
	20/40 mins	3 Oral test — 4 sections, all to be passed. Foreign language dictionaries allowed.

Examining board: Pitman Examinations Institute (PEI)

Title	Length of Examination	Format and Regulations
Basic Secretarial Group Certificate	See Tables 3.1, 4.1 and 7.1 where appropriate	All parts to be passed within 12 months. 1 Shorthand 60 wpm. 2 Elementary typing. 3 Choice of: English (elementary); English for business communication (elementary); English for office skills; English language NCE (intermediate); English as a foreign language (higher intermediate). 4 Any other PEI subject at elementary level or above excluding shorthand theory Stage 1.
Secretarial Group Certificate	See Tables 3.1, 4.1 and 7.1 where appropriate	All parts to be passed within 12 months. 1 Choice of: Shorthand/typewriting (intermediate); Shorthand speed (100 wpm) + 20 wpm typewriting transcription speed test — shorthand based. 2 Typewriting (intermediate). 3 Secretarial practice (intermediate). 4 Choice of: English (intermediate); English for business communications (intermediate); English language NCE (higher intermediate); English as a foreign language (advanced); Bookkeeping and accounts (intermediate);

Table 2.1 continued

Title	Length of Examination	Format and Regulations
		Commerce (intermediate); Foreign language (intermediate); Audio typewriting (intermediate); Word processing; Systematic notetaking.
Higher Secretarial Group Certificate	See Tables 3.1, 4.1 and 7.1 where appropriate	All parts to be passed within 12 months. 1 Choice of: Shorthand/typewriting (advanced); Shorthand speed (120 wpm) + 22 wpm typewriting transcription speed test (shorthand based). 2 Typewriting (advanced). 3 Secretarial practice (advanced). 4 Choice of: English (advanced); English for business communications (advanced); English for the secretary; English for office skills (intermediate); word processing theory and practical. 5 Choice of: Audio/typewriting (intermediate); Commerce (intermediate); Book-keeping and accounts (intermediate first class); English language NCE (advanced first class); Word processing theory and practical.

Examining board: Royal Society of Arts (RSA)

Title	Length of Examination	Format and Regulations
Diploma in Office Studies	See Tables 3.1, 4.1, 6.1 and 7.1 where appropriate	Minimum of 3 core subjects — Communication in business, Arithmetic, Office practice + 1 of the following — Audio-typewriting, Book-keeping, Shorthand 1, Spoken English, Typewriting, Word processing. Candidates may also enter — Civics, Computer literacy and information technology, Background to business, Computers in data processing, Statistics.

Table 2.1 continued

Title	Length of Examination	Format and Regulations
Diploma in General Reception	See Tables 3.1, 6.1 and 7.1 where appropriate	Minimum of 4 core subjects – Reception skills, Communication in business, Office Practice, Typewriting OR Audio-typewriting OR Word processing + 1 of the following – Ordinary certificate in spoken English, Arithmetic, Background to business, Word processing. Candidates may also enter – Audio-typewriting, Book-keeping, Computers in data processing.
Diploma in Secretarial Studies	See Tables 3.1, 4.1, 5.1 and 7.1 where appropriate	Minimum of 3 core subjects – Communication in business, Background to business OR Economics, Office practice OR Secretarial duties + 1 from Accounting, Office practice, Typewriting. Candidates may then enter any of the above or Cost accounting, Computers in data processing, Law and public administration, Shorthand 80/100 (typed transcript), Shorthand-typewriting, Word processing.
Diploma in Business Studies	See Tables 3.1, 4.1, 5.1 and 7.1 where appropriate	Minimum of 3 core subjects – Communication in business OR Economics, Arithmetic OR Statistics OR Accounting + options as for Dipl. in Sec. Studies above.
Diploma in Office Studies (Pilot scheme)	See Tables 3.1, 4.1, 6.1 and 7.1 where appropriate	Core subjects – Communication in business, Arithmetic (business & commercial), Computer literacy and information technology. Options – Audio-typewriting, Typewriting skills, Word processing, Book-keeping/accounting, Shorthand-transcription, Computers in data processing, Modern languages. Mainly in-course assessment + activity based syllabus.
Diploma in Distribution (Pilot scheme)	See Tables as above	As above except Arithmetic (distribution).

Table 2.1 continued

Title	Length of Examination	Format and Regulations
Certificate for Secretarial *Linguists*	Oral/aural Written paper – 3 hrs	Entry requirement – A level. Comprehension, use of telephone, translation, conversation, background. All work to be typed. Summary in English of foreign language passage. Translation into English. Translation into the language. Letter in the language.

Diploma for Personal Assistants	6 parts – Playing of tape + 2.75 hrs to work
	           3 hrs
	           3 hrs
	           3 hrs
	           3 hrs
		1 Office skills applied.
		
		 2 Economic and financial aspects.
		 3 Personnel and functional.
		 4 Legal aspects.
		 5 Communications.
		 6 Oral.

Diploma for Bi-Lingual Secretaries	Oral/aural Paper 1 – 3 hrs Paper 2 – 3 hrs	Entry requirement – degree in a modern language. Comprehension, use of telephone, translation, conversation and interpreting. All work to be typed. Translation into English. Translation into foreign language. Summary, letter and draft report.

Examining board: Scottish Business Education Council (SCOTBEC – now SCOTVEC)

Scottish Certificate in Office Skills	See Tables 3.1 and 4.1 where appropriate	2-year part-time or 1-year full-time course. Certificate awarded to candidates passing: Communications 1; Office practice 1 + 3 of the following (within 3 sessions): Shorthand – I, II or III; Audio typewriting – I or II; Reception; Record keeping; Calculations for the office; Introduction to micro-computers; Elements of Scottish law; Modern language I; Gaelic I.

Table 2.1 continued

Title	Length of Examination	Format and Regulations
Secretarial Certificate	See Tables 3.1 and 4.1 where appropriate	Entry requirement — O level English or equivalent. Certificate awarded to candidates passing: Communications II: Office practice II: Typewriting II or III + 1 of the following: Audio typewriting II; Accounts; Business information; Elements of agriculture; Shorthand II or III; Modern language II; Gaelic II (suitable for candidates wishing to proceed to membership of the Association of Medical Secretaries).
Scottish National Certificate in Secretarial Studies	See Tables 3.1 and 4.1 where appropriate	2-year part-time or 1-year full-time course. Entry requirements — O level English or equivalent + 3 other subjects at the same level of Stage 1 SCOTBEC Group Cert. Certificate awarded to candidates passing: Communications II; Office practice II; Typewriting II or III (in 3 sessions) + 2 of the following: Shorthand II or III; Audio typewriting II; Accounts; Business information; Data processing; Business computing practice; Elements of agriculture; Legal secretarial practice; Medical office practice; Modern language II; Gaelic II; Introduction to behavioural sciences; Introduction to industrial relations.

Table 2.1 continued

Title	Length of Examination	Format and Regulations
Scottish National Diploma for Agricultural Secretaries	See Tables 3.1 and 4.1 where appropriate	2-year full-time course. Entry requirement — min. SCE O grade in English or equivalent + 3 other subjects at same level. Entry to 2nd year with Scottish Cert. or Scottish National Cert in Secretarial Studies. Diploma awarded to candidates passing the following 9 subjects: Communications II; Office practice II; Typewriting II or III; Accounts or business information; Elements of agriculture; Farm office administration; Applied agriculture; Farm business analysis and control.
Diploma for Medical Secretaries	See Tables 3.1 and 4.1 where appropriate	2-year full-time course. Entry requirement — min. 4 SCE O grade passes (including English) or equivalent. Diploma awarded to candidates passing SCOTBEC examinations in: Medical shorthand-typewriting *or* Medical audio-typewriting + 4 papers set by Association of Medical Secretaries, Practice Administrators and Receptionists.
Scottish Higher National Certificate in Secretarial Studies	See Tables 3.1 and 4.1 where appropriate	2-year part-time, 1-year full-time course. Entry requirement — 3 Higher grade passes or Secretarial Certificate or equivalent. Certificate awarded to candidates passing: Communications III; Office administration I; Typewriting III (or shorthand/audio/typewriting/word processing module) + 2 of the following (in 3 sessions): Shorthand III (if not chosen above); Office administration II; Business information; Business environment; People and organisations; Law and the office; Information processing; Gaelic III; Modern language III.

Table 2.1 continued

Title	Length of Examination	Format and Regulations
Scottish Higher National Diploma in Secretarial Studies	See Tables 3.1 and 4.1 where appropriate	2–3-year full-time course. Entry requirement Secretarial Certificate or SNC or 3 SCE Higher grade passes (including English) + 2 O grade passes or equivalent. Candidates will be awarded the Diploma after passing: Year 1 – Communications III; Office admin I; Shorthand; Typewriting. Year 2 – Business information; Office admin II; Shorthand/typewriting + passes in 3 of the following: Business environment; People and organisations; Law and the office; Information processing; Gaelic III; Modern language III.
Scottish Higher National Diploma in Secretarial Studies with Languages	See Tables 3.1 and 4.1 where appropriate	As above. Additional entry requirement at least 1 language at SCOTBEC Stage II or SCE Higher grade or similar. Candidates must also pass examinations in 2 languages at min. Stage 111.
Diploma for Graduate Secretaries	See Tables 3.1 and 4.1 where appropriate	Entry requirement – Degree or equivalent + interview by college. Diploma awarded to candidates passing: Office administration; Shorthand; Typewriting + 2 of the following: Modern language A Stage III; Modern language B Stage III; Business information; Business environment; Law and the office.

PREPARATION FOR AN EXAMINATION

The chapters dealing with each specific skill will give more detail on how to prepare for, and take, each skill examination. Here we make some general observations relevant to all the skill examinations.

The best possible preparation for any practical skill examination is to:

1. Practise as often as possible. Frequent short practice sessions are more beneficial than one long period a week and should start right from the beginning of your course. As new operations or points of theory are introduced in your lessons, include them in your practice.

2. Proof-read all your work most thoroughly. Undetected errors are the cause of very many lost marks. This skill should be a part of your normal routine at the completion of each piece of work, again starting from the first lesson.

3. Read as widely as possible to increase your understanding of the theory aspects of your course and test yourself on past theory questions. This is also necessary for any specialist field for which you are studying.

4. Read as much as you can in the shorthand system you are learning, as this increases your vocabulary of outlines. Also try to write down a variety of passages from books, radio and television.

5. Read the book in this series concerning Communication, as the secretarial skills rely heavily on a good command of written English, including spelling and other grammatical points.

6. Work on as many past examination papers and varied tasks as possible. In the immediate time before your examination, work to the time limits imposed by the examining board.

HINTS ON TAKING THE EXAMINATION

1. The most important point is to read all the instructions for the whole examination and for each individual task most carefully, at least twice, and then follow every one of them.

2. As already stated, poor proof-reading is a major cause of lost marks. Besides checking your own work, some papers present tasks which include deliberate errors to be identified and corrected. This is often more difficult on a VDU but you can adjust the brightness to your own preference. The following chapters also give hints to help you with the different skills.

3. If permitted, have a dictionary with you and use it if you are in any doubt about a word. Also have all the necessary tools with you, including spare pens or pencils.

4. If you are asked to perform a given number of operations or state a certain number of facts, do the correct number − no more and no less than required. If two shorthand passages are required, ensure that you transcribe two of the same speed.

5. Check carefully that you hand in the correct pieces of work, i.e. shorthand notes which correspond to the transcripts, all the tasks in typewriting and combined skill examinations and print-outs requested for word processing.

6. If your equipment develops a fault, report it to the invigilator immediately. A note must be made to inform the examiner and it should be possible to move to another machine. Above all, keep calm.

Chapter 3   Typewriting

A. GETTING STARTED

Typewriting is a skill which can be self-taught from one of the many comprehensive textbooks. However, this often leads to the formation of bad habits which are extremely difficult to correct. Better progress is usually made within a group, with the guidance of an experienced teacher familiar with the requirements of both the business world and typewriting examinations.

EQUIPMENT

A wide variety of typewriters can now be found in colleges and schools. While many establishments retain some manual machines, the number of electric and electronic machines continues to increase; golf-ball typewriters are not usually found in colleges and schools. The "touch" of the keyboard varies between machines and you should try several to find one that suits you. If you are buying a machine it is essential to try several models thoroughly to find one that suits your touch. You need one which has a fully adjustable tabulator.

Electronic machines may be used in examinations, but you are not allowed to use the memory facility as it would give you an unfair advantage. Automatic justifying of the typing can cause problems with spacing and is best avoided.

It is obviously an advantage if you have a typewriter at home for your practice. However, most colleges and schools encourage students to practise when machines are available and you should take advantage of any opportunity to improve your skill. In most localities it is also possible to hire a machine.

Examinations should be taken on a machine with which you are very familiar and which you have been using for some time. It also needs to be in good working order, with a good quality ribbon. A new ribbon can be extremely difficult to correct acceptably and a very faint one might lead to marks lost for indecipherable characters.

The layout of the keyboard differs in some foreign countries and students learning to type in any other language should use the appropriate keyboard. However, these are not available in many colleges and you may have to use an adapted QWERTY keyboard.

If you are working on your own, buy a book which includes practice material on all aspects of the syllabus to which you are working. Examining boards publish detailed information on each syllabus and regular reports are issued which highlight the weaknesses and strengths of the candidates during the year.

TECHNIQUE

While typing, always pay attention to good posture, with your back supported, your feet on the floor and wrists held flat, not sagging. Develop good habits from the start, keeping your eyes on the copy and away from the keyboard and typing point. Attention to these points will help you to develop accuracy and speed, will minimise fatigue and lead to a higher degree of skill.

Typewriting is a skill, and practice is a vital ingredient to success. You should aim for accuracy first with an even rhythm, giving each key strike equal time. After early keyboarding is complete, your practice should include the manipulation of other machine controls as they are introduced during your course. Always proof-read each piece of practice undertaken as this can highlight persistent problems which need concentrated practice, such as jumping capitals caused by incorrect timing of the shift key. Always read through the original document before starting to type, noting the instructions and any content or layout problems.

A good standard of English and the ability to spell are important and you should keep a dictionary handy for checking when necessary. Calculations on line and character spacing must also be accurate to produce a high standard of presentation. This can cause difficulty if a student is weak at basic mathematics.

B. ESSENTIAL PRINCIPLES

This section gives advice on the **examiners'** criteria which form the basis of their marking schemes and then goes into more detail as follows:

1. Examiners' criteria
2. Display points
3. Document layouts
4. Foreign language typewriting
5. The examination
6. Speed/accuracy tests

1. EXAMINERS' CRITERIA

Typewriting examiners consider the most important criteria are: following instructions, accuracy, consistency and production speed, with the aim of producing "mailable" copy. These points are the basis of their marking schemes.

What do the examiners mean by the term "mailable copy"? They are looking for a standard of work which an employer could mail to his customers. So, it must be accurate, any corrections must be made neatly and the presentation should be first class.

You should study your textbooks to ensure that you are familiar with the terms used. For example, an instruction may read "use shoulder headings in closed caps". You must, therefore, be able to identify the headings concerned and present them in the style requested.

Good presentation on the paper and, where applicable, good judgement in the choice of paper size, will gain marks, especially with an instruction such as "display attractively". This expertise can only be gained from practice involving a variety of documents and paper sizes.

Instructions

Examiners' reports always comment on the frequency with which candidates do not follow, or misinterpret, instructions. The instructions given by an examiner represent those from an employer, and it is most important that every one of these is followed, even if it appears to contradict the rules you have been taught. The document may otherwise be rendered useless in the office and in an examination you will be very heavily penalised. For example, the style of headings or width of margins etc. is often specified by words such as "use paragraph headings" or "left margin of 38 mm". Where an instruction has more than one part, each part carries separate marks. You should read through the instructions at least twice and then read through the question *before* starting to type.

The PEI examinations sometimes include an instruction to "display attractively" or "to best advantage". Here, candidates are expected to use their expertise and to vary capitals, underscoring and line spacing effectively, so that the important points are highlighted. Present the display in the centre of the page. Your teacher should guide you when these instructions apply. Most examining boards do not allow you to alter their questions and you must comply with the use of capitals etc. in the printed question given. For example, "follow the layout indicated" does not give you licence to make any changes to the given display.

Some teachers and students believe that an examiner will give all the necessary instructions concerning the layout of specialist questions, such as legal documents, and it is therefore not necessary to teach or to practise them. This is *not* true. Instruction and practice on the whole range of displays included in the syllabus will give the student a much better chance of producing high-quality work within a reasonable time.

Accuracy

In all examinations, proof-reading is essential. You should check every page of work *before* it is removed from the typewriter. It can be very difficult to align a correction after returning the page to the machine. You are recommended to check your work at convenient points, such as after each paragraph or display. This will highlight any errors quickly and provide a better opportunity to make an acceptable correction. Recheck at the end of each page. Resist the temptation to let your eye skip quickly across the page immediately after typing; such a practice fails to pick up all the errors and takes no account of instructions, omissions etc. So, always check against the original question.

Examiners' reports comment repeatedly on poor standards of correction, with all methods and at all levels of ability. Correcting does take time and it is often found that the accurate student, even if a little slower manipulating the keyboard, may complete a question in less time. When you correct errors, do so neatly. Examiners will accept any form of correcting — erasers, liquids, self-correcting ribbons or correcting paper — but they do penalise every time an original error is visible, or when carbon copies are not corrected or if the paper is damaged, i.e. a hole has been made. Examining boards emphasise that correcting papers do not always make an acceptable correction as the white surface may rub off to expose the error, and they stress that the correcting liquids must be used sparingly. Examiners and employers dislike large areas "painted out". Squeezing and spreading can be effective ways of making a correction where just one character has been omitted or added, but you will be penalised if characters are touching.

While you are generally allowed to use a dictionary during an examination, it does take valuable time to look up each word. You should therefore have a good command of spelling. Despite having the correct version on the paper in front of them, a surprising number of candidates still manage to mis-spell words, often without realising it. This shows that they do not copy correctly, that their spelling is weak and that they do not proof-read. The examination questions do not contain spelling errors unless stated, in which case you are expected to identify and correct them.

Consistency

Examiners look for consistency in display, punctuation, use of figures, etc. You cannot automatically follow the style of the question as this may not be consistent, but you are expected to apply the "rules" you have been taught.

You should check the question for any apparent inconsistencies as you will be penalised for any in *display*, such as line spacing, punctuation or centring. Numbers should be typed as words or figures consistently throughout a task. Each document must be presented in one consistent style throughout. In the absence of any instructions on the style of display, you must decide this before you start to type and keep to it.

One form of consistency with which many candidates become confused is *open* or *standard punctuation*. Many marks are lost by candidates mixing punctuation styles within a question. You must keep to one style, regardless of the method used in the question paper.

Where a word has an *alternative form of spelling*, you can choose to use one which differs from that in the question, but your use must be consistent. Alternatives include:

realise/realize	grey/gray
organise/organize	medieval/mediaeval
modernise/modernize	despatch/dispatch
adviser/advisor	by-law/bye-law

However, most words have only one correct form, such as:

auxiliary   enterprise   merchandise
supervise   revise   analyse

Production speed

Typing speed is not assessed on practical examination questions. The minimum speed given on the examination syllabus (and in Table 3.1) is a guide to the ability needed to complete the paper within the time limit. Marks are deducted in proportion to any work not completed. Some boards add a final "distinction" question, which can only be attempted when all others are completed.

At least one board, the RSA, now consider that the completion of the paper is essential to gain a pass. They have introduced pilot schemes at all levels which will ultimately replace their existing examinations and marking scheme. The rate of production now assumes greater importance, but accuracy and consistency are still essential.

2. DISPLAY POINTS

Margins

Examiners generally stipulate the minimum size of margins that they are prepared to accept. On A5 landscape and A4 paper, 25 mm is the usual minimum for left, top and bottom margins, 13 mm is the minimum on the right. With A5 portrait paper the left margin may be 13 mm. You are strongly advised to allow above the minimum, while making best use of the paper. An instruction may state that margins may be below the normal minimum, e.g. down to 13 mm on A4. You can be fairly certain that the question will be a tight fit on the page.

Wherever the exact size of a margin is stated, this must be accurately presented. For instance, on some documents a "dropped head" is required, usually of 50–75 mm. Or, an instruction for "a left margin of 38 mm" is given. If the instruction states "minimum" or "at least", then you may provide more.

The right margin should never be wider than the left and you should aim to keep it as even as possible. You may need to divide a long word at a line end and this must be achieved between syllables or at an existing hyphen. Many employers and examiners dislike word division and this should be kept to a minimum. Occasionally a justified margin is required and any error in attempting this will be heavily penalised. Examiners' marking schemes have not yet taken full account of facilities on modern electronic equipment and you are advised to avoid justifying where it is not demanded.

Line spacing

Line spacing causes some difficulties, especially with one and a half or double line spacing. The only reason for inserting extra line spacing between paragraphs is to show clearly the start and end of each paragraph and this is only necessary with block paragraphs. With all other styles, and where headings or numbers separate the paragraphs, the division is clear. Some confusion is apparent between the number of clear lines which need to be inserted and the number of carriage returns which are physically made. You do need to be very familiar with these terms.

Punctuation	There are two acceptable styles of punctuation — open or standard. You need not follow the method shown unless an instruction is given. You must be very sure of where punctuation is necessary for grammatical accuracy and where it may be inserted/omitted depending on the style chosen. For example, full stops after numbers in a list are omitted with open punctuation, but any punctuation on the end of each item must remain.
Abbreviations	Take time to become familiar with the most commonly-used abbreviations, including the often confused sh/shall and shd/should. You should generally expand abbreviations unless instructed to retain them. Any abbreviations in the name of a company must be retained as this would be the form in which the company is registered. In addresses, Rd, Ave, etc. must be typed in full, but county names may remain abbreviated. Candidates frequently lose marks for expanding these incorrectly.
Correction signs	Manuscript signs also need to be learned. Care should be taken to identify all amendments involving these signs and to render them in the correct form. These manuscript and typescript changes form part of the examiners' instructions and are therefore heavily penalised if not followed. A dash is frequently confused with a hyphen, indicating a student's lack of ability in English grammar or lack of understanding of the text.
Headings	Marks are frequently lost by candidates who cannot distinguish between headings by name — e.g. paragraph, shoulder and side/marginal headings — or who present them incorrectly, i.e. no line spacing after shoulder headings. In the absence of any instructions on capitals, it is advisable to follow copy, while also ensuring that related headings are typed in a consistent style. Headings *not* in capitals should be underscored.

3. DOCUMENT LAYOUTS

Letters

Since business letters make up a large part of a secretary's typing, they are included in all examinations. Practice should be varied to include letters of different length, style, content and complexity. You should be alert to the words "enclose" or "attach" and ensure you indicate these in the normal manner. Marks are very frequently lost for this omission.

Most examining boards accept fully-blocked documents, especially for letters, and this style is recommended for examinations as it can be produced quickly and it minimises display faults. However, you may be instructed to use another layout or to deviate from the fully-blocked display by insetting a portion. *Instructions always over-ride typewriting "rules"* and must be obeyed. The most common alternative in letter layout is the semi-blocked style (which can be used with open or standard punctuation).

Urgent, confidential, personal and the attention line are frequently omitted from the envelope or, if shown, are incorrectly positioned.

Memoranda

Memoranda are also frequently presented in examinations, so again you should practise on a variety of these and note any enclosures or attachments. While the basic details are retained, the layout varies considerably both between companies in business and between examination boards. Your tutor will ensure that you practise the necessary layouts and, if you are not provided with printed memorandum paper, that you are able to produce your own headed style quickly and correctly.

Continuation sheets

Documents often extend to more than one page, and you must number the second and subsequent pages in a consistent manner and position. Continuation pages of letters and memos must be typed on plain paper, not headed, and they require additional information. Besides numbering the pages, you must repeat the date and the name of the addressee, as it appears on the first page. Some examiners, such as the LCCI, also require a repeat of the reference. Your textbook will show the layout to be used for different letter displays.

Footnotes

You should be familiar with the commonly-used footnote signs and how to type them. Remember to raise them above the typing line in the text. A footnote should always be in single-line spacing, with a clear line between consecutive footnotes. A line ruled between an article and any footnote must extend the full width of the longest typing line.

Forms

Examiners continue to comment on poorly completed forms. You should look at each form closely before inserting it into your typewriter. Decide the point at which each piece of information should be inserted and follow the capitalisation of the question. Typed insertions must not cut through lines or boxes and deletions are best achieved with continuous X, carefully aligned over the information. You are *not* expected to type on the signature line.

To display a form, study the question carefully so that you can decide on the line spacing, alignment and most suitable display. Consider the details to be inserted in each position and allow sufficient space. Lines should be typed in one consistent style, either underscoring or continuous dots. Single-line spacing is too narrow for either typed or handwritten details to be added and should not be used. For neatest presentation, typed lines must not extend beyond dotted lines, which should all finish at the right-hand margin.

Another popular form display is the *tear-off slip*. The tear-off line must extend from edge to edge of the paper, not just between margins, and be produced with continuous hyphens. Some textbooks suggest just two lines above and below the tear-off, but this often results in a poorly balanced document and must be treated as a minimum. Consider whether each part of the document would be well balanced after they were separated.

Cards

Typing on A6 cards is included in some examinations set by the RSA and SCOTBEC Boards. These cards can be difficult to correct and may slip in the typewriter. The minimum acceptable margins are 13 mm. Ruling may be included and also typing on both sides of one card is common. Careful planning is important for best use of the card.

Figures and financial terms

Instructions are sometimes given to retain words/figures "as copy". Generally, examiners accept the ruling: one as a word and all other numbers consistently as figures, but they prefer a number which starts a sentence to be presented as a word. Figures should never be divided at line ends and they must be very carefully checked.

A list of numbered points may be aligned with units under units or fully blocked to conform with the style of the document. Roman numbers may be aligned to the right or left consistently.

Decimal points must always be shown, e.g. 15.97, 7.30 pm. Millions and thousands may be shown by a comma or space, provided each is used consistently. When shown first, the £ or other symbol must be close to the figures. This means that with items of different lengths you cannot fully block and align vertically at the same time.

A knowledge of accounting makes the typing of financial statements easier. You should not guess a badly written figure, but check the totals to determine it. There are several forms of layout but all require the display of evenly-spaced columns with units, tens etc. aligned. The double underlining of totals must be less than half a line space apart. The more advanced typist will be able to adjust the margins, column spacing and line spacing to fit the statement attractively on one sheet of paper.

Tables

The variety of tables is endless, but the more practice done beforehand the greater the chance of coping successfully in an examination. Poor positioning on the page loses marks.

Within a question, you must keep to one style of display. It is quicker to produce the blocked style when this is acceptable. An instruction to centre a main heading does not force you into using a centred display throughout. However, centred column headings must lead to *consistently* centred columns. The spacing between the columns, with or without ruling, *must* be equal.

Many candidates produce a well-typed table which they then spoil with badly executed ruling. Ruling must be carefully done with a fine black pen or by use of the underscore key. Pencil ruling is not accepted without a specific instruction and poor or incomplete ruling will be heavily penalised. Examiners accept a mixture of ruling, e.g. horizontal lines by machine and vertical lines in black pen. Whatever system is used, the lines must be straight, parallel and neatly joined. If a table appears on a carbon copy, it should be ruled separately. Never divide a table between pages.

Tables are sometimes presented with vertical or oblique (diagonal) headings. You should learn how to type these accurately and practise several examples to become familiar with them. You must retain the style of the rest of the table, either blocked or centred, but never mixed.

Charts

Charts do not usually involve much typing but are very time-consuming to produce, so such questions are best left to last. They usually require the use of basic skills such as centring, ruling, column display and line spacing, together with following instructions, capitalisation etc. Some include vertically-presented information.

You should study a chart fully, dividing the display into sections, then analysing each section. Rule in black ink, unless instructed otherwise, and where particular sizes are stipulated these must be followed, e.g. an instruction for a space of 51 mm, or a box 38 mm × 25 mm, requires exact sizes. If the words "at least" or "minimum" are included, it is advisable to increase such measurements a little if space permits.

Flow charts include variously shaped symbols, representing activities. These shapes are important and are not the result of poor ruling by the examiners!

A rough practice to determine the size of a shape and how any wording would best fit into it can prove extremely valuable. Size is not usually important, but lines must not touch the typing. It is also possible to produce a neat chart by drawing it first, then adding the wording, or by drawing the shapes on a backing sheet to put behind your typing paper. Within diamonds and triangles, centred display is easier; other shapes may, however, be block-centred, so the consistency rule may not be rigidly applied.

Programmes

Sometimes a question is included in the form of a programme, and several examining boards favour the four-page leaflet style. You should study the question to decide the best approach and layout. The front is usually a heading or brief description to be displayed. Pages 2 and 3 may sometimes be treated as A4 landscape, or on other occasions as separate A5 sheets. A good balance on the page is important, so plan where possible to adjust your display so that pages 2 and 3 start and finish together.

Meetings documents

You will find it helpful to be familiar with the procedures and terms used in formal meetings, perhaps through your Secretarial Duties or Communications lessons. An agenda or chairman's agenda, perhaps with a notice of meeting, may be displayed in blocked or centred style. Good presentation on the page is important. As with any list of numbered points, you should check for the highest number and allow sufficient character spaces to include it in your display. Note whether each item finishes with a punctuation mark or not and allow a clear line space between items. Note also that the expansion of Hon is Honorary.

Minutes can be displayed in a variety of styles and practice on several different displays would be useful. The list of members present sometimes requires alphabetical rearrangement by the surname. The numbering systems vary and the styles of heading differ. You should be familiar with the use of an Action column, separating it from the minutes by at least 3 character spaces, and align items accurately.

Legal and specialist documents

A variety of specialist documents, including literary and legal documents, may be presented in an examination and can cause problems to students who have not tackled them before. Obviously, on a course designed for specialist secretaries, a considerable amount of practice is done on the relevant documents from an appropriate textbook; but *all* students should include practice on specialist documents during their studies.

4. FOREIGN LANGUAGES

Some textbooks include a small amount of practice in a foreign language and this is very useful for all students. Some examination questions include foreign names or expressions, which it may prove beneficial to understand. Accents are often included, for example in a menu, but numerous marks are lost by students omitting them.

Single subject examinations are not available in Great Britain but the group certificates involved are detailed in Tables 1.1 and 2.1. Practice on past examination papers is essential, as also is very thorough proof-reading. You should learn as many useful business phrases as possible so that you can incorporate them, as necessary, in your answers. Further information is given in Chapter 6 for audio-typewriting in foreign languages.

5. THE EXAMINATION

Secretarial duties and office practice exams may include *theoretical* questions on typewriting equipment. In more recent times, these questions have largely given way to those on word processing and audio-typewriting.

Table 3.1 provides a guide to the main *practical* typewriting examinations available in Great Britain and indicates the length, content and complexity of each.

You must use the 5 or 10 minutes reading time effectively. If this is not included in the examination procedure, take that time to study the paper fully before starting to type. Plan to start with the familiar, shorter and most straightforward questions, in order to gain confidence and diminish your nervousness.

Examinations generally consist of a number of varied questions, which carry a different proportion of the marks available. Many boards publish the number of marks allocated to each question and some students like to determine the ratio of time available to marks allocated. For example, if 120 minutes are allowed for a paper, a question carrying 25 per cent of marks would be allocated one-quarter of the time, i.e. 30 minutes. This can be used as a rough guide but should not be taken too strictly as some questions require more planning time than others.

Before starting to type a document, read the instructions and question very carefully. This will bring to your attention points such as consistency, insertions, etc.

Questions are presented in typescript or manuscript. *Elementary* papers present copy in clear and simple form. In every paper you will find a letter and a variety of other documents, one of which may require at least one carbon copy.

In *intermediate* and *advanced* papers you are expected to be much more aware of typewriting rules, and questions may not be presented in a consistent form. They may involve altering the layout or style from the copy shown. It may be necessary to extract information from a document to present in the finished answer, perhaps in an amended form. Specialised documents may be included and some papers include questions which require you to identify and correct spelling, typewriting or English grammar faults.

In order to be successful in a practical typewriting examination you must gain at least 50 or 60 per cent of the available marks (depending on the examining board). If you gain sufficiently high marks, you may be awarded a credit or distinction.

Many *group certificates* include typewriting as a single subject or combined with other skills, and again the emphasis is on producing accurate "mailable" documents. Often you are required to compose the documents from given information. It is difficult, and requires much practice, to compose at the typewriter. Tables 1.1 and 2.1 (pp. 00 and 00) give details of the group certificates available.

6. SPEED/ACCURACY TEST

Where a speed or accuracy test forms part of a practical typewriting examination, it is generally done first. This means that you may still be rather nervous and inclined to make more mistakes than usual. Do not rush straight into the passage but, rather, start a little more slowly and build up to your natural speed.

Examiners generally stipulate a minimum speed for an endorsement of the candidate's certificate. They do not all assess speed test results in the same way; but the most favoured methods are to take the passage up to a given number of errors only (usually 6 or 7), or to take the passage as a whole but deduct so many words per minute for each mistake. If you should make too many mistakes in the first two or three lines, the RSA allow you to start again and discount your first attempt, but it will have taken up part of the time allocated. You should never overtype – it wastes time in speed tests and can incur additional penalties. If you make a mistake, complete the word and continue. Do not have a second attempt at any word. Any attempt to correct errors will result in disqualification. The accuracy test included in the SCOTBEC papers forms part of the practical examination. Speed tests are taken separately with the PEI and their layout instructions must be followed.

Table 3.1 Format and content for typewriting examinations
Examining board: London Chamber of Commerce and Industry (LCCI)

Title	Level	Length of Examination	Format and Regulations
General information: Dictionaries are allowed			
Typewriting	Elementary	90 mins	Display of 5 business documents from printed or handwritten originals. Minimum recommended speed 25 wpm.
Typewriting	Intermediate	120 mins + 10 mins optional speed test	Display of 5 business documents from printed or handwritten originals. Minimum recommended speed 35 wpm.
Typewriting	Advanced	150 mins + 10 mins optional speed test	Display of 5 documents of business or specialised nature from handwritten or printed originals. Minimum recommended speed 45 wpm.

Examining board: Pitman Examinations Institute (PEI)

Title	Level	Length of Examination	Format and Regulations
Typewriting	Elementary	90 mins + 5 mins reading time	Display of documents from typed or handwritten originals of 5 tasks, including a copying test. Dictionaries are NOT allowed. Minimum recommended speed 25 wpm.
Typewriting	Intermediate	120 mins + 5 mins reading time	Display of documents from typed or handwritten originals of 5 tasks, including a copying test. Dictionaries are NOT allowed. Minimum recommended speed 35 wpm.
Typewriting	Advanced	150 mins + 5 mins reading time	Display of documents from typed or handwritten originals of 6 tasks, including a copying test. Dictionaries ARE allowed. Minimum recommended speed 50 wpm.

Table 3.1 continued

Title	Level	Length of Examination	Format and Regulations
Typewriting	Speed test	10 mins	Copy-typing test with minimum speed of 35 wpm, line by line. Error tolerance 2% assessed to nearest word per minute. Dictionaries are NOT allowed.

Examining board: Royal Society of Arts (RSA)

General information: Dictionaries are allowed

Typewriting	Stage I	110 mins + 10 mins reading time	Display business documents from typed or handwritten originals; completion of a form. 5 or 6 questions. Minimum recommended speed 25 wpm.
Typewriting Skills	Stage I	120 mins	Display 6 business documents from type-script/manuscript; completion of a form. All questions must be completed to gain a pass.
Typewriting	Stage II	140 mins + 5 mins speed test + 10 mins reading time	Display business and general documents from typed or handwritten originals. 5 or 6 questions. Minimum recommended speed 35 wpm.
Typewriting	Stage III	140 mins + 5 mins speed test + 10 mins reading time	Display of business and specialised documents, including charts, from typed or handwritten originals. 5 or 6 questions. May include spelling, typing or English grammar errors to be corrected. Minimum recommended speed 50 wpm.

Table 3.1 continued

Examining board: Scottish Business Education Council (SCOTBEC)

Title	Level	Length of Examination	Format and Regulations
General information: Dictionaries allowed			
Typewriting	Stage I	120 mins + 10 mins speed test	Display business documents from typed or handwritten originals. Minimum recommended speed 25 wpm.
Typewriting	Stage II	150 mins + 10 mins speed test	Display business documents from typed or handwritten originals. Minimum recommended speed 35 wpm.
Typewriting	Stage III	150 mins + 10 mins speed test	Display business and specialised documents from typed or handwritten originals. Minimum recommended speed 50 wpm.

Examining board: Welsh Joint Education Committee (WJEC)

General information: Dictionaries allowed

Title	Level	Length of Examination	Format and Regulations
Typewriting	Elementary	90 mins + 10 mins reading time	3 or 4 questions, including letter and envelope. Recommended speed 20 wpm.
Typewriting	Stage I	120 mins + 10 mins reading time	5 or 6 questions, including letter and envelope. Recommended speed 25 wpm.
Typewriting	Stage II	150 mins + 10 mins reading time	5 or 6 questions, including letter and envelope. Recommended speed 35 wpm.
Typewriting	Stage III	150 mins + 10 mins reading time	5 or 6 questions, including letter and envelope. Recommended speed 50 wpm.

RECENT EXAMINATION QUESTIONS

A selection of questions from the various boards is now given taken from recent examination papers and including a variety of document displays. You may wish to attempt them as extra practice. The next section presents suggested displays for these questions.

Question 1 On the A4 headed paper provided, type the following letter in semi-blocked style. Take one carbon copy on the flimsy paper provided. Address an envelope.

Mr T Davidson, Manager, Rover Travel Agency, Highbridge Rd., Stirling FK10 4EA

Dr Mr Davidson   Subject Heading: Sales Conference

Further to our meeting yesterday, we are pleased to confirm the arrangements & costs for the sales conference of Insurance Enterprises Ltd to be held in our Castle Suite

The accommodation to be provided for the fifty delegates & their wives will be double/twin bedded *(from 14 to 17 June 1984.)* rooms with private bath/shower. As agreed, our special conference rates will apply & these are as follows:

u/c   50 delegates at residential delegate charge of £24-10 each per day   £4,365

u/c
each   50 delegates' wives at special charge of £22-00 per day   3,300
                                                                                                     £7,665

These charges are inclusive of:
VAT & service charge
Hire of conference Suite & facilities   *(TYPIST use single spacing for list.)*
Bed & breakfast from 14 to 17 June
Dinner – 14th & 15th June
u/c   Special function – dinner dance – 16th June
morning Coffees, lunches & afternoon teas for delegates

We hv. noted that you wish the seating to be arranged in theatre style; the 4 syndicate rooms will be used &
stet   equipment reqd. will be an overhead projector, film projector, video recorder & television. Nearer the time you will provide us with a list of the delegates so that we
NP   can allocate rooms & prepare name *tags* plaques. We look forward to receiving confirmation of this reservation.

Yrs sincerely, Roger Wyman
Asst. Manager

TYPIST – inset margins for display.

(SCOTBEC, Cert. for Hotel Receptionists, May 1984)

31

Question 2 This personal letter is to be typed on plain white paper. Correct the grammatical errors.

Stoodleigh
Newton Ave
Rugby CV21 3XR

Mr L G Parker FRPS
6 Sandford Sq
Newbold
Rugby CV21 3PS

Dear Leonard

Thanks for yours of 21 June & for reminding me th. you need to get the Agenda done soon in order to keep within the Club's Rules. Here is my ideas about the Agenda — you may like to change it ~~around~~ around.

INSET Agenda.
Double (or 1½)
line-spacing.

Sp. Caps

AGENDA
of General Meeting of Potter's Photographic Club

Wednesday 11th July 1984

1 Apologies
2 Minutes of Meeting 18 April 1984
3 Matters Arising
4 Exhibition 8 September 1984:   Final Plan
5 Resignation of Darkroom Secretary
6 Any Other Business

It is a great pity that Ken O'Regan is leaving us. You can rely on Mollie and I to make the presentation at the /end of the\ meeting. The 'Thank You' card is enc., ~~suitably~~ suitably inscribed.

On reading the Minutes, I have ~~noticed that there are a couple of discrepancies~~ decided to alter two or three minor items as follows:

MINUTE		ACTION

4.3.1   It was agreed ⟨*unanimously*⟩ that the Exhibition
would open at 1430 hours. Committee
members would act as Stewards on a
rota basis, *to be agreed.*   *MDT*

4.3.2   Security matters were discussed at
length and a Sub-Committee *was* elected,   LMC
subject to agreement.   FLT

6.1   Ms Kendall ~~informed the Committee~~ *confirmed*
that the description of the (Praxicat) *CAPS*
~~radiotropic lens~~ should be amended
to read:-

Filter size: 52 mm , Lever: 138° angle

Minimum focus: 0.6 m
Price: £69.95 (complete)   ALK

Perhaps Nicholas cd. check
these items and take the final
Draft into the Typing Agency   *l.c.*
next week.   He has produced
a ~~very good~~ *excellent* newsletter and   *u.c.*
has helped the Club in a variety
of ways. No doubt someone will
propose a vote of thanks.

I hope Gina has recovered
from the twins' visit and will
be at the meeting next week.

          Yours,

(RSA, Typewriting III, June 1984)

From Mr T B Younger   To Ms F Greenwood   Ref TBY/JS

CONFERENCE DELEGATES

I give below the list of conference delegates, as requested.

		Dept
MANCHESTER	Miss K Pearce	Accounts
	Mrs A Waters	Buying
	Mr L Wilkinson	Sales
	Mr M Morrison	Sales
	Mr S W Salisbury	Advertising
	Ms W Revell	Personnel
LIVERPOOL	Mr A Andrews	Sales
	Mr S Donaghue	Accounts
	Miss A McPhie	Buying
	Miss Q Eversley	Buying
	Mrs Z Vickery	Personnel
GLASGOW	Mr D H Browne	Sales
	Mr K Shivani	Accounts
	Miss R England	Personnel
	Mr D McMorris	Buying
EDINBURGH	Miss L McPherson	Sales
	Mrs A Coventry	Buying
	Mr W Gallagher	Sales
DUBLIN	Miss A O'Donnelly	Sales
	Mr W Thornton	Accts.
	Mrs P Kerry	Personnel
PLYMOUTH	Miss A Noakes	Advertising
	Ms B Underwood	Accounts
	Mr E Hector	General Office
PARIS	Mme B Gironde	Sales
	Mlle A Duval	Personnel
	Mme K Molière	Personnel
FRANKFURT	Herr E Braun	Accounts
AMSTERDAM	Mme JP Hôtesse	Accounts

Example

NAME	BRANCH	DEPARTMENT
Andrews, Mr A	Liverpool	Sales
Braun, Herr E	Frankfurt	Accounts

(RSA, Typewriting III, Autumn 1984)

Question 4 Type the following invitation and reply slip. Centre each line of the invitation, and make use of capital letters, etc to make the display attractive.

The Chairman and Directors of Greens and
Benako Cosmetics

request the pleasure of your company at the

JONKAI and his Silk World Fashion Show

in celebration of the launch in Greens of the new

BENAKO SILK COSMETICS and JONKAI FASHION

Monday, 23 July, 10.30 for 11.00 am at the

Grand Hotel, Piccadilly, London, W1

10.30 am Coffee
11.00 am Jonkai Fashion Presentation   Admittance by Ticket Only

Demonstration of Benako's new Silk Make up, Bakenaki (caps)
flower arrangement and traditional japanese music.   uc

Mrs/Miss* ....

Address   .. . .   —   .   .   .

          .   .   .   .   —   .   —   .   .   —   .   .

request** .... tickets to the Jonkai and his Silk
World Fashion Show at the Grand Hotel at
10.30 am on Monday, 23 July.

* Delete as applicable
** Please fill in the number of tickets you require
and return this slip to Miss L M Johnson,
3 Winchester Studios, London Road, London W1C 3QJ.
Your tickets are complimentary and will be sent to
you by return.

(PEI, Intermediate Typewriting, 220T)

Question 5 If required, left margin may be less than 25mm (1 inch) but not less than 12mm (½ inch).

Summary of balance sheet as at 31 December 1983 *Closed caps with underscore*

	1983		1982	
	£	£	£	£

Assets Employed *Closed caps - no underscore*

Fixed Assets

u.c. Housing properties:				
Established Schemes	16,040,195		11,619,349	
Schemes in Progress	3,412,380		3,269,886	
		19,452,575		14,889,235

Less:

Property Equity	217,642		247,434	
Housing Association Grant	11,003,830		6,955,104	7,202,538
		11,221,472		7,786,697
		8,231,103		2,131
Housing Properties		3,231		
Office Furniture		8,234,334		7,788,828

Current Assets

Sundry Debtors	224,149		115,226 t/s	
Cash at Bank, in				
l.c. Hand and On Deposit	62,122		26,331	
	£286,271		£141,593	

close up

Less:

Current Liabilities				
Sundry Creditors	239,918		122,966	
Bank Overdrafts	60,280		256,866	
	£300,198		£379,832	
		(13,927)		(238,239)
		8,220,407		7,550,589

Less: and Renewals

Repairs/Provisions		332,823		231,538
		£7,887,584		£7,319,051

Typist: All total lines should be the full width of the relevant column.

(RSA, Typewriting III, Spring 1984)

Question 6

PRICE INDICES – Sp. Caps.
Centre.

The index of retail prices for items for July 1983
was 336.5 (Jan ~~is~~ 1974 = 100). This represents an increase
NP of 4.2 percent over the previous ~~twelve~~ 12 months. [The tax a
price index (TPI) for July was 174.3 (Jan 1978 = 100). This
represents an increase of ~~3.1~~ 3.1 per cent over the previous 12 months.

MONTH	TPI – in full		RPI – in full	
	1982/~~83~~3	% increase over 12 months	1982/3	% increase over 12 months
July	169.8°	9.6	8.7	323.0
Aug	169.0	8.7	8.0	323.1
Sept	168.9	9.4	7.3	322.9
Oct	169.9	7.4	6.8	324.5
Nov	170.9	6.7	6.3	326.1
Dec	170.5	5.8	5.4	325.5
Jan	170.6	5.2	4.9	325.9
Feb	170.7	5.7	5.3	327.3
March	171.9	4.8	4.6	327.4
April	171.8	3.5	4.0	332.5
May	172.7	3.2	3.7	333.9
June	173.2	3.1	3.7	334.7
July	174.3	3.1	4.2	336.5

Double line spacing

TYPIST – Horizontal ruling only
Centre tabulation headings

(SCOTBEC, Diploma for Graduate Secretaries, June 1984)

37

Question 7 Type the following tabular matter in single-line spacing, keeping to the display shown in the draft. Pencilled ruling is not acceptable.

ELECTRICAL EQUIPMENT

Insulated enclosures: Corrosion and ~~impact~~ (impact) resistant; (also)→ resistant to wide variation in temperature.

Reference	Dimensions		Price £
	External	Internal (168)	
DOP 12	191 × 191 × 131	175 × 175 × 115	13.50
JET 15	281 × 191 × 131	265 × ~~~~ × 115	15.25
RAM 19	381 × 191 × 131	366 × 168 × 115	17.50
FOB 23	560 × 281 × 131	~~~~ (536 × 258 × 115)	18.75
CAN 27	560 × 380 × 181	536 × 357 × 165	22.00

Cable reeling units: Standard portable models. Automatic cable rewind after use. Fitted with 13 amp and 5 amp socket.

Reference	Cable length (mm)	Cable size	Price £
J 4265	15.25	0.75 3 core	63.00
M 3810	18.50	1.25 3 core	~~~~ (69.50)
S 5119	27.75	1.25 3 core	77.25

Extension cable reels: Best quality 3 core cable, impervious to grease, oil, and water.

Reference	Cable length	Cable rating	Price £
D 2051	15 m	13A	12.50
F 3122	18 m	5A	25.25
H 3376	27 m	5A	£1.00

(LCCI, Higher Typewriting, March 1984)

38

Question 8 Type the following table, ruling appropriately.

sp caps / us

l, Weekend Bargain caps & us

Metropolitan Hotels Ltd

Special Weekend Bargain Breaks

Price List *

tns skt

To	From						
	Eastwood	Westwood	Northgate	Southgate	Burnham	Welham	Middlecroft
	£	£	£	£	£	£	£
Newtown	27.50	30.50	28.30	–	28.10	24.90	23.10
Oldham	25.40	26.40	23.60	26.80	31.80	24.60	25.80
Posttown	24.20	24.60	22.40	27.40	32.20	25.20	26.40
Anytown ‡	22.20	25.40	22.60	23.00	28.00	21.00	22.20
Hightown	25.00	27.00	23.60	21.80	26.20	22.60	20.60
Lowtown	27.30	–	25.30	30.10	34.70	28.30	29.30
Maincity	26.00	29.00	26.80	20.60	26.20	23.20	22.00

* Inclusive of 2nd class rail fare & hotel costs.
‡ No direct train service on Sundays.

(PEI Advanced Typewriting 3/6T)

Question 9 Type on A5 paper. Retain oblique headings.

For the Investment-Minded

Caps and u/score

Thickness of existing insulation	Typical cost of additional 4" layer	Typical additional annual saving	Years to recover outlay	Annual saving as a percentage of outlay
0"	£72	£67	0.9	107%
1"	£26	£67	2.6	38%
2"	£14	£67	4.8	21%
3"	£9	£67	7.5	13%

The table shows the savings as a percentage of yr. annual cash outlay. It shows th. is the thinner yr. insulation, the better the investment of topping it up.

close up

(RSA, Typewriting III, June 1983)

40

Question 10   Use A5 paper. Retain vertical layout of items where shown. Rule as shown. You may use left and right margins of less than ½".

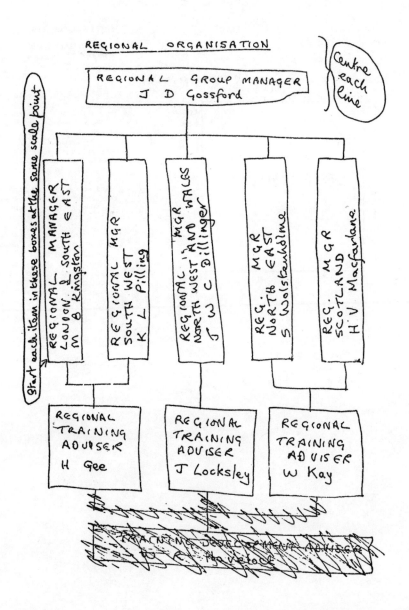

(RSA Typewriting III, Autumn 1983)

41

Question 11 Fold a sheet of A4 paper in half to form a leaflet of A5 size. Type the following conference information according to the instructions given using the fully-blocked style of layout.

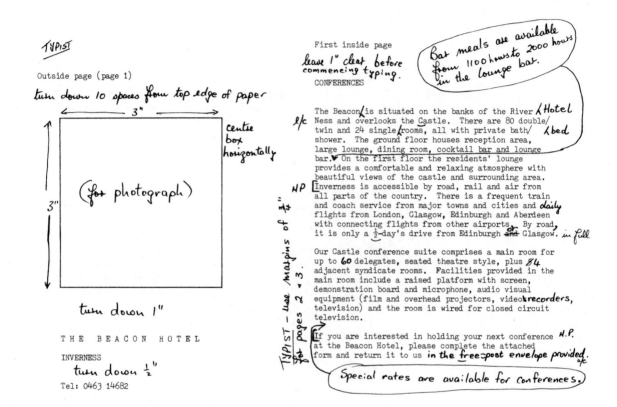

TYPIST

Outside page (page 1)

turn down 10 spaces from top edge of paper

← 3" →

(for photograph)

3"

centre box horizontally

turn down 1"

THE BEACON HOTEL

INVERNESS
turn down ½"

Tel: 0463 14682

First inside page

leave 1" clear before commencing typing.
CONFERENCES

Bar meals are available from 1100 hours to 2000 hours in the lounge bar.

l/c The Beacon ⟨Hotel is situated on the banks of the River ⟨Hotel Ness and overlooks the Castle. There are 80 double/ twin and 24 single⟨rooms, all with private bath/ ⟨bed shower. The ground floor houses reception area, large lounge, dining room, cocktail bar and lounge bar.✔ On the first floor the residents' lounge provides a comfortable and relaxing atmosphere with beautiful views of the castle and surrounding area.

NP Inverness is accessible by road, rail and air from all parts of the country. There is a frequent train and coach service from major towns and cities and daily flights from London, Glasgow, Edinburgh and Aberdeen with connecting flights from other airports. By road, it is only a ½-day's drive from Edinburgh and Glasgow. in full

Our Castle conference suite comprises a main room for up to 60 delegates, seated theatre style, plus 84 adjacent syndicate rooms. Facilities provided in the main room include a raised platform with screen, demonstration board and microphone, audio visual equipment (film and overhead projectors, video recorders, television) and the room is wired for closed circuit television.

If you are interested in holding your next conference N.P. at the Beacon Hotel, please complete the attached form and return it to us in the freepost envelope provided.

Special rates are available for conferences.

TYPIST - use margins of ¾"
for pages 2 & 3.

42

second inside page

To: Reservations Manager
    The Beacon Hotel
    INVERNESS

    Tel: 0463 14682

We are interested in holding a conference at the
Beacon Hotel and wish further particulars.

Name ....

Designation ....

Company . . .   .

Address .   .   .   .

   .   .   .   .

Dates .   .   .   .

No of delegates   .   .   .   .   .   .

Special requirements .   .   .   .   .   .

   .   .   .   . ~ .

   .   .   .   .

Signature .   .   .   .

Date ....

(SCOTBEC, Cert. for Hotel Receptionists Stage II, May 1984)

Question 12 Type the following on one sheet of plain A4 paper.

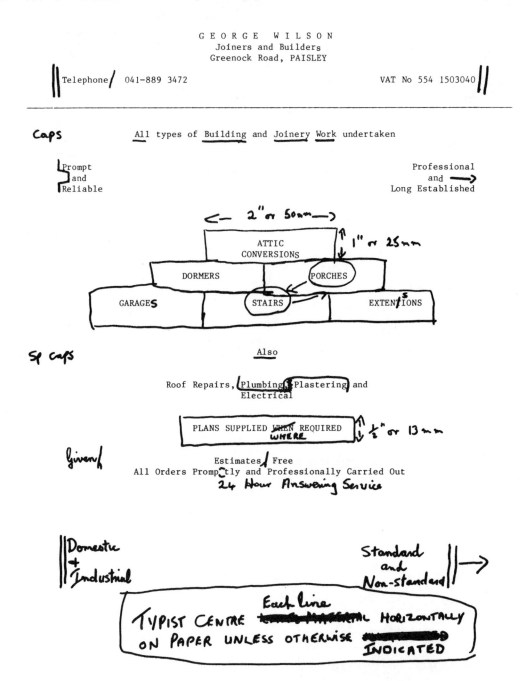

G E O R G E   W I L S O N
Joiners and Builders
Greenock Road, PAISLEY

Telephone/ 041-889 3472   VAT No 554 1503040

Caps

All types of <u>Building</u> and <u>Joinery</u> <u>Work</u> undertaken

Prompt
and
Reliable

Professional
and
Long Established

<- 2" or 50mm ->

1" or 25mm

ATTIC
CONVERSIONS

DORMERS

PORCHES

GARAGES

STAIRS

EXTENTIONS

Sp caps

<u>Also</u>

Roof Repairs, Plumbing, Plastering and
Electrical

PLANS SUPPLIED WHEN REQUIRED
WHERE

½" or 13 mm

Given

Estimates/ Free
All Orders Promptly and Professionally Carried Out
24 Hour Answering Service

Domestic
+
Industrial

Standard
and
Non-standard

TYPIST CENTRE Each line HORIZONTALLY
ON PAPER UNLESS OTHERWISE INDICATED

(SCOTBEC, Typewriting III, June 1984)

44

Question 13

PRAXI GROUP LIMITED

GROUP ENVIRONMENTAL COMMITTEE

Meeting to be held on Tuesday, 18 June 1985, at 1400 hrs
in the Small Committee Room, Head Office

A G E N D A

1 Apologies for absence.
2 Minutes of the last meeting held on Friday, 26 April 1985
   (previously circulated).
3 Matters arising from the minutes of the last meeting.
4 General progress report by the Chairman.
5 Untidy sites on the co's property: Report by Mr Rushie on

   5.1 Land to east of railway bridge, Stockley site.
   5.2 Land at the junction of Green Lane and main
        warehouse, Dursfield.
     5.3 Canal bank, Windsor Works, Borley.
6 Potential use of 5 hectares of land to the south
   of the staff car park on the McMurdo factory site
   —report by Miss Pradesh.
7 Landscaping of area surrounding the playing fields
   ~~and ablutions block~~ at the staff recreation ground
   —report by Mrs Gentry.
8 Tipping of rubbish by Konvic Plastics plc on land adjacent
   to the Head Office car park.
9 Selection of Cttee member to attend a ~~environmental studies~~
   conference in Los Angeles on 'Industrial
   Approaches to Environmental Care' in December '85.
10 Results of 'Keep it Tidy' campaign — report by
11 Mr Covak.

10 Proposed visit of staff from Tirot et Cie SA,
   Lyons.

12 (AOB.) in full

13 Date of next meeting.

B J DILLON
SECRETARY

To Mr W Armstrong
    Mr K Covak
    Mrs E Gentry
    Miss T Pradesh
    Mr K D Rushie
    Ms P Timming

Question 14 Please change paragraph headings to marginal (ie side) headings.

CAPS
→ (Minutes) of the ~~mtg~~ meeting of the Buying ~~Cttee~~ Committee held on 11 June 1984 at 1430 hrs at Praxiteles House, Adam St, London, WC2N 6AJ.

<u>Present</u> Mr W Connolly (Chairman)

(TYPIST: Type these 6 names in alphabetical order in one column)

Mr G Bayley   Mrs J Simpson
Mr J Harwood   Miss J Yates
Mr T Weirs   Mr P Stephens

1) APOLOGIES   There were no apologies for absence.

2) MINUTES   These had been circulated. They were approved & the Chairman signed them.

3) MATTERS ARISING   Mr Harwood reported that a decision on the purchasing of a Word Processor wd be reached before the next mtg. He was still awaiting the views of the Study Group.

lc 4) NEW PRODUCTS Advertising literature had been
modern/ received on / filing aids. It was hoped samples of these wd be available for consideration by the Cttee at the next mtg.

5) STORAGE It was suggested by Mr Weir that the storage space allocated to the Buying Cttee shd be extended. It was agreed that Mr Stephens wd report at the next mtg on what might be available.

7̶6̶) DATE OF NEXT MEETING   25 July 1984

8̶7̶) ANY OTHER BUSINESS Mr Bayley indicated his
additional/ wish to resign from this Cttee because of ⋀ departmental responsibilities. ~~That~~
run on stet He informed the Cttee that ~~subject~~ to the Cttee's approval, Mr Julian Sheppard had agreed to join the Cttee in his place. The Cttee agreed that Mr Sheppard shd attend the next
NP mtg. // Miss Yates informed the Cttee that she would be on holiday on the date of the next mtg.

6) BUDGET Mr Simpson reported that the
uc finance Cttee were considering increasing the allowance set aside for the
trs purchasing of ~~travel~~ samples of new products.

(RSA, Typewriting III, June 1984)

Question 15 Type the following Deed on plain A4 paper, leaving a left margin of 2″ (51 mm) minimum width. Do not insert any additional punctuation marks. Use double (or 1½) line spacing.

THIS DEED OF APPOINTMENT is made the [Leave space 2½″ (63mm)] day of July   One thousand nine hundred and eighty four BETWEEN FELICITY SARAH GREY of 92 Hillcrest Road Boston in the County of Lincolnshire and GERALD ERNEST FURNEAUX of 3 Charwell Row Boston aforesaid (hereinafter called "the Appointors") of the one part and WILLIAM HARVEY PURKISS of 3 Charwell Row Boston aforesaid Solicitor (hereinafter called "the New Trustee") of the other part

(1) This Deed is supplemental to the Will dated the Sixth day of August One thousand nine hundred and fifty three of (3 Almond Mews Boston) late of (ARTHUR JAMES GREY) [trs] aforesaid who died on the First day of August One thousand nine hundred and fifty six and whose said Will was proved in the Principal Probate Registry by the Appointors being the Executors therein named on the Thirtieth day of September One thousand nine hundred and fifty six

(2) The Appointors desire to appoint the New Trustee to be an additional trustee of the said Will

(3) The property subject to the trusts of the said Will consists of the property described in the Schedule hereto

(4) It is intended that the said investments described in the Schedule hereto shall forthwith be transferred into the names of the Appointors and the New Trustee

NOW THIS DEED WITNESSES that the Appointors in exercise of the power given by the Trustee Act 1925 [1928 stet] and of every other power enabling them hereby appoint the New Trustee to be a trustee of the testator's said Will and jointly with the Appointors IN WITNESS WHEREOF the parties hereto set their hands and seals the day and year first before written

SCHEDULE HEREINBEFORE REFERRED TO

(TYPIST — Insert list of Stocks and Shares written on next page at this point)

SIGNED SEALED AND DELIVERED)
by the said FELICITY SARAH)
GREY in the presence of   )   — [Single-line spacing as shown]

SIGNED SEALED AND DELIVERED)
by the said GERALD ERNEST)
FURNEAUX in the presence of)   —   "

SIGNED SEALED AND DELIVERED)
by the said WILLIAM HARVEY)
PURKISS in the presence of)   —   "

(Details to be typed after 'SCHEDULE HEREINBEFORE REFERRED TO': and before SIGNED SEALED — etc (FIGURES + DATES as shown))

£4690.75	12¼% Exchequer Stock 1986
£4500	10% Treasury Stock 1993
£2685.35	9½% Treasury Stock 1999
600	Strand Bank plc Ordinary £1 Shares
1300	Praxiteles Insurance plc Ordinary £1 Shares
1535	Worth Alliance Ordinary 33⅓ Pence Shares
3850	Adelphi Trust Special Bond Fund
5000	Imperial Oil 9% Convertible Unsecured Loan Stock 1995/2000

(Align these share titles please)

(RSA, Typewriting III, June 1984)

47

TYPE THE FOLLOWING WILL, ALL MATERIAL UNDERSCORED
HAS TO BE TYPED IN CLOSED CAPS. DO NOT INSERT ANY
EXTRA PUNCTUATION, + TYPE ALL ABBREVIATIONS IN FULL

I Miss Helen Littleton residing at 20 Windsor Avenue
Perth being desirous of settling the succession to my my
Means # and Estate Do Hereby Bequeath and
[Dispone]
Dispone the dwelling house owned by me at 15 Idcratio Street
to Miss Ann Grant residing of 12 Johnstone Street
Duncan

Perth and to Miss Margaret Grant residing at 12 Johnstone

Street aforesaid, equally between them or to the survivor
of them + I Bequeath and Dispone the whole Heritable
residue of my said Means + Estate Heritable Heritable
+ Moveable real + personal of whatsoever kind +
wheresoever situated together with the units titles +
uc
institutions thereof + together with also with any any
maugh   Estate over which I/have the power of disposal at the
the time of my decease equally among the said
Miss Ann Grant + Miss Margaret Grant + Miss Jean
Parker residing at 17 Broxburn Street Perth
uc of   or the survivors/the survivor of them; and I appoint
Miss   the said Miss Ann Grant/+ Miss Jean Parker my
Margaret
Grant   Executrices or the survivors or the survivor of them
my   Executrix; And I revoke all
Prior   testamentary writings; And I

consent to registration hereof for preservation;
In Witness hereof I the said Helen
Littleton have to this my will set my hand this
uc   day of
                  One thousand
nine hundred + eighty four.

Signed by the said Helen Littleton as
her last Will in the presence of us
both present at the same time who in
her presence + at her request + in the
presence of each other have
hereunto subscribed our names as
witness:-

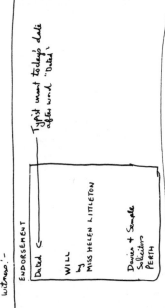

ENDORSEMENT

Dated

            WILL
              by
        MISS HELEN LITTLETON

        Davies + Semple
        Solicitors
        PERTH

* Typist leave sufficient space to insert relevant
information.

* Typist insert today's date
  after word "Dated"

D. TUTOR'S NOTES AND ANSWERS

This section gives some suggested notes and displays for the questions above. Except where explicit layout instructions have to be followed, the display shown is only *one* of the styles acceptable to the examiners.

1 Notes:

Follow the instructions for this letter and keep a consistent semi-blocked style. Decide whether you will use open or standard punctuation throughout. Insert the date and omit the words "Subject Heading". Keep date and number styles consistent. Inset the displayed portion as instructed — do not forget to return to your original margins to complete the letter.

Display:

SCOTTISH BUSINESS AGENCIES

22 GREAT KING STREET   EDINBURGH   EH3 6QH   Tel: 031-556 4691

```
Ref  RW/RHM

(date)

Mr. T. Davidson,
Manager,
Rover Travel Agency,
Highbridge Road,
STIRLING.
FK10 4EQ

Dear Mr. Davidson,

                    SALES CONFERENCE

     Further to our meeting yesterday, we are pleased to confirm the arrange-
ments and costs for the sales conference of Insurance Enterprises Ltd to be
held in our Castle Suite from 14 to 17 June 1984.

     The accommodation to be provided for the 50 delegates and their wives
will be double/twin bedded rooms with private bath/shower.  As agreed, our
special conference rates will apply and these are as follows:

     50 delegates at Residential Delegate charge
        of £29.10 each per day                          £4,365

     50 delegates' wives at Special charge
        of £22.00 each per day                          £3,300
                                                        _____

                                                        £7,665
                                                        ======

     These charges are inclusive of:

     VAT and service charge
     Hire of conference suite and facilities
     Bed and breakfast from 14 to 17 June
     Dinner - 14 and 15 June
     Special function - Dinner Dance - 16 June
     Morning coffees, lunches and afternoon teas for delegates

     We have noted that you wish the seating to be arranged in theatre
style; the 4 syndicate rooms will be used and equipment required will be
an overhead projector, cine projector, video recorder and television.
Nearer the time you will provide us with a list of the delegates so that
we can allocate rooms and prepare name tags.

     We look forward to receiving confirmation of this reservation.

                         Yours sincerely,


                         ROGER WYMAN,
                         Assistant Manager.
```

2 Notes:

As this is a personal letter and not in the usual business style, it is less formal than most letters you type and this is acceptable.

First, find and correct the grammatical (not spelling) errors before you start (there are three). Decide on layout and punctuation styles, while following all instructions for the display of the agenda and the minutes.

You should anticipate the need for a continuation sheet on a letter of this length, so make sure you finish page 1 at a logical point. Insert the required continuation sheet details and retain the margins used on page 1. Do not forget to indicate the enclosure.

Display:

```
                                    Stoodleigh
                                    Newton Avenue
                                    RUGBY  CV21 3XR

                                    25 June 1984


Mr L G Parker FRPS
6 Sandford Square
Newbold
RUGBY  CV21 3PS

Dear Leonard

Thanks for yours of 21 June and for reminding me that
you need to get the Agenda done soon in order to keep
within the Club's Rules.  Here are my ideas about the
Agenda - you may like to change them around.

        A G E N D A
        of General Meeting of Potter's Photographic Club
        Wednesday 11 July 1984

        1  Apologies

        2  Minutes of Meeting 18 April 1984

        3  Matters Arising

        4  Exhibition 8 September 1984: Final Plan

        5  Resignation of Darkroom Secretary

        6  Any Other Business

It is a great pity that Ken O'Regan is leaving us.  You
can rely on Mollie and me to make the presentation at
the end of the meeting.  The 'Thank You' card is enclosed,
suitably inscribed.

On reading the Minutes, I have decided to alter two or
three minor items as follows:

MINUTE                                        ACTION

4.3.1   It was agreed unanimously that the
        Exhibition would open at 1430 hours.
        Committee members would act as Stewards
        on a rota basis, to be agreed.            MDT

4.3.2   Security matters were discussed at length
        and a Sub-Committee was elected; subject   LMC
        to agreement.                              FLT
```

```
2

25 June 1984

Mr L G Parker FRPS

MINUTE                                        ACTION

6.1     Ms Kendall confirmed that the descrip-
        tion of the PRAXICAT should be amended
        to read:

        Filter size: 52 mm
        Lever: 138° angle
        Minimum focus: 0.6 m
        Price: £69.95 (complete)                 ALK

Perhaps Nicholas could check these items and take the
final draft into the Typing Agency next week.  He has
produced an excellent Newsletter and has helped the Club
in a variety of ways.  No doubt someone will propose a
vote of thanks.

I hope Gina has recovered from the twins' visit and will
be at the meeting next week.

Yours




Enc
```

3 Notes:

Read the instructions on this memo very carefully: many candidates misinterpreted them in the examination. Follow the style of the example, which is given to help you. Make a rough list or number the names for the order of typing, then check again before you start.

Keep punctuation consistent, including 2 spaces or a comma and 1 space after each surname. Allow equal spacing between columns as usual.

Display:

MEMORANDUM

From Mr T B Younger   *Ref*   TBY/JS

To Ms F Greenwood   *Date* 19 November 1984

CONFERENCE DELEGATES

I give below the list of conference delegates, as requested.

NAME	BRANCH	DEPARTMENT
Andrews, Mr A	Liverpool	Sales
Braun, Herr E	Frankfurt	Accounts
Coventry, Mrs A	Edinburgh	Buying
Donaghue, Mr S	Liverpool	Accounts
Duval, Mlle A	Paris	Personnel
Eversley, Miss Q	Liverpool	Buying
Gallagher, Mr W	Edinburgh	Sales
Gironde, Mme B	Paris	Sales
Hector, Mr E	Plymouth	General Office
Hôtesse, Mme J P	Amsterdam	Accounts
Kerry, Mrs P	Dublin	Personnel
McPherson, Miss L	Edinburgh	Sales
McPhie, Miss A	Liverpool	Buying
Molière, Mme K	Paris	Personnel
Morrison, Mr M	Manchester	Sales
Noakes, Miss A	Plymouth	Advertising
O'Donnelly, Miss A	Dublin	Sales
Pearce, Miss K	Manchester	Accounts
Revell, Ms W	Manchester	Personnel
Salisbury, Mr S W	Manchester	Advertising
Thornton, Mr W	Dublin	Accounts
Underwood, Ms B	Plymouth	Accounts
Vickery, Mrs Z	Liverpool	Personnel
Waters, Mrs A	Manchester	Buying
Wilkinson, Mr L	Manchester	Sales

4 Notes:

This requires the invitation to be displayed in centred style, plus the presentation of the tear-off slip. It is a "display attractively" question (referred to earlier in this chapter) which requires you to highlight the important points in the invitation, but do make sure you follow all the instructions exactly.

Before you start to type, calculate the vertical display of each part of the document, decide on the number of lines not used and divide them between top/bottom margins and before/after the tear-off line so that the whole document and each separate part are well-balanced.

Note the use of the 12-hour clock and use of footnotes.

As the use of capitals, underscore etc. is a personal decision, the tutor's suggested answer is only one of many acceptable presentations. question.

Display:

                    The Chairman and Directors of

                    GREENS and BENAKO COSMETICS

              request the pleasure of your company at the

         J O N K A I   A N D   H I S   S I L K   W O R L D   F A S H I O N   S H O W

              in celebration of the launch in Greens of the new

              BENAKO SILK COSMETICS AND JONKAI FASHION

                  Monday, 23 July, 10.30 for 11.00 am

              AT THE GRAND HOTEL, PICCADILLY, LONDON, W1

         10.30 am Coffee
         11.00 am Jonkai Fashion Presentation   ADMITTANCE BY TICKET ONLY

                  DEMONSTRATION OF BENAKO'S NEW SILK MAKE UP,
         BEKENAKI FLOWER ARRANGEMENT AND TRADITIONAL JAPANESE MUSIC

- -

         Mrs/Miss* ....

         Address ....

                 ....

         request** .... tickets to the Jonkai and his Silk World

         Fashion Show at the Grand Hotel at 10.30 am on Monday,

         23 July.

         *   Delete as applicable

         **   Please fill in the number of tickets you require and
              return this slip to Miss L M Johnson, 3 Winchester
              Studios, London Road, London W1C 3QJ. Your tickets
              are complimentary and will be sent to you by return.

5 Notes:

The instruction regarding margins should indicate to you that this may be a tight fit across the page, especially with Pica type.

As the columns are totalled, the figures must be aligned, so take great care with each number. Column spacing must be equal, but note the right-hand brackets which add to the width of some columns. Lines ruled in each column must be the same width, and line spacing above/below lines must be consistent. Calculate the vertical and horizontal displays before starting in order to get the best presentation on the page. Check all figures carefully before removing your work from the machine.

Display:

SUMMARY OF BALANCE SHEET AS AT 3¹ DECEMBER 1983

	1983		1982	
	£	£	£	£
ASSETS EMPLOYED				
Fixed Assets				
Housing Properties:				
Established Schemes	16,040.195		11,619,349	
Schemes in Progress	3,412,380		3,269,886	
		19,452,575		14,889,235
Less:				
Property Equity	217,642		247,434	
Housing Association				
Grant	11,003,830		6,955,104	
		11,221,472		7,202,538
Housing Properties		8,231,103		7.786,697
Office Furniture		3,231		2,131
		8,234,334		7,788,828
Current Assets				
Sundry Debtors	224,149		115,262	
Cash at Bank, in				
Hand and on Deposit	62,122		26,331	
	£286,271		£141,593	
Less:				
Current Liabilities				
Sundry Creditors	239,918		122,966	
Bank Overdrafts	60,280		256,866	
	£300,198		£379,832	
		(13,927)		(238,239)
		8,220,407		7,550,589
Less:				
Repairs and				
Renewals Provisions		332,823		231,538
		£7,887,584		£7,319,051

6   Notes: Again look through this carefully to ensure you follow all the instructions. While vertical ruling is shown, it must not be included and "centre headings" determines the style of the whole table. You need to find the expanded version of TPI and RPI before you can calculate your table.

The initial paragraphs make vertical centring more difficult, but it can be achieved if you practise them first, within the set margins.

Display:

```
                            PRICE  INDICES


        The index of retail prices for items for July 1983 was 336.5
   (January 1974 = 100).  This represents an increase of 4.2 per
   cent over the previous 12 months.

        The tax and price index (TPI) for July was 174.3 (January
   1978 = 100).  This represents an increase of 3.1 per cent over
   the previous 12 months.
```

MONTH	TAX AND PRICE INDEX		RETAIL PRICE INDEX	
	1982/3	% increase over 12 months	1982/3	% increase over 12 months
July	169.0	9.6	323.0	8.7
August	169.0	8.7	323.1	8.0
September	168.9	7.9	322.9	7.3
October	169.9	7.4	324.5	6.8
November	170.9	6.7	326.1	6.3
December	170.5	5.8	325.5	5.4
January	170.7	5.2	325.9	4.9
February	171.6	5.7	327.3	5.3
March	171.9	4.8	327.9	4.6
April	171.8	3.5	332.5	4.0
May	172.7	3.2	333.9	3.7
June	173.2	3.1	334.7	3.7
July	174.3	3.1	336.5	4.2

7 Notes:

There are three separate tables here and you are asked to keep to the style shown. You must check all the tables to find the column and table width and align them all, in blocked style, as shown. This means that spacing between columns will not be equal on all tables.

Be very careful when ruling to ensure that the lines are exactly as shown on the question.

Display:

ELECTRICAL EQUIPMENT

Insulated enclosures: Corrosion and impact resistant; also resistant to wide variation in temperature.

Reference	Dimensions		Price £
	External	Internal	
DOP 12	191 x 191 x 131	175 x 175 x 115	13.50
JET 15	281 x 191 x 131	265 x 168 x 115	15.25
RAM 19	381 x 191 x 131	366 x 168 x 115	17.50
ROB 23	560 x 281 x 131	536 x 258 x 115	18.75
CAN 27	560 x 380 x 181	536 x 357 x 165	22.00

Cable reeling units: Standard portable models. Automatic cable rewind after use. Fitted with 13 amp and 5 amp socket.

Reference	Cable length (mm)	Cable size	Price £
J 4265	15.25	0.75 3 core	63.00
M 3810	18.50	1.25 3 core	69.50
S 5119	27.75	1.25 3 core	77.25

Extension cable reels: Best quality 3 core cable, impervious to oil, grease, and water.

Reference	Cable length	Cable rating	Price £
D 2051	15 m	13A	12.50
F 3122	18 m	5A	25.25
H 3376	27 m	5A	41.00

8 Notes:

The table may be centred or blocked throughout — i.e. block or centre: To, From, vertical headings, and signs.

Allow equal spacing between columns, which you will notice are also equal in width. Note the spelling of Posttown. Retain 2nd in the footnote.

Rule carefully, avoiding the "From" heading area.

The display is presented in blocked style.

Display:

METROPOLITAN HOTELS LTD

SPECIAL WEEKEND BARGAIN BREAKS

PRICE LIST*

To	From						
	Eastwood	Westwood	Northgate	Southgate	Burnham	Welham	Middlescroft
	£	£	£	£	£	£	£
Newtown	27.50	30.50	28.30	–	28.10	24.90	23.10
Oldham	25.40	26.40	23.60	26.80	31.80	24.60	25.80
Posttown	24.60	24.20	22.40	27.40	32.20	25.20	26.40
Anytown[‡]	22.20	25.40	22.60	23.00	28.00	21.00	22.20
Hightown	25.00	27.00	23.60	21.80	26.20	22.60	20.60
Lowtown	27.30	–	25.30	30.10	34.70	28.30	29.30
Maincity	26.00	29.00	26.80	20.60	26.20	23.20	22.00

* Inclusive of 2nd class rail fare and hotel costs.

‡ No direct train service on Sundays.

9 Notes:

Diagonal (oblique) headings always make centring more difficult and require careful planning beforehand. Note that in this table the headings are wider than the columns (a point which must always be checked). Again, columns may be blocked or centred throughout. Rule before completing the diagonal headings. You will find it easier to align the start of the diagonal headings if you put a light pencil line across and remove it after typing, or draw a line on a backing sheet for guidance.

Vertical centring is not essential but can be done if you practise the paragraph beforehand, but this takes precious exam time.

Display:

FOR THE INVESTMENT-MINDED

The table shows the savings as a percentage of your annual cash outlay. It shows that the thinner your insulation is, the better the investment of topping it up.

Thickness of exist-ing insulation	Typical cost of additional 4" layer	Typical additional annual saving	Years to recover outlay	Annual savings as a percentage of outlay
0"	£67	£72	0.9	107%
1"	£67	£26	2.6	38%
2"	£67	£14	4.8	21%
3"	£67	£9	7.5	13%

10   Notes:

The instruction on margins again indicates a tight fit on A5 paper. Study the display carefully and you will see that you can treat it as follows.

The first box should be centred horizontally. The vertical boxes are treated just like vertical headings in a table. Then the final three boxes are an equal distance apart, centred across the page and under their relevant vertical sections. This is not as difficult as it sounds but needs careful calculation and planning.

The items in the vertical boxes must be blocked, so for consistency all the other boxed items should be blocked. Line spacing within the boxes must be consistent, with a clear line below the headings. You must not type close up to the lines and ruling must be accurate so check each line carefully (lines between boxes are frequently forgotten).

Display:

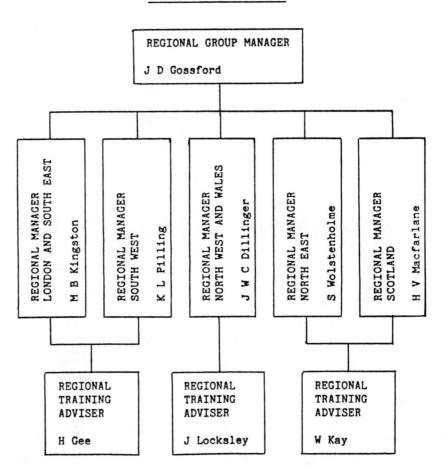

11 Notes:

The tutor's answer for this 4-page programme does not include a display of the front page, which consists of an accurately ruled square and a little typing carefully positioned as instructed. The display of pages 2 and 3 are shown. Ideally, these should be arranged to start and finish on the same line, with the margins as instructed. Consider the display of both pages before starting with page 2. On page 3 the address should be in single line spacing with the lines for completion in double spacing and all finishing at the same point.

Display:

CONFERENCES

The Beacon Hotel is situated on the banks of the River Ness and overlooks the castle. There are 80 double/ twin and 24 single bedrooms, all with private bath/ shower. The ground floor houses reception area, large lounge, dining room, cocktail bar and lounge bar. Bar meals are available from 1100 hours to 2000 hours in the lounge bar. On the first floor the residents' lounge provides a comfortable and relaxing atmosphere with beautiful views of the castle and surrounding area.

Inverness is accessible by road, rail and air from all parts of the country. There is a frequent train and coach service from major towns and cities and daily flights from London, Glasgow, Edinburgh and Aberdeen with connecting flights from other airports. By road, it is only a half-day's drive from Edinburgh or Glasgow.

Our Castle conference suite comprises a main room for up to 60 delegates, seated theatre style, plus 4 adjacent syndicate rooms. Facilities provided in the main room include a raised platform with screen, demonstration board and microphone, audio visual equipment (film and overhead projectors, video recorders, television) and the room is wired for closed circuit television.

Special rates are available for conferences.

If you are interested in holding your next conference at the Beacon Hotel, please complete the attached form and return it to us in the Freepost envelope provided.

To: Reservations Manager
The Beacon Hotel
INVERNESS

Tel: 0463 14682

We are interested in holding a conference at the Beacon Hotel and wish further particulars.

Name ....

Designation ....

Company ....

Address ....

....

Dates ....

Number of delegates ....

Special requirements ....

....

....

Signature ....

Date ....

12 Notes: This is an unusual document which should be considered in parts. It includes the letter heading, the justified sections, centred lines and the ruled boxes. Calculate the line spacing to be used throughout the document. Centre the information on the page and where instructed justify to the longest of the centred lines (which effectively forms the margins). Rule very carefully.

Display:

G E O R G E   W I L S O N
Joiners and Builders
Greenock Road, PAISLEY

Telephone   041-889 3472   VAT No   554 1503040

ALL types of BUILDING and JOINERY WORK undertaken

Prompt   Professional
and   and
Reliable   Long Established

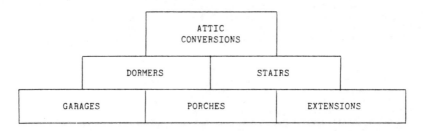

A L S O

Roof Repairs, Plastering, Plumbing and
Electrical

PLANS SUPPLIED WHERE REQUIRED

Estimates Given Free
All Orders Promptly and Professionally Carried Out
24 Hour Answering Service

Domestic   Standard
and   and
Industrial   Non-standard

13 Notes:

An agenda is a list of numbered points, so start by checking whether you need to allow space for typing double figures. Be consistent with punctuation style, i.e. after numbers, initials etc., but note that full stops are shown at the end of items. Item 2 1985 and Item 9 '85 must be typed in the same style. Keep the line spacing between items consistent and allow the normal space for signature.

Display:

PRAXI GROUP LIMITED

GROUP ENVIRONMENTAL COMMITTEE

Meeting to be held on Tuesday, 18 June 1985, at 1400 hrs
in the Small Committee Room, Head Office

A G E N D A

1   Apologies for absence.

2   Minutes of the last meeting held on Friday, 26 April 1985 (previously circulated).

3   Matters arising from the minutes of the last meeting.

4   General progress report by the Chairman.

5   Report by Mr Rushie on untidy sites on the company's property:

    5.1 Land to east of railway bridge, Stockley site.

    5.2 Land at the junction of Green Lane and main warehouse, Dursfield.

    5.3 Canal bank, Windsor Works, Borley.

6   Potential use of 5 hectares of land to the south of the staff car park on the McMurdo factory site - report by Miss Pradesh.

7   Landscaping of area surrounding the playing fields at the staff recreation ground - report by Mrs Gentry.

8   Tipping of rubbish by Korvic Plastics plc on land adjacent to the Head Office car park.

9   Selection of Committee member to attend a conference in Los Angeles on 'Industrial Approaches to Environmental Care' in December 1985.

10 Proposed visit of staff from Tirot et Cie SA, Lyons.

11 Results of 'Keep it Tidy' campaign - report by Mr Covak.

12 Any Other Business.

13 Date of next meeting.

B J DILLON
SECRETARY

To Mr W Armstrong   Miss T Pradesh
    Mr K Covak   Mr K D Rushie
    Mrs E Gentry   Ms P Timming

14 Notes: You need to change the style of these minutes to use side (marginal) headings, but keep the capital style. The word "Minutes" is the only one in capitals in the main heading.

Alphabetical order of names should be by surname, as usual, but it is not necessary to put the surname first in this list. Where the item numbers have brackets (one or a pair), they must be shown.

Display:

MINUTES of the meeting of the Buying Committee held on 11 June 1984 at 1430 hours at Praxiteles House Adam Street London WC2N 6AJ

Present   Mr W Connolly (Chairman)
           Mr G Bayley
           Mr J Harwood
           Mrs J Simpson
           Mr P Stephens
           Mr T Weirs
           Miss J Yates

1) APOLOGIES   There were no apologies for absence.

2) MINUTES   These had been circulated. They were approved and the Chairman signed them.

3) MATTERS ARISING   Mr Harwood reported that a decision on the purchasing of a Word Processor would be reached before the next meeting. He was still awaiting the views of the Study Group.

4) NEW PRODUCTS   Advertising literature had been received on modern filing aids. Ht was hoped samples of these would be available for consideration by the Committee at the next meeting.

5) STORAGE   It was suggested by Mr Weir that the storage space allocated to the Buying Committee should be extended. It was agreed that Mr Stephens would report at the next meeting on what might be available.

6) BUDGET   Mr Simpson reported that the Finance Committee were considering increasing the allowance set aside for the purchasing of trial samples of new products.

7) DATE OF NEXT   25 July 1984.
    MEETING

8) ANY OTHER BUSINESS   Mr Bayley indicated his wish to resign from this Committee because of additional departmental responsibilities. He informed the Committee that, subject to the Committee's approval, Mr Julian Sheppard had agreed to join the Committee in his place. The Committee agreed that Mr Sheppard should attend the next meeting.

                           Miss Yates informed the Committee that she would be on holiday on the date of the next meeting.

15   Notes: Legal documents have distinctive style and wording. You have several instructions concerning the style, so measure your left margin and space on the first line accurately. Follow punctuation and capitalisation exactly.

The date 1925 (line 25) must remain in figures as part of the title of the Act — consistency with other dates is less important here.

The final three attestation clauses should not extend beyond the mid-point of your typing line.

A continuation sheet is clearly needed and should be numbered. The body of the document should extend to the second page, so that the signature clauses are not separated from the content of the document. You must, therefore, be careful when deciding on your page division.

Display:

THIS DEED OF APPOINTMENT is made the

         day of July One thousand nine hundred and

eighty four BETWEEN FELICITY SARAH GREY of 92

Hillcrest Road Boston in the County of Lincolnshire

and GERALD ERNEST FURNEAUX of 3 Charwell Row Boston

aforesaid (hereinafter called "the Appointors") of

the one part and WILLIAM HARVEY PURKISS of 3

Charwell Row Boston aforesaid Solicitor (hereinafter

called "the New Trustee") of the other part

(1) This Deed is supplemental to the Will dated

the Sixth day of August One thousand nine hundred

and fifty three of ARTHUR JAMES GREY late of 3

Almond Mews Boston aforesaid who died on the First

day of August One thousand nine hundred and fifty

six and whose said Will was proved in the Principal

Probate Registry by the Appointors being the

Executors therein named on the Thirtieth day of

September One thousand nine hundred and fifty six

(2) The Appointors desire to appoint the New

Trustee to be an additional trustee of the said

Will

(3) The property subject to the trusts of the said

Will consists of the property described in the

Schedule hereto

(4) It is intended that the said investments

described in the Schedule hereto shall forthwith be

transferred into the names of the Appointors and

the New Trustee

2

NOW THIS DEED WITNESSES that the Appointors in

exercise of the power given by the Trustee Act 1925

and of every other power enabling them hereby

appoint the New Trustee to be a trustee of the

testator's said Will and jointly with the Appointors

IN WITNESS WHEREOF the parties hereto set their

hands and seals the day and year first before

 ritten

 CHEDULE HEREINBEFORE REFERRED TO

 4690.75   12½% Exchequer Stock 1986

£4500   10% Treasury Stock 1993

£2685.35   9½% Treasury Stock 1999

600   Strand Bank plc Ordinary £1 Shares

1300   Praxiteles Insurance plc Ordinary £1

           Shares

1535   Worth Alliance Ordinary 33½ Pence Shares

3850   Adelphi Trust Special Bond Fund

5000   Imperial Oil 9% Convertible Unsecured

           Loan Stock 1995/2000

SIGNED SEALED AND   )
DELIVERED by the said   )
FELICITY SARAH GREY in)
the presence of   )

SIGNED SEALED AND   )
DELIVERED by the said   )
GERALD ERNEST FURNEAUX)
in the presence of   )

SIGNED SEALED AND   )
DELIVERED by the said   )
WILLIAM HARVEY PURKISS)
in the presence of   )

18 Notes:

This question does not give as many instructions as question 16 so you would need to be familiar with the style of legal documents. They are usually typed in double-line spacing with a wide left margin of 38 or 51 mm, but the final clause should be single spaced.

You also need to know how to endorse a document. Fold your document in half vertically before typing the endorsement on the front.

Display:

Dated   22 March 1984

WILL

by

MISS HELEN LITTLETON

Davies & Semple
Solicitors
PERTH

I MISS HELEN LITTLETON residing at 20 Windsor Avenue Perth being desirous of settling the succession to my Means and Estate DO HEREBY BEQUEATH and DISPONE the dwelling house owned by me at 15 Horatio Street Dunoon to MISS ANN GRANT residing at 12 Johnstone Street Perth and to MISS MARGARET GRANT residing at 12 Johnstone Street aforesaid, equally between them or to the survivor of them and I BEQUEATH and DISPONE the whole residue of my said Means and Estate Heritable and Moveable real and personal of whatsoever kind and wheresoever situated together with the Writs Titles and instructions thereof and together also with any Estate over which I may have the power of disposal at the time of my decease equally among the said Miss Ann Grant and Miss Margaret Grant and Miss Jean Parker residing at 16 Broxburn Street Perth or the survivors or the survivor of them; And I appoint the said Miss Ann Grant Miss Margaret Grant and Miss Jean Parker my Executrices or the survivors or the survivor of them my Executrix; And I revoke all prior testamentary writings; And I consent to registration hereof for preservation; IN WITNESS hereof I the said HELEN LITTLETON have to this my Will set my hand this

       day of   One thousand

nine hundred and eighty-four.

SIGNED by the said HELEN)
LITTLETON as her Last Will)
in the presence of us both)
present at the same time)
who in her presence at her)
request and in the   )
presence of each other   )
have hereunto subscribed)
our names as witness:-

E. COURSE WORK – A STEP FURTHER

This chapter has been designed to help you to be successful in any examination which includes typewriting. It is not intended to replace your textbook or teacher, but rather to increase your awareness of the content of the examinations and of the best methods you can use in preparing for them.

To be a competent typist you should be able to adapt to all kinds of equipment, and therefore you should use the different machines available in the college. Employers often do not appreciate the problems of changing from one kind of typewriter to another and expect you to be equally able to work with them all. You may be required to take a test at an interview and could be faced with anything from an old manual to the latest electronic machine.

Visits to office equipment shops and exhibitions, either local or national, will help you to keep up with the developments and to try the full range of equipment available.

Typewriting is an extremely useful skill and forms a part of numerous office jobs – clerical, secretarial and administrative. A good qualification can help to secure a wide variety of posts, depending on your age, ability, experience and ambition. Some top students, holding advanced certificates or a group qualification, start with a secretarial post and then progress to a very responsible personnel, supervisory or administrative position. An advanced certificate can be the basis of further training, such as the teaching certificates of the RSA or Joint Examining Board or a full-time teaching course.

FURTHER READING

Past examination papers and copies of all the syllabuses may be purchased from the boards (see p. 2–3 for addresses).

There are many textbooks for typewriting at all stages and you will need to use one which covers the whole of the syllabus you are following. The most commonly used in colleges are:
Typing First Course, Drummond & Scattergood. McGraw-Hill
Applied Typing, Drummond & Scattergood. McGraw-Hill
Universal Typing Series, Edith MacKay, Pitman
Typewriting exercises are also included in the Monthly *Memo, 2000* and *Teeline* magazines.

Within this series of *Exam Guides* there are several other secretarial books especially the *Business Communication* and *Office Practice and Secretarial Administration* titles.

Chapter 4   Shorthand

A. GETTING STARTED

It is possible to learn a variety of shorthand or speedwriting systems. Shorthand uses symbols to represent the words phonetically, and *Pitman* and *Gregg* are the most common systems in the English-speaking world. It is generally easier to achieve high speeds with shorthand rather than with the alphabetically-based systems of speedwriting, but the major advantage of speedwriting systems is the short time in which they can be learned. *Teeline* is becoming very popular and is really a combination of the two. It is based on the alphabet, is quick to learn and produces accurate transcriptions. It is also possible to use a machine to take dictation. This is called stenotyping and is often used for Court work because speeds of 200 wpm plus can quite easily be achieved. However, the machines are expensive and few colleges offer tuition on them. Data writers have been developed from these, using micro-processors to automatically display work on a word processor screen in order to edit.

Anyone setting out on a shorthand course will need a quick mind, a good standard of English and also determination and motivation. A good shorthand writer needs to recall outlines and recognise vocabulary, have the ability to retain words while listening to others, and to work under pressure.

As with most skills, it is important to begin with the right tools. You will require either a shorthand pen or soft pencil for taking notes. For some systems of shorthand a ball-point pen may be suitable, but an ink pen is ideal for those systems which require both thin and thick lines to be written, and high-speed shorthand writers usually recommend them. It may take a little time to get used to the technique of writing with a pen but, whatever you use, you must use the minimum pressure possible as this will help you to achieve high speeds.

The quality of your notepad is also important. You will require a lined pad of paper over which your pen or pencil will glide easily. You should avoid cheap absorbent paper. A shorthand notebook is also designed to make it easy to turn over the pages while writing, and a spiral-bound pad will help the paper to lie flat.

As well as your chosen textbook, a shorthand dictionary will be useful, as will a small notebook for revision purposes, into which you can enter phrases and short forms as you encounter them. Even the position you adopt when writing is important in order to avoid fatigue. If possible, rest your pad on a desk and have both feet on the floor with your back well supported. The arm you are not using for writing should be placed on the desk to take your weight.

Establish good writing habits at the outset and this will facilitate reading back your notes. The need for neat, accurate shorthand cannot be over-emphasised. Your notes should be of consistent size, but do not *draw* the outlines, rather let the pen flow lightly over the page. You may find it useful to rule a margin on the left-hand side of the page for additions or alterations. Some people find they can achieve higher speeds by ruling a line down the centre of the page and using the left-hand column first and then the right; it is suggested that this method reduces the movement of the hand across the page. This is, of course, a matter of personal choice. Always try to adopt a similar format for your notes, i.e. put addresses or instructions regarding the number of copies in the same position at the start of a piece of work. This could help you to avoid missing any vital instructions as you will immediately know where to look for them. A line at the end of a piece of work to separate it from the next is a good idea and a light line drawn diagonally through your notes after they have been transcribed will save any confusion. The date at the beginning of each day's notes will also help to locate a piece of work if there should be a query about it.

Table 4.1 shows the format of the various shorthand examinations available.

Table 4.1 Single subject examinations — format and content for shorthand examinations

Examining board: London Chamber of Commerce and Industry (LCCI)

Title	Level	Transcription Time	Format and Regulations
General information:	*Dictionaries are allowed*		
	Not all examinations offered at each series		
	(*wpm — words per minute)		
Shorthand English/ French/ German/ Spanish	50/60 wpm*	28/34 mins	4 min passage at each speed, 1 passage only to be transcribed.
Shorthand English/ French/ German/ Spanish	70/80/90/ 100 wpm	40/57 mins	4 min passage at each speed, 1 passage only to be transcribed. Endorsed certificate for typed transcript.
Shorthand English/ French	110/120/130/ 140/150 wpm (no 140 wpm French)	78/107 mins	1 passage of 3 mins and 1 of 2 mins at each speed, 1 speed only to be transcribed. Endorsed certificate for typed transcript.

Examining board: Pitman Examinations Institute (PEI)

Title	Level	Transcription Time	Format and Regulations
General information:	*Only Pitman systems accepted — no longhand or mixture of systems allowed. 1 or 2 speeds may be submitted on payment of additional fee. Transcripts must be in ink or typewritten. 3% error tolerance.*		
	(*spm — syllables per minute)		
Shorthand	50/60/70 wpm	30 mins	3 mins dictation at each speed. Business letter or passage of business or general interest.
Shorthand	80/90 wpm	50 mins	1 passage of 2 mins, 1 of 3 mins at each speed. Letter or passage of business, general or social nature.

Table 4.1 continued

Title	Level	Transcription Time	Format and Regulations
Shorthand	100/110/120/ 130/140/150/ 160/170/180/ 190 wpm	60 mins at 100 + 6 mins for each additional 10 wpm	2 passages of 3 mins each. Letter or passage of general, business, literary or political nature.
Shorthand	200 wpm +		By special arrangement with the Institute.
Shorthand theory	Stage I	Length of exam − 45 mins	95% accuracy required. New Era only − theory tested up to Ch. 15 of New Course, Ch. 22 of Commercial Course, Ch. 27 of Modern Course, Ch. 29 of Instructor, Ch. 27 of Modern Course and Chs 1 to 23 and part of Ch. 29 of Instructor. Theory or dictation approach.
Shorthand theory	Stage II	Length of exam − 45 mins	Entire theory − New Era and Pitman 2000. Theory or dictation approach.
French shorthand	70/85/100 spm*	50 mins + 5 mins reading time	4 mins dictation consisting of 2 passages (max. 2.5 mins) − at least 1 business letter. Transcription must be typewritten but accents may be added in ink. 80 marks for transcription, 20 for typing. Pass marks 70 and 16. Dictionaries allowed.
Legal shorthand	80/90/100/ 110/120 wpm	50/72 mins	2 passages at each speed (max. 3 mins). Letters, case notes, summaries or reports of legal nature.
Legal shorthand	130 wpm +		By special arrangement with the Institute.

Title	Level	Transcription Time	Format and Regulations
Shorthand for journalists	100/110/120/ 130/140/150 wpm	40 mins at 100 + additional 4 mins for each 10 wpm	4 min continuous passage in field of journalism.
Medical shorthand	80/90/100/ 110/120 wpm	50/72 mins + 5 mins reading time after dictation	2 passages (max. 3 mins). Material includes letters, case notes, summaries and reports of medical nature. Dictionaries allowed at 100 wpm +.
Medical shorthand	130 wpm +		By special arrangement with the Institute.
Systematic notetaking		Length of exam — 60 mins	Dictionaries allowed. 520 words dictated in 4 mins. Verbatim notes not required but shorthand advisable. Candidates to provide heading and sub-headings and reduce passage to one-third as a summary. Verbatim notes will result in disqualification.
Typewriting transcription (shorthand based)		27 mins max.	200 words dictated at 80 wpm + 200 words of prepared shorthand for transcription within allowed time.

Table 4.1 continued

Examining board:	**Royal Society of Arts (RSA)**

General information:	Dictionaries are allowed. All examinations begin with a warm-up passage which is not transcribed. All transcriptions must be in ink or typewritten. Not all examinations offered at each series. (*nwpm — notional words per minute i.e. passages are based on a syllabic content of 1.4 per word. A 3 min passage at 50 wpm may not therefore comprise 150 words but slightly more or less — hence the term 'notional'.)

Title	Level	Transcription Time	Format and Regulations
Shorthand	80/100 wpm	80/90 mins (45 mins for typewritten transcription)	2 or 3 passages at each speed. 1 speed only to be transcribed. Total dictation — 8 mins.
Shorthand	120/130/140 wpm	100/110 mins (45/50 mins for typewritten transcription)	2 or 3 passages (max. 4 mins) at each speed. 1 speed only to be transcribed. Total dictation — 8 mins.
Shorthand transcription	Stage I — 50/60/70 nwpm*. Stage II — 80/90/100 nwpm. Stage III — 110/120/130 nwpm	60 mins	3 mins 'core' passage at irregular speed plus 3 mins at chosen speed. Up to 100 may be handwritten or typed, speeds over 100 must be typewritten. Recording supplied by RSA. Word processors may be used on application. 3 elements to be passed in each passage 1. completion of task, 2. acceptable standard of accuracy, 3. acceptable presentation.
Medical shorthand	80/100/120 wpm	80/100 mins (50/60 mins for typed transcript)	Total dictation — 8 mins, passages not exceeding 2 mins at 80, 3 mins at 100 and 4 mins at 120.

Title	Level	Transcription Time	Format and Regulations
Shorthand in a foreign language (French/ German)	80/100 spm	80 mins	2 letters of 3 mins. Transcription must be typewritten.

Examining board:	**Scottish Business Education Council (SCOTBEC)**

General information:	*Dictionaries are allowed. All examinations begin with a warm-up passage which is not transcribed. Transcripts must be typewritten — 85 marks allocated to transcription, 15 to typing. Only 1 speed to be submitted. Not all speeds offered at each series.*

Title	Level	Transcription Time	Format and Regulations
Shorthand	60/70 wpm	60 mins	3 passages (max. 3 mins) at each speed. Total dictation — 6 mins.
Shorthand	80/90/100 wpm	70 mins	3 passages (max. 3 mins) at each speed. Total dictation — 7 mins.
Shorthand	110/120/130/ 140/150/160 wpm	80 mins	3 passages (max. 4 mins) at each speed. Total dictation — 8 mins.

Examining board:	**Scottish Examination Board**

General information:	*Dictionaries are allowed. No alterations allowed to original shorthand notes. Transcription must be typewritten. All examinations begin with warm-up passage which is not transcribed. Only 1 speed may be submitted.*

Title	Level	Transcription Time	Format and Regulations
Shorthand	60/70/80/90 wpm (optional paper for Sec Studies O level)	75 mins	2 passages of 3 mins at each speed.

Table 4.1 continued

Title	Level	Transcription Time	Format and Regulations
Shorthand	100/110/120 wpm (optional paper for Sec Studies – Cert of 6th Form Studies)	70/75 mins	2 passages of 3 mins at each speed.

Examining board: **Teeline Education Limited**

General information: *96% accuracy required. Distinction awarded for 99/100%. Dictionaries are allowed.*

Title	Level	Transcription Time	Format and Regulations
Teeline	50/60/70/ 80/90/100/ 110/120/ 130/140 wpm	30/38 mins 47/55 mins 64/68 mins 72/76 mins	3 passages of 2 mins at each speed, 2 of the 3 passages to be transcribed. Longhand in the notes will be penalised.

Examining board: **Various regional boards**

Title	Level	Transcription Time	Format and Regulations
Shorthand	Stages I, II and III		On application to the Boards.

Examining board: **Welsh Joint Education Council**

General information: *Dictionaries are allowed. All examinations begin with warm-up passage which is not transcribed. Transcriptions must be handwritten in ink or typewritten.*

Title	Level	Transcription Time	Format and Regulations
Shorthand (English/ Welsh)	40/50/60 wpm	50/60 mins (40/50 mins for typed transcription)	2 passages of 3 mins.
Shorthand (English/ Welsh)	70/80/90/100/ 110/120/130 wpm	90/125 mins (70/90 for typed transcription)	3 passages – max. 3 mins up to 110, 4 mins at 120/130 wpm. Total dictation – 8 mins.

B. ESSENTIAL PRINCIPLES

This section gives advice on the essential principles for success in various types of shorthand examination and is divided into the following:

1. Shorthand theory examinations.
2. Shorthand speed examinations.
3. Shorthand in a foreign language.
4. Specialised shorthand (legal, medical, journalism).
5. Miscellaneous examinations (transcription speed test, systematic notetaking).

The next section (C) then consists of recent examination questions for you to attempt, preferably by enlisting the help of a friend so that they can be dictated unseen. Notes and answers are then presented to these questions in section D.

1. SHORTHAND THEORY EXAMINATIONS

The *Pitman Examinations Institute* is the only board offering this type of examination and obviously the emphasis is on accuracy and a high standard of penmanship rather than on speed. The Stage I examination is only for New Era shorthand and is really just a progress test which follows the same form as Stage II but does not include all the theory (see Table 4.1). The Stage II examination may be taken in New Era or Pitman 2000. You may choose to take a written paper which requires the transcription of 50 selected words from longhand into shorthand which should be freely vocalised, plus a written passage of 150 words to be put into shorthand. Alternatively, you may choose the dictation approach examination which consists of a passage of approximately 120 words dictated in 3 minutes, 10 shorthand outlines together with their meaning, which must be placed in the correct position in relation to a line and have at least one vowel sign added, and a shorthand passage to be transcribed into longhand.

To be successful you will need to study your textbook carefully chapter by chapter. If possible, use a book with a key which will give you both the text and the shorthand for each passage. You can then practise writing your notes from the text and check that your outlines are correct. Any mistakes should be written out again, and used as a drill until you can write them automatically. Ideally, you should then take the passage down from dictation, perhaps waiting a day or two, just to make sure nothing has been forgotten. No two people learn in the same way or at the same speed, and you must ensure that one rule is learned before proceeding to the next unit of your book, and short forms should be learned thoroughly as you go along.

If you work through the book in this way, your theory should be as near perfect as possible. Don't be tempted to miss out exercises: they are all designed to help you and should all be attempted. Repetition is the only way to achieve accuracy and you should expect to be tested on a wide range of theory. If you are using one particular textbook in class, you may find it helpful to work from a different one at home. Sometimes something explained in a slightly different way will clarify a point for you.

Another good way to improve your theory and penmanship is to practise copying from written shorthand; drill books are ideal for this. Reading from printed shorthand will also help you and you should do this frequently. After attempting the examination questions in the next section, compare your results in the two types of examination and decide which you prefer. Your centre should be able to give you the option of taking either.

2 SHORTHAND SPEED EXAMINATIONS

Preparation

Shorthand is not a subject that can easily be self-taught and it is also difficult to improve your speed without the discipline of class tuition. However, with the use of a cassette recorder, a stop watch and some determination, it can be done. Whether you are trying to work alone or attending a full-time college course, there are various things you should do in order to be successful in a shorthand examination.

(a) Ensure that you have a thorough grounding in the shorthand theory

Revise from your textbook, taking extra time over any particular aspect which you find difficult. It is helpful to have a book with a key. You can then practise either transcribing or reading from the written shorthand, or put the passages into shorthand yourself from the text. In either case you can then carefully check your work and concentrate on the outlines which caused you trouble. Test yourself on any short forms in each chapter until you are sure you know them perfectly.

(b) Practice taking dictation and transcribing it from a variety of sources

It is probably easier at lower speeds to work from timed readings and you will have had plenty of practice with these if you are attending classes. Most schools and colleges will also lend out cassettes to supplement your class work, and you should prepare your own if working alone. Try to take down the passage at the first hearing. In class you will probably have prepared certain words and phrases before a passage is dictated, but make sure you are also confident at taking down unprepared passages. After the first hearing, check your work carefully and practise writing any words that you did not know. Continue playing the cassette over and over again, gradually building up your speed and accuracy until you are writing it with ease. In *Pitman* shorthand, try to only insert essential vowels, as writing too many will slow you down. If your position writing is accurate, you should not need many vowel signs. Some practice every day is also important and will be more rewarding than a long burst once a week.

It is also a good idea to work on passages which are longer than those you are likely to be given in the examination. This will improve your stamina for writing and help you over the notoriously difficult middle portion of a passage. You should also practise turning over the pages of your shorthand notebook quickly and quietly during dictation so that precious seconds may be saved. The best way to do this is to gradually slide the page you are writing on upwards from the left-hand corner. You will then be in a position to start writing on the first line of the next page as you finish on the last line of the page you are using.

At higher speeds, news broadcasts, party political speeches etc. on the radio or television are useful additional practice, especially if you can record them in order to check your transcription. Even taking down personal telephone messages or writing out your shopping list in shorthand will help you. Use shorthand at every opportunity. In any spare moment, write down a sentence or list of words at random. Put the words into correct shorthand and use these as a drill to write them accurately again and again, faster and faster. If one of these words then appears in an examination passage, it will be written automatically, thus helping your speed.

(c) Study any literature in the shorthand system you are studying	This will improve your theory and phrasing and expand your vocabulary, much as it would if you were learning a foreign language. By reading *printed* shorthand, a student's speed in *written* shorthand can improve. If an outline is familiar to you, you will write it faster, so it is important to practise reading fluently from printed shorthand. This can be an enjoyment rather than a chore, as several excellent novels are available in shorthand for bedtime reading.
(d) Read a good English grammar textbook	So often a candidate's inability to write correct English means the difference between passing and failing a shorthand examination. Section E at the end of this chapter gives some suggested texts for improving your English presentation.
(e) Become familiar with business terminology	You should ensure that you are familiar with business terminology. In whichever field you choose to work there are various topics such as company reports, insurance matters etc. which are bound to crop up, and these are all favourite topics for shorthand examinations. Reading the financial section of the newspaper will help you gain this information. You should also be aware of the various documents, office equipment and procedures used in the office. The wider your knowledge of business affairs, the more sense you will be able to make of the dictation and the easier you will find it.

If you prepare thoroughly for the examination, you will be able to approach it with confidence. A shorthand examination is rather unique in that you only have one chance to take down the spoken word and so a calm, confident approach is essential. Only attempt a speed that is within your capabilities, but remember that it is important to be able to write at higher speeds for short periods. Then you do not need to panic if you feel you are being left behind. Keep the words in mind, speed up your writing, and you should easily catch up by the end of the sentence. Do not worry either if your outlines are not absolutely perfect. You are being tested on your ability to *transcribe* accurately and if you can read back the occasional dubious outline you will not be penalised.

The examinations at lower speeds will tend to use the 700 common words. You will not be required to write long, complicated sentences, but vocabulary and sentence structure will become progressively harder at higher speeds. To achieve higher speeds you must, where this is applicable, make full use of short forms, intersections and phrasing.

The new RSA shorthand/transcription examination is designed to be more realistic and to raise standards especially at lower speeds. Stage I aims to give students an idea of what to expect from a shorthand examination and is only a first step in becoming a competent shorthand writer. The common 'core' passage is dictated at an average speed of approximately 55 wpm and so a candidate who can only just take dictation at 50 wpm will struggle and ideally students should be able to tackle passages at 60 to 65 wpm before attempting this examination. The same applies at Stages II and III.

Before the dictation

If you have a few minute to wait before the examination begins, write out a few drills and practise them to loosen up your hand and to help you to relax. Listen carefully to any instructions given by the reader, and make sure that you follow the instructions on the answer paper. It may be important that you do not transcribe passages at different speeds or forget to cross out passages that you do not want marked. A transcription could be ignored if written in pencil when the instructions state ink, so do go prepared with plenty of spare pens and pencils.

During the examination

It is important to concentrate and to remove all other thoughts from your mind. This does not mean that you should listen to each word in isolation, however. It is essential to understand the *sense* of the passage being dictated and this is one of the secrets of a good transcription. If you have fully understood the passage, you will not make foolish errors and you will be able to make intelligent guesses if you do have a gap in your notes. Do remember that an incorrect outline is probably better than no outline at all, as otherwise you may not be sure how many words are missing.

However hard-pressed you are during the dictation, always insert full stops. The person reading will undoubtedly drop their voice at the end of a sentence and it is imperative that you write it down. You will find that most examination passages could be read in one of two ways, depending on where the full stop is inserted. Other punctuation should not be written at this stage, but inserted during transcription. If you do have ample time, a slightly larger space than usual between outlines could indicate a comma, parenthesis, etc. The examiner will expect to be able to see the logic of your punctuation and this goes for paragraphing too.

Always take care when writing "a" or "the" in your notes. Many students seem to guess at which to use, but it is essential that you use the correct word if you want to avoid losing marks. Similarly, you should take particular care with your word endings, e.g. price and prices.

Sometimes you may realise that you have written something incorrectly in your notes. Try to rectify this immediately rather than rely on your memory, as this may prove unreliable. Either circle the incorrect notes and re-write (if necessary in the margin) or, where appropriate, place a vowel sign to avoid confusion when transcribing. If your system of shorthand has similar outlines for two words, make sure you know how to differentiate between them.

It is very often the small words that let candidates down when transcribing, so although difficult at speed, do make an effort to take extra care over such words as:

of off for on at in has is it but who with that to
too or your out our no not.

The transcription	Take your time when transcribing, whether by hand or on the typewriter. You will find you have plenty of time for the transcription *and* for reading through the finished passage. If the transcription is handwritten, try to make it as neat as possible. In particular, clearly differentiate between upper- and lower-case letters, since many styles of handwriting do not make the difference obvious. The examiner will not spend time trying to decipher a squiggle, and letters written to look like either an "a" or an "e" will be counted as wrong. Eventually the new RSA shorthand transcription examination will have to be typewritten at Stages II and III but there will still be the option to hand write at Stage I. A handwritten transcription must, however, be presented in a similar way to a typed transcript, i.e. well laid out, with no obvious corrections or alterations and paragraphs and punctuation clearly shown. Correcting fluid could be used but a correcting biro will produce the neatest work. When transcribing, there are many things you should bear in mind.
(a) Spelling	In those examinations where dictionaries are allowed, there is little excuse for spelling errors, so expect to be penalised stringently. Do not be tempted to guess − always look a word up if in any doubt. Occasionally, however, a dictionary will not help, for example, when you have no idea how to begin spelling a word. Also, a dictionary may not be permitted in your examination, in which case you should obtain the list of 200 words compiled by PEI which are commonly mis-spelled and which occur frequently in examination passages. The 40 words which show the *highest error frequency* are given overleaf, plus a few additional words which candidates seem to find difficult.
Note:	Although "enquiry" and "inquiry" are given as correct in most dictionaries, "enquiry" is usually the form that will be dictated and seems to be the modern acceptable version. You would be well advised to use this form. There are also many words which are frequently muddled or are *homophones*. Again, either check in your dictionary for the correct spelling or make sure you are aware of the differences between such trap words. Some additional examples are given in Chapter 6 − Audio Typewriting.

accommodate
accommodation
acquaintance
acquainted
acquire
acquisition

beginning
believed

certainly
coming
conscious
correspondence
correspondent

definite
disappointed

especially
expenses
extremely

friend

immediately
independent

losing
lying

necessary
unnecessary
noticeable

occasion
occasional-ly
occasioned
occurred

planning
precede
preceding
privilege

referred
reference

scarcely
secretaries
separate
separately
sincerely
surprising

transferred
transference

truly

undoubtedly
usually

valuable
view

adviser
bankruptcies
buffet
catalogue
develop-ment
dialled
enrol
foresee
initiative
leisure
recurrence
shrewd
voucher
warehouse

accept/except
affect/effect
advice/advise
allusion/illusion
bare/bear
born/borne
capital/capitol
check/cheque
choose/chose
council/counsel
draw/drawer (especially
chest of drawers)
ensure/insure
extensive/intensive
impassable/impassible (especially
medical students)

impressed/imprest
manner/manor
meter/metre
passed/past
pear/pair/pare
peace/piece
practice/practise
principal/principle
program/programme
role/roll
sight/site/cite
sole/soul
some/sum
their/there

(b) Separate/combined words	Other words are often written separately when they should be combined, or are incorrectly combined. You should be familiar with the following:

Separate words	Combined	Hyphenated
at least	anyone	by-law
every day	commonplace	part-time
in spite of	copyright	reply-paid
per cent	everything	time-table
thank you	farewell	up-to-date
	forthcoming	
	loudspeaker	
	overdue	
	payroll	
	percentage	
	turnover	
	whatsoever	
	worthwhile	

(c) Abbreviations

Apart from the commonly-accepted abbreviations such as Mr and Mrs, Dr and etc, and when writing sums of money or the date in figures rather than words, it is probably safer to write everything else in full. You should not be penalised for doing this but could lose marks if you abbreviate something that the examiner wishes to be written in full.

(d) English grammar

Perhaps the most common mistake in written English is the use of the apostrophe. You can be almost certain that one or more will be needed in your examination passage, so don't just ignore them. Make sure you have really mastered their use with the aid of your grammar book. Other weaknesses include the use of hyphens and question marks. The omission of the latter is often just carelessness. There is often confusion too about when to use capital letters. If in doubt it is better to use a capital letter. You will be penalised for omitting them but not for additional use of capitals as long as they are used sensibly, e.g. Bank Manager and Head Office would be accepted, even if not required by the examiner.

The RSA shorthand/transcription examination gives punctuation and paragraphs during the dictation at Stage I but candidates at Stage II and III must insert their own.

If you do have a gap in your notes or you cannot read an outline, do not alter other words in an attempt to make sense of the passage. This could incur further penalties. It is better just to leave a space in your transcription in the hope that you may be inspired to insert the correct word when you read through the finished passage.

Finally, proof-reading is essential for ensuring that the passage makes sense and that you have not omitted words or lines. Check against your shorthand notes, making sure that you have not inadvertently written shall for should, will for would, that for this, this for these, or can for could, etc. Students often write the wrong word while having a perfectly correct outline in their notes and these must then be counted as errors. Take particular care if a word occurs twice in the passage, as you could have skipped a few lines by moving to the second outline in your notes. Also check that you have been *consistent* in your transcription, in the use of words or figures, in the use of words or symbols, and in constructing sentences in which the verb and subject agree. Often a plural is used instead of a singular word, and vice versa.

A typewritten transcription must be typed according to the instructions, paying particular attention to required margins and line spacing. Corrections may be made by any acceptable method and you should follow the normal procedure for a typewriting examination. However, it is primarily your *transcription* that is of interest to the examiner and the standard of typing required is probably not as high as that required for a typewriting examination. Nevertheless, only a certain number of errors will be acceptable in order to have your certificate endorsed for a typewritten transcription. Filling in gaps in handwriting, overtyping or poor erasures are quite unacceptable and will be penalised, as will inconsistency in paragraph or punctuation style.

FOREIGN LANGUAGE SHORTHAND EXAMINATIONS

Obviously there are similarities between success in these examinations and in English shorthand speed examinations, and you will undoubtedly have started by progressing through a series of speed examinations before tackling foreign shorthand examinations. However, as well as being thoroughly prepared in the shorthand theory, your ability in the language must be equal to that stated in the syllabus or you will be struggling with the vocabulary. As well as practising dictation as often as possible, read a wide range of literature in the foreign language, preferably including as many business letters and documents as possible. Ideally, try to spend your holidays in the country whose language you are studying in order to become as fluent as possible.

French shorthand

The most common errors made in these examinations are with word endings which sound alike but which are spelled differently, as in the case of many plural and feminine forms. Here the context will help you, but a knowledge of gender will be necessary. Always check carefully that subject, verb and adjective endings agree. Other problems may arise over the various nuances of pronunciation, e.g. the difference between "é", "er", "ez" and "ais". Similarly, errors are often made over "l'é" and "les". A thorough knowledge of the language is therefore essential in order to be able to differentiate between them. Hopefully you will be taking dictation from someone whose voice and accent are familiar and this may help you to avoid such errors. Needless to say, accents always cause problems and must be learned with each new word.

German shorthand

The majority of errors are those made by forgetting to put a capital letter for all nouns, or by wrongly using a capital letter for "sie", "ihre", etc. Sometimes, especially with unfamiliar vocabulary, you may mistake a noun for a verb, so when reading back do check the sentence structure carefully to see whether you have already written the verb. The use of the umlaut also causes problems and, just in case you have misheard or made a mistake in your notes, careful checking afterwards is again important.

A good grammatical knowledge is, of course, essential. Pronunciation is usually fairly easy to follow, with the only problem, other than those already mentioned, being when and when not to combine words. A date or year always seems to be included, so do make sure you can write these with confidence.

Spanish shorthand

There are fewer pronunciation traps in Spanish than with many other languages, but remember that although a word sounds similar to its English equivalent, the spelling may well be different, e.g. la tarifa/tariff, ilustrar/illustrate. A date or number is usually included in one of the passages and you should make sure you are confident at writing these.

Welsh shorthand

Welsh shorthand is slightly different and should perhaps not be included as a foreign language because those taking this examination will probably use Welsh as their first language. However, speaking fluently does not always mean writing accurately and care must be taken when transcribing.

SPECIALISED SHORTHAND

There are many professions where the language is rather specialised and, with the introduction of courses for medical and legal secretaries and for journalists, there are now shorthand examinations in these three areas. Other courses might be welcomed by employers in such fields as engineering, but whatever the subject is there will be a new vocabulary to learn, and in the case of medicine this can seem quite a formidable task. Normally there is a dictionary of terminology for the various professions and it is important to look up new words as they occur in your studies or your work. A transcription is more likely to be accurate if the meaning of the passage is clear. Some shorthand books for specialist outlines are also available — see the list at the end of this chapter.

Apart from the specialised vocabulary, there is little difference between preparing for one of these examinations and for a standard speed examination. The section on speed examinations should therefore be read and a similar procedure followed, using suitable material.

Legal shorthand

Only a few colleges offer courses for legal secretaries at present, but do not be deterred if you cannot find a special course. If this is a subject which interests you, acquire good basic secretarial qualifications and, with some research, a basic legal vocabulary can be self-taught without too much difficulty.

If possible, try to gain some work experience in a lawyer's office, as the best way to learn any new vocabulary is to see it used in context. You may only be given mundane tasks such as copy-typing, filing, or the proof-reading of wills, leases and conveyances. These tasks will still be very useful for seeing at first hand how the legal terms are used, and they will help you become familiar with the rather archaic word formations used in the various documents. You could also approach a local firm of solicitors for a selection of the various forms used relating to conveyancing, land registry, legal aid, etc. By studying these, both vocabulary and understanding will improve. Passages relating to legal matters are also included in shorthand magazines, and there are some helpful books written for the legal secretary (see the final section of this chapter). The main areas to study include conveyancing, litigation, divorce, company law, wills and probate, including trusts, and tax laws, etc.

Shorthand for journalists

Special courses for journalists are relatively new, but if journalism is your chosen career it is important to be able to take fast, accurate notes – a cassette recorder may not always be available. Journalists aiming for high speeds must make good use of phrasing wherever possible, but stick to established phrasing principles given in your textbooks, such as the omission of small words. High-speed writers do not have any special short cuts, and if you try to invent your own you could run into trouble when transcribing. Some topics are frequently reported, especially in the local press, e.g. council meetings, sports events, and magistrate and county court proceedings, and a newcomer will probably be given such assignments. Some legal terminology and knowledge of court and meeting procedure is necessary; political words and phrases would also be useful. Accuracy is naturally vital: a mistake could be embarrassing or even lead to legal action.

As journalism covers such a wide range of subjects, perhaps the best way to practise is to read other reporters' material, both in the local and national press. With the help of a friend or by using a cassette recorder, you can practise notetaking, speed building and transcription in the normal way.

Medical shorthand

Some people may be able to tackle this subject alone, but the majority of people aiming for a career in this field will almost certainly need to enrol in a medical secretary's course, to study subjects other than shorthand and typewriting, and to obtain an appropriate qualification such as the Medical Secretary's Diploma. Not only is the medical vocabulary extremely extensive and difficult, but the syllabic content of the words is extremely high, so you will need to work even harder to achieve high shorthand speeds. Medical shorthand at 100 wpm is the equivalent to 120 wpm in normal shorthand. Some medical shorthand examinations are now counted in syllables per minute and some boards give the names of drugs mentioned to the student before dictation. These practices are helpful to the student, but in the working world such allowances may not be made. A good speed will be required and you will be expected to recognise and to spell the majority of drug names. A college course will gradually build up your medical vocabulary and speed and enable you to write with confidence.

The medical secretary must pay particular attention to neat, accurate outlines as it is imperative to be able to differentiate, when transcribing, between such words as abrasion/operation/aberration/portion/abortion or afebrile/febrile/pyrexia/apyrexia, etc.

Obviously, it is impossible to learn every word in the medical dictionary and, however well prepared, one unknown word always seems to appear in an examination. It is a good idea to try learning shorthand outlines for everyday medical words while initially learning shorthand theory. For example, when studying the "st" sound, look up the shorthand outlines for such words as stomach, sterilisation, sternum, stool, steroids, constipated, etc. In this way, later in the course you will be writing many medical outlines automatically and can spend more time during dictation concentrating on new, more difficult words. If you have learned Latin or Greek at school, another glance at these subjects might be very helpful as root medical words stem from these two languages.

Another way to tackle new vocabulary, or as an aid to revision, is to study one part of the body at a time, say the eye. Work from a large labelled diagram and insert the shorthand outlines for all the labelled parts. List in longhand and shorthand the likely diseases of the eye, the types of equipment and drugs used and the various treatments available. This is easier than trying to learn words in isolation.

Don't, however, concentrate on the medical words in your transcription to the exclusion of all else. Many candidates make errors by misunderstanding or mis-spelling straightforward English words, e.g. *fatty* liver — a new word is often invented here. Also, many culinary words are used in medicine, e.g. nutmeg liver, and again these seem to cause difficulties. Also take care when spelling words which include "i" and "y". These are often transposed or the wrong one used, e.g. dyspepsia is written as dispepsya and colitis as colytis. There is also a tendency for American spellings to creep into the medical language, and in the examination you should be sure to use the English version, e.g. coeliac rather than celiac.

6. MISCELLANEOUS EXAMINATIONS

Typewriting transcription speed test (shorthand-based)

This examination is offered by the *Pitman Examinations Institute* and candidates must use a Pitman system of shorthand or speedwriting. Everything that has already been said about shorthand/transcription and about typewriting is pertinent, the important difference being that in this examination outlines must not be altered or longhand inserted in your notes. No preliminary transcription is allowed and each exercise must be typed on a separate sheet of paper. New paragraphs are given during dictation. Marks will be deducted if any of these instructions are ignored.

Systematic notetaking

The aim of this examination is to reduce the dictated passage to about one-third of its original length. Notes must not be taken down verbatim and the technique is to write down only the main points of the passage. The tendency at first is always to write too much and it is simply a matter of practice in being able to gauge that one page of notes will result in so many words, and to make cuts or additions as necessary.

The candidate who can produce a piece of work of the correct length at the first attempt is extremely rare. A draft is normally essential so that you can count the words and produce a final polished version. You will find that there is time enough to do this in the examination. Practise looking at passages and underlining the salient points. You should also study the communications book in this series and practise writing summaries.

C. RECENT EXAMINATION QUESTIONS

This section includes a selection of examination papers set by various boards for you to attempt. Dictation for most of the secretarial certificates and diplomas is given on tape and as it is at a variable speed and may include alterations to be made, examples are not included as they would be unrealistic. If you are unable to practise from tapes available from your college, they may be obtained from the various boards at a small charge.

Ideally, try to find a friend to dictate the passages to you unseen or, failing this, use a cassette recorder yourself. For someone who has not dictated work before, it may take a few attempts to achieve the correct reading speed. A stop watch with second and minute hands is easier to use than a digital one, but whichever type you are using start by trying to read one word per second, i.e. 60 wpm. Once this can be done confidently, slightly increase the speaking rate to 80 wpm, aiming to read the 0.25 min mark in the passage at 15 seconds, and so on. Only a little practice will be needed to be able to read at a good steady pace.

Students attempting theory and miscellaneous papers should follow the instructions at the head of the paper.

Question 1

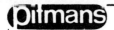

PITMAN SHORTHAND

Theory Stage I

PITMAN
EXAMINATIONS
INSTITUTE

This paper must be returned
with the candidates work.

No   _155 S_

PAST PAPER

Time allowed: 45 minutes

_Outlines for the fifty selected words which form the first part of the test
should be written beneath the words they represent. They should be freely
vocalised (with the exception of short forms and contractions), and position
must be observed. All essential vowels should be inserted in the continuous
matter which forms the second part of the test. You may use all practical
phrasing._

_The whole examination must be written in ink (not pencil) on this working
paper. Any work on separate paper will not be examined._

* * * * * * *

Candidate's Name ....

* * * * * * *

remarkable   assumed   honestly   white   councillor   never

....

welding   improvement   black   green   objected   ordinary

....

situation   election   session   arrangement   third   harm

....

grab   doubt   before   Thursday   children   prompt   sweeter

....

principle   taxation   friend   impose   women   scale   fences

....

intentional   propriety   memorandum   guard   replied   shelf

....

finger   around   opinions   record   depends   owner   describe

....

shrink   wife   station   corner   explain

....

The Chairman in the course of his speech in moving the adoption of the

....

report and accounts said: "The past year has been a good one. In these days,

....

when exports are so vital to the country, it is pleasing to note that our

....

sales overseas have risen by nearly fifty per cent. We have invested a

....

large sum in new factory and office buildings and much of our old machinery

....

has been replaced. Our work force has increased and the varied menus every

....

day in the new canteens enable everyone to enjoy a good meal at an economic

....

price."

....

Question 2

THIS DICTATION SHEET MUST NOT BE HANDED TO CANDIDATES.
IT MUST BE RETURNED TO PITMAN EXAMINATIONS INSTITUTE,
GODALMING WITH THE WORKED PAPERS.

P I T M A N   2 0 0 0   S H O R T H A N D

THEORY STAGE II

DICTATION APPROACH

(1) The following is to be dictated in three minutes by
the teacher in the invigilator's presence. The
teacher should hand the sheet back to the invigilator
immediately after the dictation and leave the room.

Dear Mr Brown

Thank you for your letter dated 26 June informing us
that the parcel we had posted // to you on 28 May   ½
had not arrived. This is to let you know that we
have repeated your ∫ order and this time dispatched   1
it by Road Services Company Limited. We are certain
that they will deliver to your // factory before   ½
the end of this week. Please note that our offices
and works will shut for the annual holiday ∫ during   2
the second and third weeks in August. All orders
placed by 30 July will be filled and dispatched
prior // to our closure. Please check your stocks   ½
in good time to avoid disappointment. With my
kindest personal regards,

Yours sincerely ∫   3

J/GF/BAH

2055 DS (2000)

 2 0 0 0 S H O R T H A N D

THEORY STAGE II

(Dictation Approach)

PITMAN
EXAMINATIONS
INSTITUTE

This paper must be returned
with the candidates work.

No 2055 DS (2000)

Time allowed: 45 minutes

The whole examination must be written _in ink_ (not pencil) on this working paper.

Any work on separate paper will not be examined.

Candidate's Name ....

(1) Dictated passage to be written below in Pitman 2000 shorthand (in ink) on
the lines to the right of the ruled margin. No transcript is required.

(2) Copy the following shorthand outlines on the line below, writing them in
ink in their proper positions in relation to the line. Add at least one
vowel sign in every outline.

quote	positively	usual	girl	exhausted	obvious

mineral	expenditure	incomplete	discovery

(3) Transcribe the following passage in ink on the lines below.

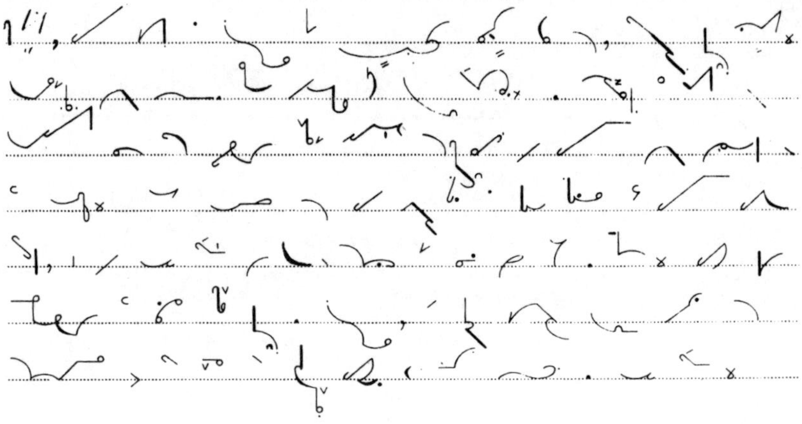

Question 3 180 words to be dictated in three minutes.

(Ways of protecting the office or home against burglary)

Minutes

During the past year over one million crimes were recorded which
½ may have been prevented / had more care been taken by the
½ general public. A large proportion of these crimes / were
committed by amateurs.

The following important points should always be borne in mind
½ when / making premises safe against thieves.

1 A minimum amount of money should be kept in the // office or
home. Petty cash should be locked away and cheque books and bank
½ cards / placed in safe but separate places. Doors and windows
½ should be locked and fastened before / buildings are vacated
and if homes are unoccupied in the evenings, lights should be
½ left / on. Ladders should be locked up and not left lying
2 about to provide access to // first floor rooms.

At home, milk and newspapers should be cancelled when going
½ away. If / possible the police, a friend or a neighbour should
½ be asked to keep an eye / on the house.

Burglar alarms, however, can be very useful and the local crime
½ prevention / officer is always willing to give his help and
3 advice on all matters of security. //

Question 4

MINS.

MINS.

Dear Mr. Jones,

You will have already heard from our editor that, if expenses
¼ can be kept at a reasonable / level, we would be willing to accept your manuscript for publication. We have now had
½ an estimate of the cost / and have given it very careful consideration. In its present form the published price of the
¾ book would be over / nine pounds per copy. We have in mind a maximum of seven pounds, and therefore offer the
1 following suggestions for] reducing costs so that it can be published at that price.

The illustrations should be
1¼ limited to twenty in number / for the whole publication and should not be printed in colour. The colour process is expensive,
1½ and although it would / considerably increase the attraction, we think that any resulting sales would be less
1¾ than if the books were sold at / a lower price. Will you kindly make a selection of any illustrations you desire to retain in black and
2 white.]

Also, it would be advisable to cut down the length of the actual text. With the intention of
2¼ assisting you, / we have asked our proof reader to suggest some alterations to bring the pages to the number required.
2½ He considers / the subject matter in chapter thirteen might either be left out completely or included in a shorter form as
2¾ part / of chapter seven. He has made certain notes in pencil on several pages to indicate where
3 the number of] words might possibly be reduced without affecting the value of the text. We must stress that these are
3¼ only suggestions and / are put forward for your approval or rejection. When you are revising the text will you please
3½ endeavour to reduce / the number of pages to about three hundred. For this purpose, it is estimated that there will be
3¾ roughly seven / hundred words on each of the pages.

We are sending the manuscript to you today by registered post.

4 Yours sincerely,]

(London Chamber of Commerce and Industry, June 1984)

92

Question 5 One hundred and ten words per minute. (Seventy minutes allowed for transcription.)

The oblique lines, /, mark the division of time, but the reader must not make a pause when they occur, unless the sense requires it. The double lines, //, mark the completion of each minute.

Passage A

"DO I REALLY NEED A MICRO?"

A question which the small or medium-sized business man, and even the executive in major
¼ companies, is increasingly being pressured to ask is: "Should I buy / a micro-computer?"

All around people are telling him that this is the age of the micro. On television he sees
½ computers which can, at the press of / a button, answer almost any question; he reads of computers that can play chess at any level of ability. His children are learning about comput-
¾ ers for school / examinations and have no doubt also become addicted to computer-based games.

1 Little wonder that under such pressure he should begin to feel that he is the odd // one out and in danger of being left behind in the business race. Little wonder indeed that he does not
¼ ask himself the one question he should / have asked at the outset—"Do I really *need* a computer?"

½ If his aim is simply to get hands-on experience of computing, then even the smallest model / will provide useful practice. For £100 he can buy a computer that will plug into a TV set, as
¾ well as a printer to which / he can couple it. But he will soon discover that there are strict limitations to what a small micro with limited CPU power and program storage capacity
2 can // do.

Many, for example, have a limited amount of internal storage and it is all too easy to fill
¼ it up. The first sign that the unit's / memory space is used up is normally an "error" report, which can cause some natural misconceptions. Some small computers are, admittedly, more
½ easily expanded than others, and it / may be a good idea if business requirements are likely to change, to start with a configuration which can be expanded readily.

¾ One can, for instance, easily / fit a memory board to some micros and most units can be
3 expanded to store data on floppy discs or even on the later generation of hard discs. //

(SEB 1983, Cert. 6th Year Studies)

Question 6   420 syllables to be dictated in three minutes.

(Une enquête révèle les inégalités de salaire
des secrétaires en Europe)

Minutes

Une enquête a été menée récemment sur les
salaires de quelque deux mille secrétaires
¼ d'Europe. Cette enquête, / qui porte sur les
dactylographes, secrétaires spécialisées et
secrétaires de direction de huit pays d'Europe,
½ révèle / les inégalités de salaire qui
existent en France. Elle indique aussi très claire-
¾ ment l'énorme différence / entre les salaires
selon les pays. Les secrétaires suisses sont de
très loin les mieux payées ; les anglaises, par
1 contre, // arrivent toujours en dernier avec un
salaire vraiment très bas.

Pour faire la comparaison, les salaires bruts ont
¼ été / calculés en francs français et pour
mener à bien l'enquête, il a fallu calculer le
½ salaire net (déduction faite des charges /
sociales et des impôts). Mais le pouvoir d'achat
d'un salaire net varie énormément selon le pays. Il
¾ a donc fallu ajuster / les salaires nets au coût
de la vie, se référant au coût de la vie en
France.

2 Les trois pays d'Europe où les dactylographes //
sont les mieux payées sont la Suisse, la Belgique et
l'Allemagne. La dactylo suisse dispose d'au moins six
¼ mille cinq cents francs / français, ce qui est
plus du double de ce que gagne par mois sa collègue
½ anglaise. Il est intéressant de constater qu'en /
Suisse la secrétaire spécialisée ne gagne pas
beaucoup plus que la dactylographe confirmée. C'est
¾ le pays où l'écart de / salaire entre ces deux
niveaux est le plus faible.

C'est encore en Suisse où la secrétaire de
3 direction gagne le plus. //

(RSA, 1984)

94

Question 7   Test at 110 words per minute.

(Letter from Registrar to Dr Snow regarding John Green. The drugs mentioned
are Codeine Phosphate (C-o-d-e-i-n-e P-h-o-s-p-h-a-t-e) and Salazopyrine
(S-a-l-a-z-o-p-y-r-i-n-e). Isogel (I-s-o-g-e-l) is also mentioned)

1   Dear Dr Snow

2   John Green, date of birth, four, six, sixty-three

3   Many thanks for referring this young man, who was seen in Dr Bond's Clinic
4   today. / I was given details of four years of diarrhoea, abdominal pain and   ¼
5   vomiting, diagnosed at General Hospital as Crohn's disease and treated until
6   March of this year with // Codeine Phosphate and steroids. He told me that   ½
7   at the beginning he lost a lot of weight and was quite ill. I was also told
8   that since /// May he has had no symptoms, he feels well, has had no pain   ¾
9   and bowels are opened once or twice a day, the motions being mostly formed
10 with / no slime or blood. However, as he is taking five Codeine Phosphate   1
11 tablets a day he feels that if these cease then the diarrhoea will recur.

12 On / examination today there was little for me to find. He was not anaemic,   ¼
13 nor were there masses or tenderness in his abdomen and I could not feel any //   ½
14 organs. On rectal examination there were two short blind sinuses with
15 indurated areas below them.

16 I discussed this case with Dr Bond today and he felt that /// Mr Green   ¾
17 should stop the Salazopyrine as there has been, as yet, no trial indicating
18 that this is efficient in stopping the relapse in Crohn's disease which
19 differs / from ulcerative colitis. Dr Bond thought that Mr Green should   2
20 take Isogel instead of Codeine Phosphate and I have given him a preliminary
21 supply for an immediate / start. Dr Bond also told the patient that he   ¼
22 could take the Codeine tablets if he felt he needed them for the present but
23 he should be weaned // slowly on to the Isogel, which is not a drug, and   ½
24 take that only. I have arranged for some blood tests today and will advise
25 you should /// they not be normal.   ¾

26 I should like to see Mr Green in a month's time if there is any further
27 change in his present condition.

28 Your sincerely

29 Registrar /

Question 8   384 syllables to be dictated in three minutes.

(This is about Sally, a spina bifida baby with a meningomyelocele)

Minutes

Sally was born in hospital on fifteenth August nineteen
seventy-three at oh one hundred hours. She was an
¼   unplanned, / unwanted baby. Her mother was only
sixteen years of age and unmarried. She had already
½   decided to have the baby / adopted as soon as
possible following delivery. The identity of the
¾   father was not revealed by the mother. /

Pregnancy and labour were uneventful. Sally was born
by spontaneous vertex delivery at the full term.
1   Apgar // score was eight at one minute, and ten at
five minutes. This is the method used to determine the
¼   degree of hypoxia, if / present, of the infant
immediately following birth. Optimum score is ten.

½   Sally's congenital defect was obvious / following
delivery. She was seen immediately by a paediatrician
¾   and a diagnosis of spina / bifida was made. The
meningomyelocele extended from the first to the fifth
2   lumbar vertebrae. She also had early // hydro-
cephalus and mild talipes. Her birth weight was two
point nine kilogrammes. There was no family history of
¼   spina / bifida or other neural tube defects.

Sally was put into an incubator and temperature, apex
½   beat and / respiration recorded hourly. After an
intense physical and neurological examination by the
¾   consultant / paediatrician over the next few days,
it was decided to close the meningomyelocele as soon as
3   possible. //

Question 9

1 I consider it a great honour to be chosen as your president for the
2 coming year and I will fulfil this position to the best of my ability.
3 My grey hairs do not indicate a lifetime of / service to the Union as   ¼
4 many of our previous presidents have had, and it is only as family
5 commitments have lessened that I have become involved in union work -
6 first as a committee member and then as membership // secretary.   ½

7 As many of you know, I am the deputy head of the local Infants' School
8 and have taught there for seventeen years, but my early teaching
9 experience, though brief, was in the lean post-war years, /// when   ¾
10 reception classes were 48, and other infant classes over 50, and
11 paintings were done on old newspapers. When my own children entered
12 school a few years later, school secretaries, long-retired teachers
13 and post sixth-form / girls were brought in at various times to teach   1
14 large classes, unaided by any ancillary help, because of the shortage
15 of qualified staff. How ironic that after 30 years in what has been
16 an expanding and developing / service, the children of those deprived   ¼
17 post-war children are now entering their school lives at a time of
18 cuts in educational provision, not because of a shortage of qualified
19 teachers. With 26,500 registered // unemployed teachers, this is   ½
20 hardly the case - but because of lack of financial provision at local
21 and national level.

22 Thankfully we have not experienced the drastic cuts imposed by some
23 local authorities, and every attempt has been /// made to provide an   ¾
24 adequate service within the financial constraints imposed upon the
25 authority. But the latest rate support grant settlement will ensure
26 that these standards cannot be maintained, even though Her Majesty's
27 school inspectors have made clear / the damage caused by spending cuts   2
28 already in force.

29 We now have in our infant schools fully qualified staff, smaller class
30 numbers, the introduction of scale posts and ancillary help and a
31 gradual increase in resources, plus / the setting up of teachers'   ¼
32 centres and courses for in-service training, and in many schools a
33 shift in emphasis from class teaching to group teaching in open-plan
34 units.

35 This situation will remain only if these resources // are maintained   ½

36 and teachers have reasonable conditions of service and remuneration.

37 Otherwise, as has happened with the Health Service, when economic

38 conditions improve we shall see large numbers of qualified teachers

39 leaving the profession.

40 What we do /// have is a static situation in many of our primary   ¾

41 schools with falling rolls resulting in the redeployment of staff,

42 very little or no prospect of promotion within the schools, and little

43 opportunity for young teachers to get ⌐ varied school experience, even   3

44 if they are lucky enough to obtain a job. A lot of emotive headlines

45 have appeared in the press about four year olds being brought into

46 school to play and waste public money. / The true situation was that   ½

47 we were ensuring that the "summer born" children were not deprived of

48 the whole of their first year's schooling in the infant school - a

49 privilege which some "summer born" children in village and // primary   ½

50 schools had already been receiving. We support equal opportunity for

51 all children in our schools and this led to the abolition of the

52 11-plus and the establishment of comprehensive schools. So I whole-

53 heartedly support /// the move to give all children the same early   ¾

54 school experience with their own peer group.

55 I make no apology for concentrating on the local school scene at

56 primary level, as this is my own field of experience. ⌐   4

(PEI, Shorthand for Journalists)

Question 10   Test at 80 words per minute.

(Letter from Vendor's Solicitors to Purchaser's Solicitors)

1   Dear Sirs

2   Re: Number 62, The Close - Johnson from Harris - Subject to Contract

3   Thank you for your letter of / the fourth of April with   ¼
4   enclosures. We now return one copy of your Preliminary Enquiries
5   with our replies thereto and // are obliged for the spare copies   ½
6   provided for our use. These replies are subject to our client's
7   confirmation and we /// shall write to you again in this   ¾
8   connection as soon as possible.

9   Meanwhile, we enclose Office Copy Entries which we ∫ have   1
10 received from the Land Registry. As you will see, the matters to
11 which we referred in Special Condition One / of the Contract have   ¼
12 been set out in the Property and Charges Register and we should
13 therefore be glad if // you would kindly delete proposed Special   ½
14 Condition One.

15 We confirm that the vendor agrees, upon completion, to allow the
16 purchaser /// the sum of five hundred pounds towards the cost of   ¾
17 repairs to be carried out to the property.

18 Yours faithfully ∫   2

Question 11

TYPEWRITING TRANSCRIPTION SPEED TEST

(SHORTHAND-BASED)

PITMAN
EXAMINATIONS
INSTITUTE

This paper must be returned
with the candidates work.

No. TRS-S4

CANDIDATE'S INSTRUCTION SHEET

1 Your examination will consist of two passages of shorthand.
One passage has just been dictated to you and the other is
to be found on the attached sheet.* MAKE SURE YOU SELECT
THE CORRECT PASSAGE, according to the system you used for
the dictation; otherwise you will automatically be
disqualified.

2 As soon as these instructions and the two sheets of A4 paper
have been distributed, you will be given 27 minutes in which
to make your original transcriptions of both passages, each
exercise to be started on a separate sheet of paper. You
will be told when to begin typing your transcriptions and
you should make any necessary corrections as you go. The
passing of time will be indicated to you at regular intervals
by the Invigilator. Type direct on to the A4 paper provided -
no preliminary transcription is allowed.

3 When you have completed your work make sure your name appears
on each sheet of paper you have used. Assemble the sheets
with the Entry Form on top, then your original shorthand
notes, and finally the two typed passages in their correct
order (Part I then Part II).

4 Immediately you finish, hand in your work and make sure the
Invigilator writes the time at which you started and finished
your transcriptions on the top sheet of your transcription
papers.

This sheet, together with the prepared shorthand sheet, MUST be
handed back separately to the Invigilator for return to the
Institute.

 **Pitman**

TYPEWRITING TRANSCRIPTION SPEED TEST

(SHORTHAND-BASED)

PITMAN
EXAMINATIONS
INSTITUTE

This paper must be returned
with the candidates work.

No. **TRS-S4**

DICTATION PASSAGE FOR PART I

We have pleasure in enclosing a free copy of the Monthly News, which
is a new magazine and is intended / especially for the people of our   ¼
town. *(paragraph)*

At its meeting last week, the Town Council decided that this magazine
would // help people to communicate with each other. We are very well   ½
aware that with the new large housing development which /// is taking   ¾
place in the West End at the present time, many new families are
constantly moving into the ⌐ town and this magazine will provide them   1
with all the information they will need concerning coming events, and
also full / details of local organizations. *(paragraph)*   ¼

We hope that when you have read this first issue, you will be pleased
with what // you see and that you will place a regular order. The   ½
magazine will be published every month and will cost /// thirty-five   ¾
pence. The profits from the magazine are to be given to the new fund
which has just been ⌐ set up to provide a new community centre for   2
the town, which, it is hoped, will be built in about / eighteen months'   ¼
time. *(paragraph)*

If you wish to submit anything for publication, we would be very happy
to hear from you. //   ½

TYPEWRITING TRANSCRIPTION SPEED TEST (SHORTHAND-BASED)

PART II - Passage of prepared shorthand in PITMANSCRIPT

TYPEWRITING TRANSCRIPTION SPEED TEST (SHORTHAND-BASED)

PART II - Passage of prepared shorthand in PITMAN NEW ERA

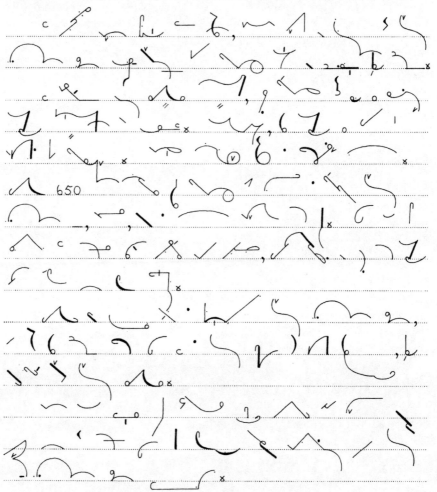

TYPEWRITING TRANSCRIPTION SPEED TEST (SHORTHAND-BASED)

PART II - Passage of prepared shorthand in PITMAN 2000

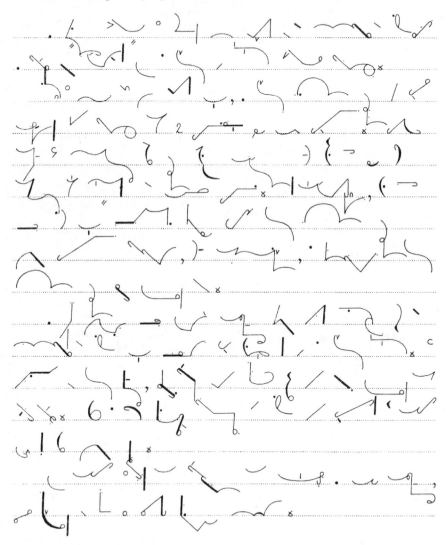

D. TUTOR'S NOTES AND ANSWERS

This section gives advice on the problem areas, difficult outlines and phrases for the papers presented in the previous section. Various systems of shorthand are covered for those papers set by boards other than PEI. Pitmanscript is included only for papers at lower speeds since it is difficult to achieve more than 80 wpm with this system.

Question 1

*short forms

'st' loop used medially where good join results

*remarkable   assumed   honestly   white   councillor   *never

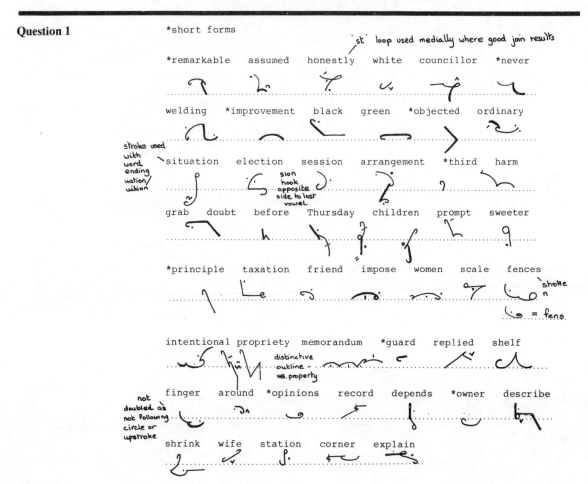

welding   *improvement   black   green   *objected   ordinary

stroke used with word ending uation/uition
*situation   election   session   arrangement   *third   harm

sion hook opposite side to last vowel

grab   doubt   before   Thursday   children   prompt   sweeter

*principle   taxation   friend   impose   women   scale   fences

stroke n

= fens.

intentional   propriety   memorandum   *guard   replied   shelf

distinctive outline - NB. property

not doubled as not following circle or upstroke
finger   around   *opinions   record   depends   *owner   describe

shrink   wife   station   corner   explain

105

do not forget to mark capital letter

The Chairman in the course of his speech in moving the adoption

of the report and accounts said: "The past year has been a good

one.   In these days when exports are so vital to the country, it

is pleasing to note that our sales overseas have risen by nearly

fifty per cent.   We have invested a large sum in new factory and

office buildings and much of our old machinery has been replaced.

The work force has increased and the varied menus every day in

the new canteens enable everyone to enjoy a good meal at an

economic price."

Some alternatives to the above could be used, e.g.

in the course of

report and accounts

fifty per cent

machinery

Question 2

Part (1)

You must be aware of the difference between personal and personnel (line 14) which is an error frequently made by candidates. The word dispatched is used twice in the passage (lines 5 and 11) and although both dispatch and despatch are acceptable in written English, be careful to write the outline in the correct position for the former as this is what was dictated. Remember to mark your shorthand notes for the capital letters required for the company name (line 6), also for the months mentioned (lines 2, 10 and 11). Take particular care when writing "offices" (line 8) as "office" would also make sense. Put in those vowels which will be needed to avoid any confusion, e.g. "filled", if written in the wrong position and not vocalised, could be mistaken for "filed" or even "folded".

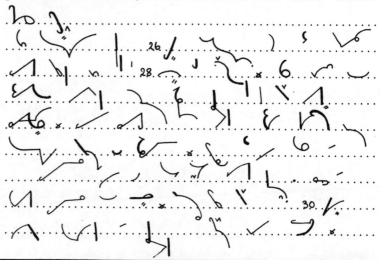

Part (2)

The second part of the paper (positioning the outlines) is relatively simple as long as you forget spelling and think phonetically. One or two of the words might cause problems, e.g. "mineral" and "incomplete" are included and many candidates have trouble placing a mainly horizontal outline when the initial vowel makes them want to write it through the line. Note that the stroke l in mineral goes through the line, not the m, and the halved pl stroke in incomplete, i.e. the first upstroke or downstroke is written through the line. Students might also be inclined to place the entire outline for "expenditure" on the line by listening to the initial vowel sound, but it is the first downstroke which is placed on the line. Make sure you show clearly where the outline is intended to be as if there is any doubt in the examiner's mind it will be marked wrong.

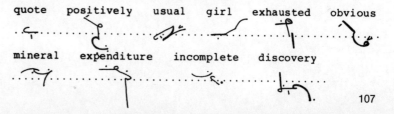

Part (3)

The final passage to be transcribed has one or two pitfalls to be avoided, but you should have no real problems if you read the outlines slowly and carefully. Employee is again included in the passage and you are also required to add an apostrophe in the correct position. Don't be tempted to write capital letters for "committees" or "conference" as these are not marked in the passage.

Other outlines which might present difficulties are "policies" which could be muddled with "police"; "product" with "predict" or "protect"; "secret" for "sacred"; and "autumn" for "time". If you know distinguishing outlines and are not hasty, there should be no need for errors of this kind. If you cannot read a particular outline, it is sensible to leave a gap and come back to it. Often the word seems obvious on second reading once you have the sense of the passage.

Below is a transcription of (3) for you to check your own attempt.

Dear George

We are holding a conference at the International Hotel this year, probably during March. Various committees will be making strong recommendations on their future policies. The employees' committee has already put forward some very useful ideas and we know that your contribution concerning our work will be listened to with interest. In the next year we should be able to achieve a definite advance with the work we have planned, but our new product will have to remain on the secret list until the autumn. We shall deal extensively with sales drives during the conference, and it would be helpful if you could relate your remarks to the particular kinds of advertising we shall need without actually mentioning the new product.

Question 3

General: Students seem to find the spelling in this passage particularly difficult and so careful note should be taken of those given below. "The" is frequently used instead of "A" in lines 3 and 7. If in doubt as to whether to use capital letters for such words as "police" (line 15) and "crime prevention officer" (lines 17/18), it is better to use them. They should be acceptable in this case. However, a capital for "local" (line 17) would not be allowed.

Common spelling errors:
amateurs
borne
thieves
cheque ('check' often used through carelessness)
separate
burglar

Difficult
outlines:

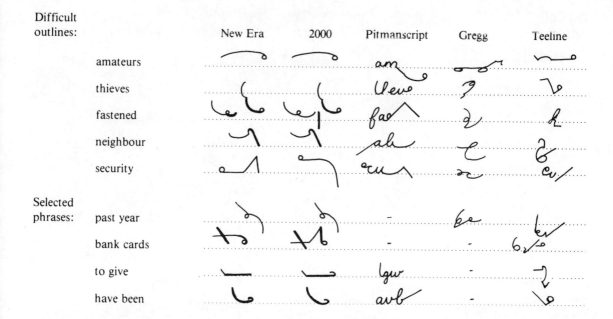

	New Era	2000	Pitmanscript	Gregg	Teeline
amateurs			am		
thieves			theve		
fastened			fas		
neighbour			ahr		
security			cur		

Selected
phrases:

	New Era	2000	Pitmanscript	Gregg	Teeline
past year			-		
bank cards			-		
to give			lguv	-	
have been			avb	-	

Question 4

General: A straightforward paper with fairly simple vocabulary. Vocalise the name fully so that there is no confusion. The major problem is the need for careful punctuation: a full stop could be inserted after "costs" in line 8; the next sentence could then run on and this would still make sense. This applies to other parts of the passage too. Both "a" or "the" could be used in several places. In Pitman shorthand, use tick "the" whenever possible. In line 2, check carefully with your notes the order of the words "already heard". These are often transposed in transcription when either word order makes sense. Do not forget the final "Yours sincerely".

Common
spelling
errors:
editor
accept
advisable
affecting (know the difference from effecting)
endeavour

Difficult outlines:		New Era	2000	Pitmanscript	Gregg	Teeline
	twenty			20	20	20
	roughly					
	pencil					
	manuscript					
	publication					
	published					
	maximum					
	expensive					
	rejection					
Selected phrases:	present form					
	shorter form					
	should be limited					
	black & white					
	number required					
	lower price					
	it would be					
	we have now					
	should not be					
	we think					
	selection of					
	700 words					
	will you please					
	number of					

General: This is an example of a topical subject being used for an examination passage, and the computer terminology should be quite familiar to all younger students and those following a secretarial course. Care is needed with the "A" in line 1; "The" would also make sense. The punctuation in this passage is particularly tricky as quotation marks, hyphens, semi-colons, apostrophes, question marks and even italics are all included. There is also a sentence beginning "But" on line 15, a sentence structure which always confuses some students. Despite "micros" being the subject of the passage, beware of writing it with a capital letter each time it occurs.

Common
spelling
errors:
executive
addicted
practice (know the difference from practise)
program (as opposed to programme)
storage
misconceptions

Difficult
outlines:

		New Era	2000	Gregg	Teeline
	executive				
	micro-computer				
BUT	computers				
	addicted				
	admittedly				
	configuration				
	generation				
	children				

Selected
phrases:

	business man				
	no doubt				
	that he is the				
	if business				
	requirements				

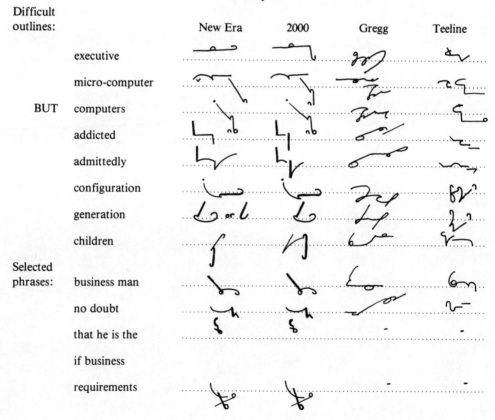

General: A passage with vocabulary which is quite easy to understand. Even if the word "enquête" is new to you, its meaning soon becomes clear. "Selon" (according to), lines 9 and 18, causes many problems. Students write this as "ce l'on" or "ce l'en". Another point to watch out for is the lower-case letters for "suisses" (line 9), "anglaises" (line 10) and "francais" (line 14) – used as adjectives. Care is necessary with punctuation, e.g. a sentence beginning with "Mais".

Common spelling errors:

comparaison	
menée	(mener – to take)
révèle	(to reveal) not to be confused with reveiller
l'écart	(difference) often written as les quarts

Difficult outlines:

	New Era	2000	Teeline
secrétaire			
dactylograph(e)			
spécialisée			
gagne			
la Suisse			
dernier			
inégalités			

Selected phrases:

des charges			
6500 francs	6500	6500	65
ce que			
ce qui est			

General: Date of birth is often written as DOB. In the examination, it is advisable to write it in full. Care is needed with the apostrophes in Bond's clinic, Crohn's disease and month's time. Drug names are given to you before dictation, so no excuse for mis-spelling these.

Common
spelling
errors:

diarrhoea
colitis
abdominal
Crohn's disease
weaned
anaemic

Difficult
outlines:

	New Era	2000
diarrhoea		
abdominal		
vomiting		
diagnosed		
Codeine Phosphate		
steroids		
symptoms		
tenderness		
sinuses		
indurated		
Salazopyrine		
ulcerative		
colitis		
Isogel		

Selected
phrases:

Crohn's disease

month's time

at the beginning

Question 8

General: The first paragraph does not contain any specialised vocabulary and should be quite simple. Punctuation should pose no problems as the passage consists of only short sentences. The date would be acceptable written in figures, as would "oh one hundred hours" and "two point nine kilogrammes". "Meningomyelocele" is more usually written as "Myelomeningocele" so ensure that you have written as dictated.

Common spelling errors:
vertex
hypoxia
congenital
paediatrician
meningomyelocele
vertebrae (correct plural ending)

Difficult outlines:

	New Era	2000	Gregg	Teeline
pregnancy				
uneventful				
spontaneous				
hypoxia				
congenital				
paediatrician				
vertebrae				
hydrocephalus				
talipes				
incubator				
temperature				
neurological				

Selected phrases:

as soon as possible				
next few days				
Apgar score				

114

General: Particular care is required with punctuation as several long, complex sentences are included. The full stop after "secretary" (line 6) should definitely be marked, otherwise it might be placed after "As many of you know" (line 7) which would also make sense. The full stop after "authority" in line 25 is also important as the following sentence begins with "But". Several apostrophes are included and you must be certain of their use.

Common
spelling
errors:

fulfil
commitments
secretary
ancillary
remuneration
emotive
whole-heartedly
peer
rolls
privilege

Difficult
outlines:

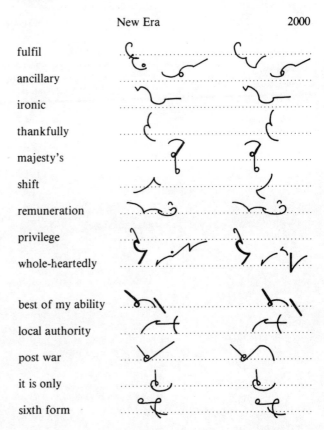

	New Era	2000
fulfil		
ancillary		
ironic		
thankfully		
majesty's		
shift		
remuneration		
privilege		
whole-heartedly		

Selected
phrases:

best of my ability		
local authority		
post war		
it is only		
sixth form		

General: A letter which includes many words and phrases relevent to conveyancing. The main problem will be knowing when to use capital letters. "Preliminary Enquiries" (line 4) has capital letters as this is the title of a form; "Land Registry" (line 10) has them as a special office; and "Special Condition One" (line 11) as a heading in the Contract. As "number" (line 2) has been dictated, do not merely write the figures but remember to include the word too. Note the use of the apostrophe (line 6).

Common spelling errors:
fourth
preliminary
Registry

Difficult outlines:

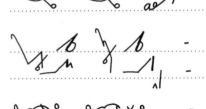

	New Era	2000	Pitmanscript
enclosures			
thereto			
Registry			

Selected phrases:

as soon as possible			
Property and Charges register			
carried out			
Preliminary Enquiries			

Question 11

Part 1

General: The second paragraph in particular contains several words with a high syllabic content and candidates may therefore find the passage difficult. Care is needed with the apostrophe at the end of paragraph three.

Words commonly
misspelled: especially
               communicate
               development
               community

Outlines for difficult words:

	New Era	2000	Pitmanscript
intended			
especially			
communicate			
aware			
concerning			
organisations			
published			
profits			

Selected phrases:

	New Era	2000	Pitmanscript
last week			
Town council			
each other			
West End			
at the present time			
every month			

Part 2

Pitmanscript

The Directors join me in thanking you most sincerely for bringing to our attention so promptly the fact that the new fire alarm system is not working.

We have today written to the manufacturers of this fire alarm system. They have promised to send their senior engineer on Monday morning of next week. Unfortunately, he is away on holiday at the present time. We are very upset that no action will be taken until then, but in the meantime, we have written to all members of the staff informing them of the new procedure to be followed should a fire occur anywhere on our premises. We enclose a copy of these instructions for your information.

With regard to the other matter which you raised with us, we have instructed all members of staff that fire doors must be kept closed, but not locked of course, at all times. As you say, this could be very dangerous indeed, and the Safety Officer, Mr James, has been asked to make inspections from time to time and to warn any staff caught fixing these doors in the open position.

Please let us know if you have any further recommendations on safety arrangements.

New Era

With reference to my telephone call of this morning, I now write to confirm that the fire alarm system installed by your company on our premises only two weeks ago does not work.

When I spoke to your Service Manager, he promised that he would send his senior engineer on Monday morning of next week. Unfortunately, this engineer is away on holiday at the present time. I must emphasize that this is a very serious matter. We have 650 employees on these premises and the lack of a proper fire alarm could, of course be a matter of life or death. While not at all happy with your company's slow response to our request, we will be pleased to see your engineer and will offer him every courtesy.

We have been able to fix up a temporary fire alarm system, and although this worked very well when a fire drill was held this afternoon, it has not been approved by the fire service.

I am in close touch with the company's trade union representative and would like to be able to reassure him that your company will do everything possible to repair our fire alarm system quickly.

Pitman 2000

The Chairman of the Company has asked me to write to all members of staff concerning the procedure to be followed if a fire should occur on the company's premises.

Many of you will already know, the fire alarm system which was installed on our premises only 2 weeks ago is not now working. We have been in touch with the manufacturers of this system and they have informed us that they cannot send their engineer until Monday of next week.

Unfortunately they can give us no guarantee at present when the fire alarm system will be working properly, so in the meantime, a temporary fire alarm system has been fixed up.

The attached leaflet gives full instructions which should be read carefully so that all members of staff know exactly what they must do should a fire occur. With regard to fire doors, it has been brought to our attention that these are being fixed in the open position. This is a very dangerous practice and staff are warned that anyone found doing this will be disciplined.

If anyone has any problem in understanding the new instructions, he is advised to contact his head of department immediately.

E. COURSE WORK — A STEP FURTHER

Whatever standard you have reached, the need for continual practice is vitally important. You must make use of phrasing and short forms where appropriate, and some of the publications mentioned below should help you both during and after your course of study. It is also a pity to abandon all theory work once you have started employment. All too often students feel they never want to look at a textbook again. Hopefully, however, you will be taking a pride in your notes and you should still try to look up any word which is new to you. It may be that the word will occur frequently in your day-to-day work and so it is sensible to start by writing it correctly. If you have achieved a good speed but find that you do not use much shorthand in your work, try to maintain your speed by using your shorthand for telephone messages, instructions, etc. and perhaps by reading shorthand magazines. Some students may feel they would like to continue their studies by taking a teacher's certificate in shorthand. Enquiries should be made to the RSA or PEI in order to find out where such courses are held.

FURTHER READING

Gem Dictionary of English Usage, Collins
Fowlers Modern English Usage, Oxford University Press

Shorthand theory and speed practice

New Era:	*Memo* Magazine; *Office skills* Magazine; *The New Phonographic Phrase Book*, by Emily D. Smith. All published by Pitman.
2000:	*2000* Magazine; *Office Skills* Magazine; *Pitman 2000*; *Speedbuilder*, This section gives practice on one RSA paper. Stage III RSA
Pitmanscript:	*Progressive Shorthand Passages* (Books 1, 2, 3, 4), by M. Quint; *Pitmanscript Graded Exercises*, by Emily D. Smith. Both published by Pitman.
Gregg:	*Gregg Speed Practice*, by E. W. Crockett; *Today's Secretary Magazine*. Both published by McGraw Hill.

Teeline:	*Teeline Shorthand Made Simple*; *First/Second Teeline Workbooks*; *Teeline Magazine*. All published by Heinemann.

Medical

Nurses' Dictionary. Published by Balliere.

New Era:	*Case History Correspondence for Medical Secretaries*, by Ruth Reynolds. Published by Pitman. *Medical Shorthand Dictation Passages*, by Irene Burgess. Published by Cassell & Co Ltd.
2000:	*Medical Words and Phrases*, by Janice Kerr. Published by Pitman.

Legal

New Era and 2000:	*A Secretary's Guide to the Legal Office*, by Annette Parry. Published by Pitman.

Chapter 5

Shorthand – Typewriting (including medical)

A. GETTING STARTED

Shorthand – typewriting qualifications are becoming popular with employers because they like to know that staff can use the combined skills of shorthand and typewriting required in most secretarial posts and they feel the qualification is more realistic than separate examinations.

Some examining bodies dictate business letters for accurate typing in a given time; others require accurate typewritten transcription of dictated matter, often incorporating short simple display and with the addition of a portion of printed manuscript tabulation, which may or may not need to be inserted into the matter. Finally, notes may be dictated for expansion into a business letter for signature. Occasionally, a correction may need to be made.

You will see from the above that *all* your skills will be required to pass this examination, but accurate notetaking is the first step to success. As stated previously, clear, tidy notes are an aid to transcription and this is particularly true where tables are being dictated. Messy shorthand will often result in messy transcription, and remember that the emphasis in this examination is on "mailable" copy at first attempt. Spelling errors, faulty punctuation, typographical errors, poor corrections and bad display will all be severely penalised and so the chapters on both shorthand and typewriting should be studied as well as the book on communications in this series. However, the majority of marks are lost because the tasks cannot be completed in the given time, an indication that students have not fully prepared for the examination.

You should aim to start typing back your notes soon after starting to learn shorthand; in fact, as soon as you have become reasonably proficient on the keyboard. It is no good learning shorthand and typewriting in isolation. The best way to begin is to start with a previously prepared shorthand passage so that you are familiar with the words. You will need to select the suitable size of paper for the material and to set appropriate margins and line spacing. This is part of the skill of a good shorthand-typist and will become easier with practice and experience. Selecting the correct paper will depend on being able to judge how much room your own notes will need. It is therefore a good idea to work out approximately how many lines of your notes will comfortably fit on to a sheet of A5 paper when transcribed. You will then know when it is necessary for you to use A4 paper.

When starting to type from shorthand notes, the inclination is to read a few words of shorthand, pause, type them, pause, and then read the next few words. However, try to avoid this stop/start action. Try from the outset to type at a steady pace, keeping your eyes on the shorthand outline two or three words ahead of the word you are typing. This may be a slow process to begin with but gradually you will find that you can read the shorthand notes as easily as longhand and can attain a good consistent speed. At first it may be better to ignore your errors, as to stop and make corrections will halt the flow of your typing. When you have completed the passage, you can ring the mistakes and, if the number is unacceptable, re-type it from your shorthand notes once again.

Once you have mastered typing back prepared shorthand, you can progress to unprepared dictation and finally begin to use carbon paper and produce envelopes.

Details of shorthand–typewriting examinations are given in Table 5.1.

Table 5.1   Single subject examinations – format and content
Examining board: **Pitman Examinations Institute (PEI)**

General information: Only Pitman systems accepted – no longhand or mixture of systems allowed.

Title	Level	Length of Exam	Format and Regulations
Shorthand Typewriting	80/100/120/ 140 wpm	43/51 mins	Dictionaries allowed. 6 mins dictation consisting of 2 passages (max. 4 mins), business letters. Electronic typewriters allowed.
Typewriting transcription (shorthand based)		27 mins max. transcription time	200 words dictated at 80 wpm + 200 words of prepared shorthand for transcription within allowed time.

Table 5.1 continued

Examining board: **Royal Society of Arts (RSA)**

General information: Dictionaries are allowed.

Title	Level	Length of Exam	Format and Regulations
Shorthand Typewriting	Stage II Stage III	150/180 mins	Dictation not at uniform speed. Tasks to type from dictation, printed material and composition from dictated notes. Corrections may need to be incorporated.
Medical Shorthand Typewriting	Stage II	170 mins	Dictation not at uniform speed. Tasks to type from dictation, printed material and composition from dictated notes. Work of medical nature. Some display work from dictation. Corrections may need to be incorporated.
Medical Shorthand Typewriting	Stage III	180 mins	2 compulsory sections. 7 to 9 tasks from dictation, dictated instructions and printed material. Work includes case notes, letters, reports, completion of medical forms, etc. Dictation by 2 people (tape supplied by RSA) at average 100 wpm.

B. ESSENTIAL PRINCIPLES

Most shorthand-typists can produce with ease all the tasks required in the shorthand–typewriting examinations, but the real test is being able to produce "mailable" copy at the first attempt under the pressure of examination conditions. This is not so easy and it is imperative that you practise carrying out tasks in a given time so that you can confidently expect to finish the paper. It is extremely difficult to reach the pass mark if you have omitted several questions.

It is also, of course, important to be really familiar with the typewriter you will be using in the examination, so try to decide which machine to use well in advance. Make sure that it is in good working order and that the ribbon does not need changing.

PREPARATION

When attempting the recent examination questions in the next section, adopt the following procedure:

1. Do not look at the reader's section of the paper until after you have finished the tasks (assuming you can find someone to dictate the paper to you), otherwise the paper cannot be tackled realistically.

2. Make good use of any reading time. You are given ten minutes to read the paper before the RSA examinations and you should be sure to put it to good use; study the topics to be dictated and the instructions to typist. There will not be a common theme to the work and letters may vary from insurance to staff matters. If you fail to take advantage of this reading time, you may rush into a task without perhaps noticing an instruction to the typist at the foot of a page of manuscript.

3. After any reading time, the tasks should be dictated. There is a preliminary passage of approximately two minutes followed by all the passages, one after the other, with an interval of half a minute between each. The preliminary passage is so that candidates can become familiar with the reader's voice and no transcription is required for this. The dictation speed will not be constant and punctuation will be indicated only by inflexion of the voice.

4. Decide which task to attempt first. Some students prefer to work methodically through the paper; others prefer to start on the question which has most marks allocated to it or the one they feel most confident to tackle.

5. Underline the instructions before beginning the task so that you do not overlook them.

6. Decide which paper to use for the chosen task. You may have been given definite instructions or may need to use your own judgement. Again this could influence the choice of task you attempt first. You may prefer to start by using the stationery stipulated, then to see what remains to be used for other tasks.

7. Check again before starting to type that all instructions regarding number of copies, references, etc. have been followed. When you have finished typing, check your work carefully against your notes before taking it out of the machine as errors and omissions are easier to correct at this stage.

MEDICAL SHORTHAND– TYPEWRITING

For the RSA examinations at Stage II you will be expected to tackle tasks varying from case notes to reports, memoranda, notices or letters of a medical nature. Medical vocabulary at this stage will not be so difficult as that required at Stage III and drug names will often be given to you on the instruction sheet. You must, however, satisfy the examiners in all three parts of the examination, i.e. transcription, letter expanded from dictated notes, and manuscript tabulation. Obviously, therefore, everything that has been said on shorthand transcription, medical shorthand and typewriting is relevant and should be studied, as well as the communications book in this series.

Stage III will include all the above and the medical vocabulary will be appropriate for a fully qualified medical secretary. It may be helpful to study the syllabus for Stage III given below as this gives details of all the learning objectives. Students do not always bother to look at this syllabus, relying on their lecturers to cover the points. However, at higher levels this can be an excellent revision aid and will ensure that nothing has been overlooked by you or your tutor.

It is impossible to state categorically which vocabulary you will require at which stage and the wider your knowledge, even at Stage II, the better. It is essential to be familiar at Stage II with all the shorthand outlines for the various consultants; the branch of medicine in which they specialise; the names of the various clinics held in hospital; all parts of the body (bones, arteries, glands, etc.). You should be familiar with the common ailments, operations, treatments and drugs, also the commonly-used abbreviations and the medical root words, prefixes and suffixes.

MEDICAL SHORTHAND-TYPEWRITING STAGE III (ADVANCED)

The Aims of the examination are

(a) to test shorthand-typewriting ability in dealing with medical vocabulary at a level appropriate to employment as a medical secretary, including work in hospitals, general practice and community medicine

(b) to encourage the ability to produce, with economy of time and materials, typewritten work that is ready for signature

It is recommended that before taking the examination candidates should have a shorthand speed in excess of 100 wpm, typewriting ability equivalent to Stage III level, a background of medical vocabulary and a good command of English language.

SYLLABUS TOPIC	LEARNING OBJECTIVES	BEHAVIOURAL OBJECTIVES
	Candidates should	In this examination candidates should be able to
1. RECORDING OF DICTATION	Have a thorough knowledge of the shorthand system and its abbreviating devices	1.1 Take continuous dictation for periods of up to 3 minutes
	Recall and write without hesitation the shorthand outlines for a wide general vocabulary and for common medical words, terms and abbreviations	1.2 Write fluently and accurately from dictation at an average speed of 100 wpm (approximately 150-170 spm)
	Generate new outlines for unfamiliar general and non-specialist medical vocabulary	
	Be accustomed to recording material of higher than normal syllabic intensity	
	Comprehend and record language of varied grammatical complexity	
	Write fluent, accurate and controlled outlines from dictation	
	Use appropriate equipment (shorthand notebook, pen/pencil etc.) effectively	
2. TRANSCRIPTION In general	Have a working command of the grammar of everyday English; be familiar with the style of medical communication	2.1 Transcribe the dictated work verbatim on a typewriter as required
	Be familiar with common medical words, terms and abbreviations	2.2 Transcribe the handwritten work/amended typescript on a typewriter as required
	Understand the common word roots underlying much medical terminology and the principles of word formation	2.3 Punctuate either as directed or so as to convey the sense of the original
	Recognise and transcribe accurately words of similar sound/structure, e.g. hypotension/hypertension, hysterectomy/hysterostomy/hysterotomy	2.4 Spell according to normal English usage
		2.5 Interpret and incorporate amendments as instructed
	Use English and medical dictionaries effectively	2.6 Interpret and render abbreviations appropriately

SYLLABUS TOPIC	LEARNING OBJECTIVES	BEHAVIOURAL OBJECTIVES
	Be experienced in using English language and medical knowledge, as necessary, to supplement an inadequate shorthand note or to decipher unclear handwriting	2.7 Complete all the work within 2½ hours from completion of the dictation
	Know when abbreviations should be retained/extended	
	Know when words dictated in full should be transcribed in abbreviated form	
	Appreciate the need for cost effective use of time and materials	
From own shorthand notes	Have confidence in their shorthand notes	
	Read their notes quickly and accurately	
	Co-ordinate shorthand reading with typewriting skills	
From manuscript	Be familiar with different styles of handwriting/amended typescript	
	Know the common manuscript correction signs and conventions	
3. MATERIALS Paper, Envelope, Carbon paper, Correcting materials, Printed forms	Know sizes and qualities of stationery and their appropriate usage	3.1 Select appropriate materials for given tasks
	Understand the importance of clean, uncreased typewritten work	3.2 Carry out the set tasks using no more printed stationery or envelopes than provided by the Board
	Know how to correct errors effectively, using appropriate correction methods	3.3 Produce and route carbon copies as indicated
	Know procedures for routing carbon copies	3.4 Make any necessary typographical corrections effectively
	Understand the need for economy in use of materials	
4. INSTRUCTIONS Explicit and implicit	Understand the importance of complying with specific instructions	4.1 Interpret and follow appropriately instructions relating to the processing of the work given in the dictation or in the candidate's instruction sheet
		4.2 Re-arrange, extract and incorporate amendments in accordance with instructions
	Understand the secretary's responsibility to recognise and carry out related tasks without explicit instruction (e.g. routing of carbon copies)	4.3 Apply instructions, once given, to all identical instances within a task and carry out related tasks without explicit instruction
	Understand the secretary's responsibility to verify facts (e.g. figures, drug dosages etc.) from information (case notes/file records etc.) supplied, without explicit instructions	4.4 Check, select and incorporate appropriately any necessary "file" details (e.g. reference, patient's name and address) from information supplied
		4.5 Indicate enclosure(s), produce/route carbon copies as implied by context (i.e. not necessarily specified in the instructions)
5. PRESENTATION OF TYPEWRITTEN WORK In general	Understand the importance of clear and systematic presentation of the material, for effective communication	
	Understand the importance of precision and accuracy in medical work	
	Understand the need for adaptability, e.g. in conforming to "house style"; and appreciate that conventional styles may on occasion be over-ridden by the originator's particular requirements	
	Be familiar with the layout of standard medical documents and forms	
Layout Headings (horizontal and vertical) Paragraphing, Footnotes Columns, Tabulation	Be fully conversant with blocked, indented and centred styles of layout	5.1 Select and use appropriate layout styles for given tasks
		5.2 Use any of these layout styles as instructed
		5.3 Follow a specified/demonstrated layout
Punctuation	Be conversant with "open" and "full" styles of punctuation and fully conversant with one of them	5.4 Select and use *one* of these punctuation styles
		5.5 Select appropriate material and allocate to correct location(s) on forms provided; position material correctly

126

C. RECENT EXAMINATION PAPERS

This section gives practice on one RSA paper. Stage III RSA examples are not given as dictation is on tape. If you are unable to practise from tapes supplied by your college, they may be obtained from the RSA at a small charge. For advice on reading the passages, see "Recent Examination Questions" in Chapter 4.

Question 1
(for candidate)

THE ROYAL SOCIETY OF ARTS
EXAMINATIONS BOARD
SINGLE-SUBJECT EXAMINATIONS

S 277   SHORTHAND—TYPEWRITING, STAGE II
THURSDAY, 21st JUNE 1984
TWO AND A HALF HOURS ALLOWED

Instructions to Candidates

You have TEN minutes to read through this question paper before the start of the examination, during which time you may make notes on the examination paper.

Important – As soon as you receive this paper, read carefully the letter printed on page 4. Notes for a reply to this will be dictated to you as Passage 6.

Except where a different instruction is given, all letters should be typed on the headed paper provided, ready for signature as for despatch today. Where no special directions are given regarding display, any method, consistently used within each exercise, will be accepted.

Carbon copies should be taken only where indicated. Dictionaries (both English and Shorthand) and calculators may be used.

Candidates must satisfy the examiner in each section of the examination.

_____

PASSAGE 1 (17 marks)

A memorandum from Area Organizer to Heads of Adult Centres. Our ref: GDB/CAH.
Heading: ADULT LITERACY CLASSES

PASSAGE 2 (80 marks)

A circular letter to be signed by the Managing Director. Do not leave space
for the insertion of name and address. Leave undated. The price list on page
3 is to accompany this letter.

PASSAGE 3 (17 marks)

A letter to Cosgrave Construction Ltd, Greenbank Industrial Estate, York YO3
9TP. A carbon copy is required on the yellow paper provided. Designation:
Financial Controller.

PASSAGE 4 (12 marks)

A notice to be typed on plain white A5 paper and headed: GREENVALE HEALTH CLUB

PASSAGE 5 (24 marks)

A letter to Mr P Clewes, 2 The Paddock, Hatfield, Herts AL9 5PS.

PASSAGE 6 (50 marks)

From the dictated notes, compose and type on plain white A4 paper a reply to
the letter on page 4. Type the appropriate letter-heading for the task.

————————————————————————

NB: At the end of the examination you should put your work into the order of
the examination paper.

128

caps Praxi Canal Cruisers Ltd

s/caps Price List

uc

Starting Saturday	King Class A 8 berth	King Class B 8 berth	Queen Class A 6 berth	Queen Class B 6 berth	Princess Class 4 berth
	£	£	£	£	£
MAY 5	~~230~~	~~220~~	~~210~~	~~170~~	~~160~~
12	~~250~~	~~240~~	~~230~~	~~190~~	~~180~~
19	~~"~~	~~"~~	~~"~~	~~"~~	~~"~~
26	~~320~~	~~330~~	~~310~~	~~270~~	~~260~~
JUNE 2	280	270	260	220	210
9	"	"	"	"	"
16	"	"	"	"	"
23	310	300	290	250	240
30	"	"	"	"	"
JULY 7	"	"	"	"	"
14	"	"	"	"	"
21	350	340	330	280	270
28	"	"	"	"	"
AUG 4	"	"	"	"	"
11	"	"	"	"	"
18	"	"	"	"	"
25	340	330	320	270	260
SEPT 1	280	270	260	220	210
8	260	250	240	200	190
15	240	230	210	180	170
22	210	205	200	150	140
29	160	155	150	140	130

ALL PRICES SUBJECT TO VAT AT CURRENT RATE

lc

N.B 8 berth Boats are £30 less if only 6 persons book
6 " " " £20 " " " 4 " "
(This offer does not apply during ~~July~~
~~and~~ August)

TYPIST – Boat prices in double spacing
and do not use ditto marks.

129

8 Willow Crescent
EGHAM
Surrey
TW20 9TS

19 June 1984

The Manager
Magna Supermarket
Town Square
EGHAM
Surrey
TW20 3PV

Dear Sir

I have just completed my fifth year at Greenbank High School and will be returning to the sixth form in September. I feel that now my examinations are over I would like some part-time work, and I have heard that you sometimes employ young people to work on Saturdays only.

I am very interested in this type of work and would be grateful if you could let me know if there are any vacancies at the present time.

Yours faithfully

A M Rafferty

A M Rafferty (Miss)

THE ROYAL SOCIETY OF ARTS
EXAMINATIONS BOARD
SINGLE-SUBJECT EXAMINATIONS

SHORTHAND–TYPEWRITING, STAGE II

S **277** THURSDAY, 21st JUNE 1984

Passages and Notes for Dictation

(NOT to be shown to candidates)

Instructions to Reader

The following passages are to be dictated in the manner in which they would be dictated to a shorthand-typist in a commercial office, and therefore not at a uniform speed. The **average** speed of dictation is to be **80** words per minute, except where a speed of 60 wpm is indicated. To assist the reader in timing the dictation, each of the passages is divided into half-minute portions. Provided that the passage is dictated precisely within the time limit specified, the actual speed of dictation within the passage is a matter for the dictator's discretion, and the time indicators should be used only as a guide.

The marks of punctuation should be indicated by the inflexion of the voice, and must not be dictated. Care should be taken to articulate the words very distinctly.

The dictator must follow the passages **exactly** as printed. Dictation of each passage should be preceded by the title or addressee, and any instructions given. An interval of half a minute is to be allowed after the dictation of each passage.

The reader must hand these printed passages to the invigilator on the completion of the dictation.

NOTE

The dictation of the preliminary passage, of the note immediately following, and of the examination passages proper with their introductory headings must be completed within the first 20 minutes (approximately) of the two and a half hours allowed for the complete examination.

TO BE READ TO THE CANDIDATES IMMEDIATELY BEFORE THE DICTATION OF THE PASSAGES OVERLEAF.

Before each passage you will be told the title or addressee. Further instructions may also be dictated before the passage begins, but before you start typing, make sure that you have read the instructions on the printed paper handed to you by the invigilator. Addresses and references not given in the dictation are printed on that paper.

S–T II (Dict)(Summer 1984) [OVER]

SHORTHAND—80 WORDS A MINUTE

PRELIMINARY PASSAGE

Before the passages set for the examination are dictated, the following preliminary passage should be read so that the candidates may become accustomed to the reader's voice. The passage is marked up at 80 wpm; the whole of the passage need not be read.

No transcription of the preliminary passage is required, but the shorthand notes must be returned with the notes of the examination passages.

(Recruiting for the police force)

Minutes

⅟₄   In a recent recruiting drive the police said they would like to interview well-educated, ambitious school-leavers who want to be of real help to society.

½   They believe the new generation can help considerably to solve society's new problems. Rapid social changes, more organised crime and more cunning criminals
¾   create the kinds of problem which take a good education to master.

1   In addition, there is the complexity of today's city traffic. These are all problems which call for men and women with a good educational background.

⅟₄   Policemen and women of today in their dark blue uniforms do not spend all their time patrolling the streets.

½   There are many branches of police work and many opportunities in every field so their education is never wasted. They need integrity, intelligence and, above all, the
¾   ability to think for themselves. According to the advertisements a policeman has a worthwhile, rewarding job with good pay and housing and a pension on his
2   retirement.

Passage 1 — 140 words to be dictated at an average speed of 80 words a minute

(A memorandum)

Minutes

Please note that from the term beginning September nineteen eighty-four, in addition to our usual range of courses we will be offering adult literacy classes at all six centres.

½ These classes will be widely advertised in the two weeks / prior to enrolment and I would stress the need for accepting enrolments by telephone. Although this is not our normal practice, the prospective students' learning difficulties may prevent them from completing the application form.

1 There is no fee for the // courses, which will be staffed by volunteers who have been trained at the local College of Education. There is, however, a shortage of volunteers, as this work is normally done in very small groups, with each teacher taking just
½ two / or three students. If, therefore, you know anyone who might help us with this worthwhile work, please let me know.

[INTERVAL OF HALF A MINUTE]

Passage 2 – 240 words to be dictated at an average speed of 80 words a minute

(A circular letter)

Minutes

Dear Sir or Madam

Thank you for your interest in our canal cruising holidays. We hope you will decide to holiday with us this year, but as we are already receiving enquiries
½ for next season we would advise you to / book as soon as possible.

Not only are there no price increases for nineteen eighty-four, but the price for some weeks has actually been reduced. If you are able to take your holiday in
1 either June or September, you // will effect great savings.

Canal cruising is fun for the whole family. The children will enjoy helping to steer the boat and learning to operate the locks. You will pass through beautiful, unspoilt countryside at a leisurely pace,
½ and if / you wish to stop and explore, there are villages and shopping centres within walking distance of the canal.

Our marina is ideally situated to give you a choice of different routes, whether your cruise is for one week
2 or two. //

I enclose a price list, and would like to point out that our prices are fully inclusive. There are no hidden extra costs. Fuel, bedding and car parking are all included, and you are welcome to bring your family
½ pet / free of charge.

Our friendly staff will be pleased to answer any questions you may have and to give you every assistance in planning your cruise, so please telephone or write without delay and ensure a memorable holiday.

3 Yours faithfully //

[INTERVAL OF HALF A MINUTE]

Passage 3 — 140 words to be dictated at an average speed of 80 words a minute

(Letter to Cosgrave Construction Limited)

Minutes

Dear Sirs

We have received your letter dated sixth June, nineteen eighty-four relating to delayed payments for the construction contract.

We acknowledge that certain payments have not been made according to the terms of the contract and we

½   regret / any undue delay.

In your letter you imply that it is your intention to invoke the clause relating to interest which can be charged on overdue payments. Before you make any

1   calculations we must point out that you have had // the full benefit of interest earned on the original down payment, and you have also been paid the balance of the financial agreement money, which was one million pounds. Not only is this helping to fund these overdue

½   payments but / you are earning interest on a substantial amount of money.

We should be pleased to receive your comments.
Yours faithfully

[INTERVAL OF HALF A MINUTE]

Passage 4 — 100 words to be dictated at an average speed of 80 words a minute

(A notice)

Minutes

Why not make nineteen eighty-four the year you return to fitness and good health? We have excellent facilities and our qualified staff will be pleased to plan a programme just for you.

½   Our members can exercise in the gymnasium, / swim in the heated pool or relax in the sauna. The club is open for twelve hours a day, every day of the year except for bank holidays.

The annual membership fee is one hundred pounds per

1   person, but family // membership for one hundred and fifty pounds is excellent value for money.

Call in, write or telephone for further details.

Passage 5 — 180 words to be dictated at an average speed of 80 words a minute

(A letter to Mr P Clewes)

Minutes

Dear Mr Clewes
I understand that you have expressed interest in our timber-framed houses.

We are the subsidiary of a large Swedish company and our aim is to develop and sell a wide range of houses ½ specifically designed for / the home market.

In addition to our attractive designs, and the high quality of materials used in the construction of our houses, we should point out that the insulation we use is a great improvement on the usual building 1 methods. // This results in a warm and comfortable home for much lower fuel costs.

One other main reason for choosing a timber-framed house is the speed with which the building can be erec-½ ted. From receiving your order until moving into / your beautiful new home could be as little as fourteen weeks.

I hope these brief details have impressed you, and if you would like to receive our brochure, which gives full specifications including plans of the different 2 house designs and // a price list, please send a cheque for five pounds and it will be despatched by return post.
Yours sincerely

[INTERVAL OF HALF A MINUTE]

Passage 6 — notes for reply to the letter given on page 4 of your printed paper. To be dictated at an average speed of 60 words a minute.

Minutes

Yes Saturday work available – mainly shelf filling and packing customers' shopping. Hours oh nine hundred to seventeen thirty but one week in four, eleven hundred ½ to nineteen thirty. One hour / lunch break. Rate of pay one pound seventy-five per hour. Overall provided. Discount shopping for employees. Telephone Staff Officer for interview.

(52 words)

136

D. TUTOR'S NOTES AND ANSWERS

All the sections of paper 1 are answered here. The layout of letters, etc. is, of course, only one of several acceptable styles (see Chapter 3).

Question 1
Passage 1:

General:

If you have read the instruction sheet carefully, you will know that no reference will be dictated as this has already been given to you, together with memorandum headings, so do not forget and use your own initials. You are not given instructions as to paper size so you must use your discretion here. I have chosen A4 paper and the layout is just one of several acceptable styles. Take care with the apostrophe (prospective students'). 1984 is acceptable written in words or figures, as are other numbers given. Remember that although College of Education has capital letters, local does not.

Words commonly
mis-spelled:

literacy
enrolment
prospective
volunteers
practice – know the difference from practise
worthwhile – one word, not two

Outlines for
difficult words:

	New Era	2000	Gregg	Teeline
literacy				
enrolment				
prospective				
volunteers				
worthwhile				

Selected
phrases:

term beginning

two or three

range of

Note: As this is quite straightforward it is a good warm-up passage. Some students may, however, prefer to tackle passage 2 first which has 80 marks allocated to it.

137

Display:

MEMORANDUM

To: Heads of Adult Centres   Ref: GDB/CAH

From: Area Organiser   Date: 21 June 1984

ADULT LITERACY CLASSES

Please note that from the term beginning September 1984, in
addition to our usual range of courses we will be offering
adult literacy classes at all six centres.

These classes will be widely advertised in the two weeks prior
to enrolment and I would stress the need for accepting
enrolments by telephone. Although this is not our normal
practice, the prospective students´ learning difficulties may
prevent them from completing the application form.

There is no fee for the courses, which will be staffed by
volunteers who have been trained at the local College of
Education. There is, however, a shortage of volunteers, as
this work is normally done in very small groups, with each
teacher taking just two or three students. If, therefore, you
know anyone who might help us with this worthwhile work, please
let me know.

Passage 2:

General: Pay close attention to the instructions given to you about leaving the letter undated and without a space for name and address. Often these are done so automatically that it is difficult to omit them. This circular letter obviously needs to be typed on A4 paper, as does the price list accompanying it. As always, care is needed over punctuation so as not to distort the sense of the passage.

Words commonly mis-spelled:
interest
receiving
advise − know the difference from advice
effect − know the difference from affect
steer
leisurely
countryside − one word, not two

Outlines for difficult words:

	New Era	2000	Gregg	Teeline
canal				
unspoilt				
leisurely				
marina				
memorable				

Selected phrases:

	New Era	2000	Gregg	Teeline
in our				
we hope you will				
this year				
as soon as possible				
or two				
price list				
free of charge				
without delay				

The most common mistake when typing the price list is to underline King, Class, etc., instead of realising that the lines refer to the instruction "uc".

139

Display:

Dear Sir or Madam

Thank you for your interest in our canal cruising holidays. We
hope you will decide to holiday with us this year, but as we
are already receiving enquiries for next season we would advise
you to book as soon as possible.

Not only are there no price increases for nineteen eighty-four,
but the price for some weeks has actually been reduced. If you
are able to take your holiday in either June or September, you
will effect great savings.

Canal cruising is fun for the whole family. The children will
enjoy helping to steer the boat and learning to operate the
locks. You will pass through beautiful, unspoilt countryside
at a leisurely pace, and if you wish to stop and explore, there
are villages and shopping centres within walking distance of
the canal.

Our marina is ideally situated to give you a choice of
different routes, whether your cruise is for one week or two.

I enclose a price list, and would like to point out that our
prices are fully inclusive. There are no hidden extra costs.
Fuel, bedding and car parking are all included, and you are
welcome to bring your family pet free of charge.

Our friendly staff will be pleased to answer any questions you
may have and to give you every assistance in planning your
cruise, so please telephone or write without delay and ensure a
memorable holiday.

Yours faithfully

Managing Director

Enc

PRAXI CANAL CRUISERS LIMITED

P R I C E   L I S T

Starting Saturday	KING CLASS A 8 berth	KING CLASS B 8 berth	QUEEN CLASS A 6 berth	QUEEN CLASS B 6 berth	PRINCESS CLASS 4 berth
	£	£	£	£	£
JUNE 2	280	270	260	220	210
9	280	270	260	220	210
16	280	270	260	220	210
23	310	300	290	250	240
30	310	300	290	250	240
JULY 7	310	300	290	250	240
14	310	300	290	250	240
21	350	340	330	280	270
28	350	340	330	280	270
AUG 4	350	340	330	280	270
11	350	340	330	280	270
18	350	340	330	280	270
25	340	330	320	270	260
SEPT 1	280	270	260	220	210
8	260	250	240	200	190
15	240	230	210	180	170
22	210	205	200	150	140
29	160	155	150	140	130

ALL PRICES SUBJECT TO VAT AT CURRENT RATE

NB 8 berth boats are £30 less if only 6 persons book
    6 berth boats are £20 less if only 4 persons book
    (This offer does not apply during August)

Passage 3:

General: Here again the instructions are all important as a carbon copy is required and all details regarding stationery, address etc., are given. Care again needed with punctuation, and don't forget the copy if you have to make corrections. The date and sum of money can be typed either as words or figures.

Words commonly
mis-spelled: received
    imply
    invoke

Outlines for
difficult words:

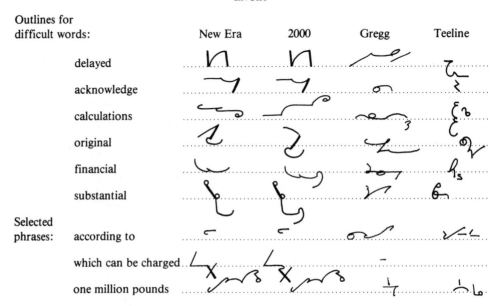

	New Era	2000	Gregg	Teeline
delayed				
acknowledge				
calculations				
original				
financial				
substantial				

Selected phrases:

according to

which can be charged

one million pounds

Display:

Our Ref   /

21st June 1984

Cosgrave Construction Ltd
Greenbank Industrial Estate
YORK
YO3 9TP

Dear Sirs

We have received your letter dated 6th June 1984 relating to
delayed payments for the construction contract.

We acknowledge that certain payments have not been made
according to the terms of the contract and we regret any undue
delay.

In your letter you imply that it is your intention to invoke
the clause relating to interest which can be charged on overdue
payments. Before you make any calculations we must point out
that you have had the full benefit of interest earned on the
original down payment, and you have also been paid the balance
of the financial agreement money, which was one million pounds.
Not only is this helping to fund these overdue payments but you
are earning interest on a substantial amount of money.

We should be pleased to receive your comments.

Yours faithfully

Financial Controller

Passage 4:

General:

This passage only merits 12 marks but they should be quite easy to obtain as all instructions are clearly given to you. Only line spacing and margins need to be chosen so that the notice is attractively displayed on the A5 paper. Punctuation is fairly simple but do not forget the question mark, and no closure of course. Again figures or words acceptable for date, sums of money, etc.

Words commonly mis-spelled:

programme (program acceptable in relation to computers only)

gymnasium

sauna

Outlines for difficult words:

	New Era	2000	Gregg	Teeline
facilities				
exercise				
gymnasium				
relax				

Selected phrases:

every day of the year				
bank holidays				

144

Display:

GREENVALE HEALTH CLUB

Why not make 1984 the year you return to fitness
and good health? We have excellent facilities
and our qualified staff will be pleased to plan
a programme just for you.

Our members can exercise in the gymnasium, swim
in the heated pool or relax in the sauna. The
club is open for twelve hours a day, every day
of the year except for bank holidays.

The annual membership fee is one hundred pounds
per person, but family membership for one hundred
and fifty pounds is excellent value for money.

Call in, write or telephone for further details.

Passage 5:

General: This letter will need careful paragraphing and care with small words such as "of" and "for", also singular and plural words.

Words commonly mis-spelled:
subsidiary
Swedish
develop
comfortable
fourteen
impressed – NOT imprest
brochure

Outlines for difficult words:

	New Era	2000	Gregg	Teeline
subsidiary				
Swedish				
specifically				
insulation				
fourteen				
brochure				

Selected phrases:
timber-framed
Swedish company
your order
as little as

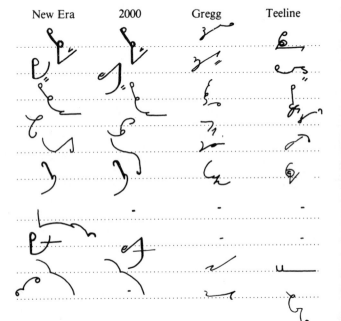

Display:

Our Ref

21 June 1984

Mr P Clewes
2 The Paddock
Hatfield
Herts
AL9 5PS

Dear Mr Clewes

I understand that you have expressed interest in our timber-
framed houses.

We are the subsidiary of a large Swedish company and our aim is
to develop and sell a wide range of houses specifically
designed for the home market.

In addition to our attractive designs, and the high quality of
materials used in the construction of our houses, we should
point out that the insulation we use is a great improvement on
the usual building methods. This results in a warm and
comfortable home for much lower fuel costs.

One other main reason for choosing a timber-framed house is the
speed with which the building can be erected From receiving
your order until moving into your beautiful new home could be
as little as fourteen weeks.

I hope these brief details have impressed you, and if you would
like to receive our brochure, which gives full specifications
including plans of the different house designs and a price
list, please send a cheque for five pounds and it will be
despatched by return post.

Yours sincerely

This is often the part of the examination which causes most problems. Candidates tend to string the notes together into short unrelated sentences. Do not be afraid to move points about in order to produce a letter in good style and to expand on the facts given in the notes. Letters will obviously vary enormously as they reflect a person's personality. However, for this particular question I feel it should have a friendly tone while remaining business-like.

Display:

MAGNA   SUPERMARKETS

Our Ref   /

21 June 1984

Miss A M Rafferty
8 Willow Crescent
EGHAM
Surrey
TW20 9TS

Dear Miss Rafferty

Thank you for your letter of 19 June asking about the possibility of part-time work in this store. We do employ young people who are still at school to work on Saturdays only and I am pleased to be able to tell you that we have a vacancy at the moment.

The work consists mainly of re-stocking the shelves and the packing of customers´ shopping. An overall is supplied by the firm.

The hours are from 0900 to 1730 for three Saturdays, and 1100 to 1930 on the fourth and one hour is allowed for a lunch break. We pay £1.75 per hour and allow a good discount on staff purchases made in the store.

I have passed your letter to our Staff Officer, Mr H Jones, and suggest you telephone him at the above number as soon as possible to arrange a convenient time for an interview.

Yours sincerely

Manager

E. A STEP FURTHER

However many examinations are successfully passed, once you are working, each new shorthand task to be typed provides a new challenge for the shorthand-typist, and by attractively displaying documents the conscientious worker will gain much satisfaction.

Efficient shorthand-typists will find there is a great demand for their skills and they should have no difficulty in speedily progressing to secretarial/personal assistant positions if they have also acquired the necessary office practice skills. There is really no limit to career prospects, for many of today's managers and executives started their working life in a secretarial position.

The book lists referred to at the end of Chapters 3 and 4 are equally relevant in preparing for shorthand−typewriting examinations.

Chapter 6

Audio-Typewriting

A GETTING STARTED

TECHNIQUE

Audio-typewriting is really a combination of skills. While it can be, and often is, "picked up" by typists without formal training, it is unlikely that a high degree of competence will result and bad habits may be formed.

Clearly, a level of typewriting ability is necessary before introducing audio equipment. There are two points at which audio training might start. Firstly, when the student has achieved a typewriting speed of 20–25 wpm, with good accuracy and some display practice. The skills of typewriting and audio-typewriting are then developed alongside each other. Secondly, later in the course, when a greater degree of typewriting skill, including a higher speed, has been achieved. Audio-typewriting can then be developed more intensively in a much shorter time.

It is a fear of many students that they would be expected to type at the speed of the dictation! This is not so, because you control the equipment, stopping and starting the recording as necessary. From the start you are aiming to achieve **continuous typing with controlled listening**.

As there is no "copy" on which to concentrate your eyes, many students find they are looking at their hands. Others fix their gaze on the page in the typewriter. Both ways can become habits and transfer to your typewriting and shorthand transcription, with adverse effects. Never look at your hands or the keyboard. Try not to watch the typing point, but fix your eyes on a point in the room or on your instruction sheet.

Your training should start with short sentences, leading on to longer ones without dictated instructions. This is also testing and training your memory. The training should then extend to various business documents and gradually bring in more dictated instructions.

You need a good command of English grammar and spelling. While dictionaries may be used in class and in most examinations, valuable time is lost each time you stop to check a word.

EQUIPMENT

There is an extensive range of audio equipment with which candidates should be familiar. It is clearly an advantage for candidates for Secretarial Duties, Office Practice and Group Certificate examinations to have used at least one form of audio equipment. During the secretarial duties/office organisation classes, you should have discussed all aspects of audio-typewriting in your examination syllabus, including centralised systems.

Table 6.1 Format and content of examinations

Examining board: **London Chamber of Commerce and Industry (LCCI)**

General information: Dictionaries are allowed.

Title	Level	Length of Exam	Format and Regulations
Audio-typewriting	Elementary	90 mins	Dictation speed 60 wpm. Transcription from recorded dictation, printed matter and manuscript.
Audio-typewriting	Intermediate	120 mins	Dictation speed 80 wpm. Transcription from recorded dictation, printed matter and manuscript.
Audio-typewriting	Higher	150 mins	

Examining board: **Pitman Examinations Institute (PEI)**

Typewriting Transcription Speed Test (Audio)	Elementary	27 mins + 8 mins preparation	Dictation speed 80 wpm. Transcription of 2 passages totalling 400 words. Error tolerance 4%. Dictionaries are not allowed.
Audio-typewriting	Intermediate 80	28 mins + 4 mins preparation	Dictation speed 80 wpm. Transcription of 2 passages totalling 400 words. Error tolerance 3%. Dictionaries are allowed.

Table 6.1 continued

Title	Level	Length of Exam	Format and Regulations
Audio-typewriting	Intermediate 100	30 mins + 4 mins preparation	Dictation speed 100 wpm. Transcription of 2 passages totalling 600 words. Error tolerance 3%. Dictionaries are allowed.
Audio-typewriting	Advanced	33 mins + 4 mins preparation	Dictation speed 120 wpm. Transcription of 2 passages totalling 720 words. Error tolerance 3%. Dictionaries are allowed.

Examining board: Royal Society of Arts (RSA)

General information: Dictionaries are allowed.

Title	Level	Length of Exam	Format and Regulations
Audio-typewriting	Stage I	100 mins	Transcription from recorded dictation and manuscript. Total 560 words.
Audio-typewriting	Stage II	120 mins	Transcription from recorded dictation and manuscript. Total 800 words. Composition from notes.
Audio-typewriting	Stage III	120 mins	Transcription from recorded dictation and manuscript. Total 1400 words. Composition from notes.
Audio-typewriting French or German	Intermediate	120 mins + 10 mins reading time	Display material from manuscript and transcription of recording at 15 spm production speed.

Table 6.1 continued

Title	Level	Length of Exam	Format and Regulations
Medical Audio-typewriting	Intermediate	150 mins	Transcription of material of a medical nature. Notes to expand into a letter. Average dictation speed 80 wpm.

Examining board:	**Scottish Business Education Council (SCOTBEC)**		

General information: Dictionaries are allowed.

Title	Level	Length of Exam	Format and Regulations
Audio-typewriting	Stage I	90 mins	Display of documents from recorded dictation and dealing with priorities.
Audio-typewriting	Stage II	120 mins	Display of documents from recorded dictation.
Medical		150 mins	Transcription from recorded dictation and manuscript. Composition from notes. Total 1400 words at average speed 100 wpm.

B. ESSENTIAL PRINCIPLES

As in other chapters, this section is arranged in parts to give advice on important areas, as follows:

1. Examiners' criteria
2. Audio-typewriting transcription
3. The manuscript
4. Composition from notes
5. Audio-typewriting in foreign languages
6. Medical audio-typewriting
7. Audio-typewriting theory
8. The examination

1. EXAMINERS' CRITERIA

Continuous typing with controlled listening must be the aim throughout your practical training. The basis of the examiners' marking schemes is largely the same as for typewriting, that is following instructions, accuracy, production speed, consistency, and producing mailable documents. You should refer to Chapter 3 for additional details.

Instructions

You will be given instructions both on an instruction sheet and during recording. All written and verbal instructions are important and must be followed, otherwise you will be heavily penalised.

The instruction sheet details the rules and the composition of the examination, gives the names and addresses you will need, and the length of each passage. It also states the type of paper you should use, number of carbon copies and the nature of the alterations and additions to be made to the text. Sometimes, difficult spelling or unusual words are shown. Use all the information given and check that you copy accurately from the instruction sheet.

Recorded instructions mostly concern layout and type style. You may be given several instructions together, e.g. heading, closed capitals, underscore. There are alternative expressions for the same signs – solidus/oblique, brackets/parentheses, full stop/sentence, quotes/inverted commas. When instructed to "open quotes", use double quote marks; if single quotes are wanted, they are usually dictated as such. There is still frequent confusion between a colon and a semi-colon, and a hyphen is frequently rendered as a dash. In some group certificates, few instructions are given as you are expected to know where to use capitals, punctuation marks, etc.

Accuracy

Accurate transcription is extremely important. Listen carefully to the ending of words. You need to understand the meaning of each sentence and the passage so that you distinguish correctly between similar sounding words. The ability to spell with minimum reference to a dictionary and to recognise the need for commas and apostrophes, correctly positioned, is important. Poor spelling and punctuation, especially the omission or incorrect positioning of apostrophes, are always among the most frequent causes of failure. Some of the most commonly mis-spelt words are listed in Chapter 4, and the PEI also produce a spelling list.

Incorrect rendering of *similar sounding* words is also a major cause of lost marks. Errors may be due to poor spelling, unclear dictation or lack of comprehension. The most frequently confused words are listed below and in Chapter 4.

accept/except	eminent/imminent
access/excess	enable/unable
addition/edition	enforce/in force
advice/advise	ensure/insure/unsure
affect/effect	era/error
ascent/assent	faint/feint
assistance/assistants	finally/finely
bare/bear	formally/formerly
board/bored	forth/fourth
born/borne	loose/lose
check/cheque	minor/miner

course/coarse	personal/personnel
compliment/complement	piece/peace
correspondence/correspondents	practise/practice
council/counsel/consul	prophecy/prophesy
current/currant	residence/residents
decease/disease	role/roll
decent/descent/dissent	site/sight/cite
dependent/dependant	stationery/stationary
device/devise	through/threw
draft/draught	to/too/two
draw/drawer	wear/ware
elicit/illicit	whose/who's
emigrate/immigrate	your/you're

Sometimes two words are written separately when they should be combined, or are hyphenated incorrectly or are combined when they should be written separately. Some examples are listed in Chapter 4.

Before removing your work from the typewriter, *proof-reading* is essential. This must include checking on grammar, punctuation and the use of capitals, spelling, accuracy, display, numbers and transcription. Many marks are needlessly lost through undetected errors.

A poor standard of *correcting* is also a major cause of lost marks. Neat and careful correction by any efficient method is accepted, but many candidates take insufficient care. You should stop and make any necessary corrections as you go along. If you use liquid paper to mask an incorrect letter, do not forget to insert the correct one!

Where you are required to compose a letter from dictated notes, you must make sure that you convey the correct meaning and tone and that nothing is omitted.

Production speed

The time allocated to most audio-typewriting examinations is fairly tight. This means that you need to type accurately and at a reasonable speed. You do *not* have time to stop and use a dictionary or to rewind the recording too many times. You should have practised passages using a variety of instructions and subject matter, and near to examinations your practice should be timed. Marks are deducted in proportion to any passages left unfinished. The time allocated does not allow for listening through without typing, or for complete re-typing of any documents.

Consistency

The same standards of consistency are expected in audio-typewriting as in typewriting. This particularly concerns the layout, capitalisation and punctuation of each piece of dictation. You are expected to use capitals for months, names, etc. without instructions and to be consistent in rendering other terms, such as "Head Office", "Marketing Manager", etc. An instruction for initial capitals is not repeated when the same word(s) recur, but you are expected to use a consistent style. Penalties are frequently incurred when candidates fail to identify these repeats.

2. TRANSCRIPTION

Your training should start with sentences and short passages, recorded in a familiar voice, to introduce you to the concept of aural "input". It will then progress to longer, varied and more complex passages, which may be dictated by different people.

Initially there is a tendency to type every word, but you must learn to distinguish between the text and instructions. At first your teacher should preview the dictation, pointing out new instructions, unusual content and common spelling faults, but you must learn to cope with these as you go along. There is no visual document to indicate the length and you must assess this from the number of words indicated or the amount of tape used.

You must use a consistent style, correctly executed, and follow all printed and verbal instructions concerning the style, layout, inclusion of a heading, additional text, details of copies and the type of paper.

Listen very carefully to the word endings and verb tenses. Also listen to the inflexion of the voice to determine the need for commas, which are not dictated. You need to understand the meaning of each sentence in order to distinguish between homophones, e.g. hear/here, or between plurals and singular words with apostrophes, i.e. secretaries/secretary's, companies/company's. Penalties *are* imposed when candidates sprinkle their work with unnecessary capital letters, commas or apostrophes. This indicates a lack of basic English competence and a failure to understand the passage.

You are expected to be consistent in the form of display you use and you should read Chapter 3 for details of the individual documents. As with typewriting, you are expected to be consistent in the use of words/figures, upper/lower case, etc. and to conform to the rules on margins, line spacing and other display points. Letters and memoranda always require a date and some boards insist on every document carrying a reference.

3. MANUSCRIPT

In the office, you may often need to combine some recorded dictation with another manuscript document. Most audio-typewriting examinations (with the exception of Pitman Examinations Institute) include a manuscript with one passage. This document will be of a comparable standard of typewriting to that of your audio examination. It may be any style of document but often it is a form, price list, table or programme to be displayed on the same or a separate sheet to the dictation.

Some examination boards, such as the RSA, do give a considerable proportion of the marks to this question and it is therefore important to complete it well. You can again refer to Chapter 3 for the display of documents.

Before starting on either dictation or manuscript, read the document fully. You should gain an understanding of the subject and it might contain useful names or spellings which occur in the dictation. Instructions may be given on the recording or the instruction sheet.

4. COMPOSITION

It is not enough to simply string the dictated notes together in sentences: you must expand them into a good business document. Your letter must convey the full and correct message, in the right tone.

Firstly, you should read several times through the letter you have to answer. Then type the dictated notes and underline the important points. Compose a draft reply, using the dictated facts. This may be done in rough by handwriting or typewriting. Avoid long, complicated sentences and words you do not fully understand. Put the information into a logical order, divided into paragraphs. Check that you have used correct spelling and complete sentences, conveyed the full message clearly and unambiguously and used the appropriate tone. This is determined by the content of the original, the message in the notes and to whom the letter is addressed. It may be giving information, replying to a complaint, conveying an apology or thanks, or answering an invitation. If you are writing to a young person, the style should be less formal and stilted than to a company.

Now you can type your letter, paying full attention to accuracy and display.

This type of exercise will be slow at first, but you should aim to complete it in about 20–30 minutes during your examination. You should refer to the *Business Communication* title in this series for help in this skill and apply the knowledge you have gained from Communications or English lectures included in your course. You can also gain from studying the letters which are dictated to you in shorthand and those you produce as typewriting exercises.

5. FOREIGN LANGUAGE AUDIO-TYPEWRITING

There are audio-typewriting examinations in French and German, which are likely to be taken by bi-lingual students.

For students following a secretarial course including a foreign language, the level of ability detailed in the syllabus should be considered an absolute minimum. At least "A" level is usually recommended and even post-graduate students find the business vocabulary extensive and challenging. Much more extensive typewriting practice in the language is obviously essential and a specialist textbook would be used which would detail the displays accepted for business documents and all the other variations from British standards. The RSA booklet *Foreign Secretarial Practice* gives details for the four languages in which they examine, together with a list of dictation instructions.

It can be difficult to distinguish spellings, plurals, etc., and an understanding of the passages is very important for accurate transcription to be achieved. Documents must be displayed in the correct style for the country.

Proof-reading must also be undertaken very thoroughly, checking for grammatical points, gender agreements, accents, spelling, word endings, punctuation etc. Misunderstanding or mishearing similar sounding words and phrases and lack of careful proof-reading are the causes of many lost marks.

Some students find that another big problem is alternating frequently between English and a foreign language, with the numerous minor differences in display etc. Such differences as the use of commas for decimal points, use of courtesy titles, different paragraph indents etc. can create problems for students entering examinations.

6. MEDICAL AUDIO-TYPEWRITING

If you wish to become a medical secretary, you should follow a specialist course, which will include tuition on terminology and where all the skills subjects will include considerable medical content. You will need a medical dictionary as well as your English dictionary.

In audio-typewriting, as in shorthand, variations in pronunciation and regional accents may cause difficulty in understanding and accurately transcribing the passages. You should become familiar with the general and common phrases as well as much specialist vocabulary and common drug names. There are many recurring prefixes and suffixes, but confusion can arise between similarly sounding words of different spelling and meaning, e.g. ilium/ileum, fibrous/fibrin, dis/dys and hyper/hypo. Extra care with listening and proof-reading should eliminate errors. Also take care if amounts such as strength or dosage of drugs are dictated.

7. THEORY

Secretarial duties and office practice textbooks include information on dictation equipment. Practical use of equipment also increases your awareness of theoretical points, as will any experience you may have of a company's individual or bank system. Most theory questions in Secretarial Duties, Office Practice and group certificates/diplomas concern the advantages/disadvantages of recorded dictation and centralised services, instructions to a dictator or inexperienced transcriber and, in group certificates, the managerial considerations.

Examination technique — how to read a question and present a full and appropriate answer — is a skill. Some part of your course, usually in the month before the examination, should be dedicated to this skill by using past question papers. Some questions are very short, requiring one word or just a sentence, while others must be answered more fully. Examiners are looking at your approach to a question as well as testing your knowledge; marks are allocated to style as well as content. Where a description is required, then an essay style answer is appropriate. If the answer can best be presented as a list of points, this is much quicker and more positive for you to compile and it is much easier for the examiner to mark. Sometimes an answer is required in the form of a business document, i.e. a memo or report. The "action" words in the questions are a guide to the style and depth of answers required. "List", "state", "select" and "specify" are best answered by detailing separate points, in sentences. "Compare" and "contrast" may be presented in one or two lists of specific comparable facts. "State", "identify" or "outline" usually involve the recall and statement of facts. "Describe", "explain" or "distinguish" require you also to show that you understand the facts. "Apply", "construct", "complete" and "advise" ask you to use your knowledge in a given situation. "With reasons" ensures that you provide some explanation to show your knowledge while "give examples" shows that you can apply your knowledge appropriately.

8. THE EXAMINATION

Theory

Make the most of your reading time before you start to write, especially if you have a choice of questions. Then read the question at least twice, underlining the main points. Plan your answer in pencil, by noting the points you wish to make; arrange these in a logical order and determine the style of answer required. Then you are ready to present your answer clearly, logically and concisely, in ink and in the style demanded, with correct spelling, grammar and paragraphs.

When you think you have finished your answer, read both the question and your answer again. Make any further additions or amendments as necessary. Put a line through your pencilled plan and leave several clear lines before going on to another question, so that you can add any other points later if time permits.

If the question is of the "short answer" type, do not spend a long time writing unnecessary detail — be concise. Multiple-choice or short questions should be quick to answer, but if you cannot think of it, move on and return to it later. Allow most time for the long questions — reading, thinking, planning and presenting each one carefully.

If your examination has a combination of question styles, such as the RSA Diploma for Personal Assistants, Personnel and Functional Aspects, allow approximately two-thirds of your time for the long questions.

The companion title in this series, *Office Practice and Secretarial Administration*, deals with the method and content to be used in answering theory questions.

Practical

The examinations vary considerably in length and content, and you should be advised by your tutor as to which one to enter. For all of them, however, it is necessary to have the typewriting or transcription speeds recommended in the syllabus.

It is possible to take an examination lasting approximately 30 minutes, consisting of just two business documents. This is ideal for candidates with a reasonable typing speed but with only limited audio experience, or for students on short intensive courses. A standard of 96 or 97 per cent accuracy is required.

More advanced examinations may last 2 to 3 hours and include a much wider variety of documents and carbon copies. A manuscript may be included and one question is presented in note form, from which you compose and type the document.

C. RECENT EXAMINATION QUESTIONS

PRACTICAL

In this section there are two complete papers from the PEI, followed by several extracts from recent audio-typewriting papers set by other boards. They have been chosen to include as wide a variety of dictated instructions as possible from several examination boards. If you can persuade someone to record them for you, or if you record them yourself, you can then use them as practice material.

AUDIO-TYPEWRITING EXAMINATION

(INTERMEDIATE 80)

PITMAN
EXAMINATIONS
INSTITUTE

This paper must be returned
with the candidates work.

No   80-15 AT

CANDIDATE'S INSTRUCTION SHEET

PAST PAPER

1   Your examination will consist of two passages of recorded dictation which
    will be either two business letters, or a business letter and a memorandum,
    a staff notice or a short business report. Below these instructions you
    will find all the information you need for this examination.

2   You will be allowed four minutes to prepare and type addresses, etc on the
    A4 paper provided, ready for the audio dictation from your machine. If a
    printed letterhead has been provided for one or both passages, you must
    use it. Make sure that you use the correct one by checking it against the
    supplementary information given below. If the letter or passage does not
    fit on to one side of the sheet, turn over and continue on the back.

3   The signal to begin will be given at the end of four minutes. You will
    then have 28 minutes to complete the transcription of the two passages.

4   You may make any corrections, alterations or re-typings you wish, but
    remember that the maximum time allowed is 28 minutes.

Supplementary information on the audio passages

Passage 1   Letter of 257 words

To: Mr S Black, 20 Mile Oak, Broadsea Bay, Kent, BR11 1LN.

From: ABC Tours, Travel House, High Street, Dover.

Date: 1 January of this year.

Please use headed paper supplied

Passage 2   A memorandum of 223 words

To: Branch Manager, Stone Heath

From: Chief Accountant, Head Office

Date: Yesterday's

Please use plain A4 paper. Type the above at the top of the sheet.

PITMAN
EXAMINATIONS
INSTITUTE

AUDIO-TYPEWRITING EXAMINATION

(INTERMEDIATE 80)

This paper must be returned
with the candidates work.

No 80-15 AT

Passages for Dictation *on to individually controlled audio machines with stop
and playback facilities. Dictation to be at a speed of 80 wpm.
Please dictate what follows in full with the pauses as indicated:*

Pitman Examinations Institute:

Audio-Typewriting Examination (Intermediate 80) 80-15 AT   *(3 seconds pause)*

UNDERLINE PASSAGE ONE: A letter of 257 words   *(3 seconds pause)*

Text begins: *(1 second pause)*

Dear Mr Black *(paragraph)*

(heading closed capitals) SEVEN DAY BREAK TO JERSEY *(paragraph)*

(capital letters) ABC *(initial capital)* Tours propose / to organize two   ½
visits to Jersey *(dash)* - one in the spring and one in early autumn. *(full
stop)* We have // reserved twenty single and ten twin *(hyphen)*-bedded rooms   ½
at the *(initial capitals)* Old Mount House, West Park. *(full stop)* /// Both   ¾
tours will leave on a Monday. *(full stop)* The *(initial capitals)* Mount
House is a luxury four *(hyphen)*-star _I_ hotel with a heated swimming pool.   1
(full stop) Each bedroom has its own private bathroom. *(full stop)* It
is hoped / that the cost of the holiday will be in the region of *(pound*   ½
sign, figures) £150. // *(full stop)* This does not include travel to and   ½
from Jersey. *(full stop)* *(open brackets)* (There may be a small /// extra   ¾
charge if you book a single room.) *(full stop)* *(close brackets)* During
the visit it is hoped to see _I_ many places of interest in Jersey. *(full   2
stop)* No doubt many people will wish to take a look at the / *(figures)*   ½
20 acre leisure site at *(initial capitals)* Fort Regent. *(paragraph)*

Travel to Jersey will be by British *(initial capital)* // Rail *(closed*   ½
capitals) SEALINK from Weymouth. *(W-E-Y-M-O-U-T-H)* *(full stop)* *(capital
letters)* ABC *(initial capital)* Tours will arrange outward travel unless ///   ¾
you wish to make your own way by air. *(full stop)* We can provide you
with full details of flight _I_ times at no extra cost. *(paragraph)*   3

As single rooms are limited *(open brackets)* (we have booked every one)
(close brackets) / if friends are willing to share a twin *(hyphen)*-   ½
bedded room, please will they emphasize this on the enclosed booking //   ½

161

form. *(full stop)* Names should also be printed clearly. *(paragraph)*

(capital letters) ABC are pleased to receive your booking at /// any   ¾

time. *(full stop)* We do not ask for full payment now but we are setting

a reserve fee of *I (pound sign, figures)* £10 per person, which is   4

returnable. *(paragraph)*

Yours sincerely

                                                    (1 second pause)

End of text for PASSAGE ONE   *(3 seconds pause)*

PASSAGE TWO: A memorandum of 223 words   *(3 seconds pause)*

Text begins: *(1 second pause)*

(heading: initial capitals, underscore) <u>Changes to Clients' Credit Cards</u> *(paragraph)*

I am sorry that you were unwell and could not / attend the *(initial*   ¼

capitals) Finance Section's monthly meeting for managers. *(full stop)*

It was agreed at the meeting to start // the central credit card   ½

scheme at once. *(paragraph)*

All managers have been asked to send in details of the costs /// for   ¾

starting such a scheme at their branch. *(full stop)* We would like to

know this in two weeks' time. *I (full stop)* At the same time please   1

could you give us some idea of a date for the start of / the scheme.   ¼

(paragraph)

As you know, under this scheme a new account card will have to be sent

to all // clients, and we feel this is a good opportunity to issue a   ½

new type of card. *(full stop)* This work /// will be put in hand soon.   ¾

(full stop) It has been agreed that the card will bear the name and *I*   2

address of the main store. *(full stop)* We feel that there may be clients

who would like their account card / to show their own branch, and this   ¼

will be done. *(full stop)* Clients may pay their accounts at any store //   ½

listed on the back of their new cards. *(full stop)* It should be made

clear to clients that receipt of /// a new type of card means that   ¾

their old cards should be cut in half and destroyed. *(paragraph)*

A draft letter *I* will be sent out soon for your comments. *(full stop)*   3

                                                    (1 second pause)

End of test for PASSAGE TWO

                                                    (3 seconds pause)

This concludes Audio-Typewriting Examination (Intermediate 80) 80-15 AT

Question 2

AUDIO-TYPEWRITING EXAMINATION

(INTERMEDIATE 100)

PITMAN
EXAMINATIONS
INSTITUTE

This paper must be returned
with the candidates work.

No 100-19 AT

CANDIDATE'S INSTRUCTION SHEET   PAST PAPER

1 Your examination will consist of two passages of recorded dictation which
   will be either two business letters, or a business letter and a memorandum,
   a staff notice or a short business report. Below these instructions you
   will find all the information you need for this examination.

2 You will be allowed four minutes to prepare and type addresses, etc on the
   A4 paper provided, ready for the audio dictation from your machine. If a
   printed letterhead has been provided for one or both passages, you must
   use it. Make sure that you use the correct one by checking it against the
   supplementary information given below. If the letter or passage does not
   fit on to one side of the sheet, turn over and continue on the back.

3 The signal to begin will be given at the end of four minutes. You will then
   have 30 minutes to complete the transcription of the two passages.

4 You may make any corrections, alterations or re-typings you wish, but
   remember that the maximum time allowed is 30 minutes.

Supplementary information on the audio passages

Passage 1   Memorandum of 313 words

TO: All Staff

FROM: Managing Director

DATE: 1 March (this year)

Please use the printed form provided

Passage 2   Letter of 287 words

TO: Messrs James & Robert, 49 Lovelace Terrace, Leeds, LS1 3XU

FROM: Pratt's Press

DATE: 27 June (this year)

Please use the headed paper provided

PITMAN
EXAMINATIONS
INSTITUTE

AUDIO-TYPEWRITING EXAMINATION

(INTERMEDIATE 100)

This paper must be returned
with the candidates work.

No 100-19 AT

<u>*Passages for Dictation*</u> *on to individually controlled audio machines with
stop and playback facilities. Dictation to be at a speed of 100 wpm.
Please dictate what follows in full with the pauses as indicated:*

Pitman Examinations Institute

Audio-Typewriting Examination (Intermediate 100) 100-19 AT   *(3 seconds pause)*

<u>PASSAGE ONE</u>: Memorandum of 313 words   *(3 seconds pause)*

Text begins: *(1 second pause)*

(Subject heading, capitals) HALF YEARLY REPORT

Some of you may have read in the national press that the *(initial capital)*
Company's half yearly profits are / down to *(pound sign, figures)* £2,000,500.   ¼
(full stop) This, as you can imagine, is in large contrast to this time last //   ½
year when the Company made a profit of *(pound sign, figures)* £6,000,000.
(paragraph)

There are of course many reasons to account for this /// change of events,   ¾
not least of which is the general recession in all branches of trade and
industry. *(full stop)* This Company has been no ⋌exception, but we have *(open*   1
bracket) (perhaps) *(close bracket)* been slow to take effective measures to
try to reduce the deficit *(d-e-f-i-c-i-t)*. *(full stop)* This / we now intend   ¼
to do, and I am afraid that some of the measures we shall be forced to take
will not be popular with // all *(initial capital)* Staff. *(full stop)* However, for   ½
the sake of the Company and the majority of the Staff, certain sacrifices will
have to be /// made. *(paragraph)*   ¾

Your *(initial capital)* Directors and I have been looking at everyone's *(initial*
capitals) Staff Record Card, and we are encouraged to see that ⋌many staff are   2
due to retire either this year or next. *(full stop)* Those who are due to
retire within the next *(word, underline)* <u>three</u> / months may leave immediately   ¼
on full pay to their normal retirement date and with no loss of pension rights.
(full stop) Those who are due // to retire within the next *(word, underline)*   ½
<u>six</u> months may leave within *(figure)* 1 month, on the same terms as above. *(full*
stop) Those who /// are due to retire within *(word, underline)* <u>twelve</u> months   ¾

164

may either leave now, with a lump sum redundancy payment or with half pay and
full ⌒ pension rights. *(paragraph)*   3

This would leave *(figures)* 500 Staff for whom I regret there will be no jobs
after 31 March next. *(full stop)* / The *(initial capital)* Accountant has worked   ¾
out full redundancy payments and these will be made on the basis of *(open
double quotation marks)* "last in // first out". *(close double quotation marks,*   ½
paragraph)

The Company very much regrets having to take this action but has no alternative.

_____

                                                        (1 second pause)

End of text for PASSAGE ONE   *(3 seconds pause)*

_____

PASSAGE TWO: Letter of 287 words   *(3 seconds pause)*

Text begins: *(1 second pause)*

Dear Sirs

Thank you for your letter of *(figures)* 24 June *(figures, insert this year)* 19..
enclosing the manuscript of a booklet / which you would like us to print for   ¼
you. *(paragraph)*

We have now had the opportunity of going through the booklet, and whilst we
are // happy to quote you a price for the printing, there are *(word)* one or   ½
(word) two additional points we need to clear before we can /// quote anything ¾
definite. *(paragraph)*

In the first place, you have given no indication as to whether you require the
booklet to have a hard or ⌒ a soft cover. *(full stop)* As you can imagine this   1
will make a considerable difference to the cost. *(paragraph)*

In the second place, although the / cover has a design, you have not indicated   ¼
whether you wish it to be in black and white or in *(word)* one or more colours. // ½
(full stop) Again, this decision will considerably affect the price. *(paragraph)*

A third point is the type of print you wish us to use and /// the size. *(full*   ¾
stop) The type does not affect in any great detail the cost, but the size will.

165

(full stop) For instance if you ⟋ use a *(figures)* 12 point type this would be   ?

cheaper than a *(figures)* 10 point, and in the same way, *(figure)* 8 point would

be / cheaper than 6 point. *(full stop)* I enclose some sample styles so that   ¼

you can choose the one you like best. *(full stop)* If I // may make a suggestion,   ½

the type best suited for this kind of booklet would be either *(initial capital)*

Diplomat or *(initial capital)* Elite, but this /// is entirely your own decision   ¾

and will not affect the *(one word)* overall price. *(paragraph)*

If you will let me have your answers to these ⟋ points I shall be very pleased   3

to give you a firm quotation and delivery date. *(paragraph)*

Yours faithfully *(turn up 1 space)*

(initial capitals) Pratt's / Press *(turn up 5 spaces)*   ¼

(initial capitals) J Pratt *(turn up 1 space)*

(capitals) DIRECTOR

                                    (1 second pause)

End of text for PASSAGE TWO   *(3 seconds pause)*

This concludes Audio-Typewriting Examination (Intermediate 100) 100-19 AT

Question 3

Instructions to the dictator

The time taken to dictate the material is at the discretion of the dictator.

Material to be dictated

I am going to dictate a Notice of Activities for a Games Complex which should be typed on a sheet of plain A4 paper.

Type your name, the name of the school or centre and the grade of presentation at the top of the reverse side of the paper.

The Notice begins with 2 headings. The first heading which should be centred in Closed Capitals and typed two inches (50 mm) from the top edge of the paper is: Kintore (spelt KIN-TORE) Academy Games Complex. (Now turn up 4 lines) The second heading which should be centred in Initial Capitals and underscored is: List of Activities for Summer Session (Dash) 1983 (Now turn up 3 lines) (The Notice should be typed in Single Line Spacing, unless otherwise indicated, and with margins of one inch (25 mm)). (The first paragraph reads) Below you will find details of activities offered to the public during the (Initial Capitals) Summer Session 1983. (Sentence) You must be a member of the (Initial Capitals) Kintore Academy Community Complex and pay a membership fee of £3 before you can take part in any of these activities. (Sentence) The cost of each activity will be £5 for a period of 10 weeks (Dash) with reduced charges for children under 16 years of age. (Paragraph) (Now turn up 3 lines and type 2 column headings in Initial Capitals and Underscored. The first heading which is to be typed at the Left Margin is) Activity (Type an asterisk after the word Activity) (The second heading which should be typed one and a half inches (38 mm) from the Left Margin is) Details (Turn up 2 lines) (Now follow details of 5 activities with the name of each activity being typed with Initial Capitals under the column heading Activity. The details which follow each activity should be typed in Block Style under the column heading Details. Turn up 2 lines between the details of each activity. The first activity is) Archery (The details are) This class will be held on Wednesdays (Left bracket) 7.00 pm to 9.00 pm. (Right bracket) (Sentence) Members will be required to supply their own equipment.

(Sentence) (The second activity is) Badminton (The details are) This class will be held on Tuesdays (Left bracket) 6.30 pm to 9.30 pm. (Right bracket) (Sentence) Where numbers are sufficient 2 classes will operate. (Sentence) (The third activity is) Football (The details are) This class will be held on Fridays (Left bracket) 8.00 pm to 9.00 pm. (Right bracket) (Sentence) Coaching from a professional football player will be available. (Sentence) (The fourth activity is) Keep Fit (The details are) This class will be held on Thursdays (Left bracket) 7.15 pm to 8.15 pm. (Right bracket) (Sentence) The class is for women only. (Sentence) (The fifth and last activity is) Table Tennis (The details are) This class will be held on Mondays (Left bracket) 7.30 pm to 8.30 pm. (Right bracket) (Sentence) There is a reduced charge of £3 for this activity. (Sentence) (Now turn up 3 lines and at the Left Margin type an asterisk followed by the sentence) Classes will operate only if at least 10 people enrol. (Now turn up 3 lines and at the Left Margin type) Further details available on request at the (Initial Capital) Complex or write to (Colon): (Now turn up 3 lines. The name and address which follows is to be typed in Single Line Spacing and in Fully Blocked Style one and a half inches (38 mm) from the Left Margin) Mr Richard Grant, Games Complex Supervisor, 258 Union Street, Kintore AB5 7SR.

(End of Question)

[60/216]

(Scottish Cert of Education, Higher Audio-Typewriting, May 1984)

[60/216]

Question 4

(Dictation time: approximately 1 minute)

(Come down 1″/25 mm) from the top edge of the postcard and centre the following address. First line CLOSED CAPITALS) STRATHCLYDE OFFICE SERVICES (Next line) 213 Bath Street (Next line
40 CLOSED CAPITALS) GLASGOW (Turn | up 2 line spaces and date the postcard. Turn up 2 line spaces) We shall be glad to call and demonstrate our latest (initial capitals) Photocopying Machine to
80 you at any time you care to arrange. (Paragraph) Perhaps you | would be good enough to let us know which day would be suitable.

(End of question)

Notice

(Dictation time: approximately 4 minutes)

(Come down 2″/51 mm) from the top edge of the paper and type the first heading in SPACED
40 CAPITALS) SUMMER IN (abbreviation) ST ANDREWS 1984 (Turn up 2 line spaces and type | the next heading in CLOSED CAPITALS) HOLIDAY COURSES AND RECREATION FOR EVERYONE (Turn up 2 line spaces and underscore the next heading) Stay one week— (dash) or any
80 number of weeks (Turn up 3 line spaces and type the following | paragraph) The St Andrews (initial capitals) Holiday Courses are now so popular we have reserved additional accommodation for the summer of 1984. (Sentence) This accommodation is situated within St Andrews itself and is within easy
120 walking | distance of the (initial capitals) West Sands and attractive shopping areas. (Sentence) The holiday courses are suitable for every age group. (Sentence) Everyone is welcome. (Sentence) Details of
160 courses are given in the enclosed leaflet. (Paragraph. Now a shoulder heading. | Type in CLOSED CAPITALS) DIETS, DOGS AND CHILDREN (Paragraph) The (initial capital) Staff are most helpful and everything will be done to meet requests for special diets. (Sentence) We regret that no dogs are
200 allowed. (Sentence) Children of 5 | years and over will be made welcome. (Paragraph) (Shoulder heading. Type with CLOSED CAPITALS) DEPOSIT (Paragraph) A non- (hyphen) returnable deposit of £5 must
240 be paid for (underline the next 2 words) each week booked in respect of every | person aged 12 and over. (Paragraph) (Shoulder heading. Type with CLOSED CAPITALS) REGISTRATION (Paragraph) Full details are contained in the enclosed (initial capitals) Application Form. (Paragraph) (Shoulder heading.
280 Type with CLOSED CAPITALS) RESERVATION (Paragraph) The enclosed form, with your deposit, | should be sent as soon as possible to:- (colon, hyphen) (Turn up 3 lines spaces) Holiday Programmes (next line) University of St Andrews (next line) 3 St Mary's (apostrophe s) Place (next line) (CLOSED
320 CAPITALS) ST ANDREWS (next line) Fife (next | line) KY16 9UZ.

(End of question).

Notice

(Dictation time: approximately 2¼ minutes)

(Come down 1½″/38 mm) from the top edge of the paper and type the first heading in CLOSED CAPITALS) NEW SCALE OF CHARGES FOR SERVICE ENGINEER (Turn up 2 line spaces and
40 type the next | heading with initial capitals and underscore) From 1 June 1984 (Turn up 2 line spaces and underline next heading) Prices given are per hour (Turn up 3 line spaces and type the items at the left-
80 hand margin | and the prices at the right-hand margin and connect them with leader dots) Basic charge
120 for travelling and labour £13.50 (Turn up 2 line spaces) Evening and night call- (hyphen) out during |
weekdays £21 (Turn up 2 line spaces) Call- (hyphen) out from 0900 hrs on Saturday morning to (next line)
160 0900 hrs on Monday morning £29 (Turn up 3 line spaces) All (initial capitals) Maintenance | Contracts will be honoured at the current price, and a new scale of charges will be presented at the time of renewal.

(End of question).   **(SCOTBEC, Audio-typewriting I, March 1984)**

Question 5

(Dictation time: approximately 3½ minutes)

(Leave a ½″/13 mm margin at the top of the page and display the name and address of Scotia Bank Limited: the letter reads) Dear Mr Graham, Thank you for your letter of 12 June 1984 and for your
50 assurance that your overdraft will be greatly | reduced by the end of this month. (Paragraph) You ask about a scheme whereby the (initial capital) Bank can arrange to pay your bills in instalments; (semi-colon) this is not really the case. (Sentence) I think you may be referring to the (initial capitals) Scotia
100 Bank Budget Account system. (Sentence) | Unfortunately, everybody gets bills and frequently one finds that in one month bills will arrive for rates, telephone, (capitals) TV licence, in addition to regular monthly payments such as mortgage, car payments and insurance. (Sentence) It is quite a lot to deal
150 with and this, of course, is when many | customers of the (initial capital) Bank tend to overdraw on their accounts. (Paragraph) We can help you out of this situation if you are prepared to open a (initial capitals) Scotia Bank Budget Account. (Sentence) All you have to do is to estimate your total annual
200 commitments, divide the total | figure by 12 and arrive at a monthly figure. (Sentence) This amount will cover all your commitments (dash) fuel, telephone, mortgage, hire purchase payments, insurance, (capitals) TV licence. (Sentence) You can even include a monthly payment towards holidays. (Sentence)
250 Once you have arrived at a total monthly amount to cover | all your commitments, we will then arrange to transfer this sum to your (initial capitals) Budget Account from your current account each month. (Paragraph) We will issue you with a special (initial capitals) Budget Account cheque book and
300 when your bills arrive, you pay them from your (initial capitals) Budget | Account. (Paragraph) I enclose a (initial capitals) Budget Account form for you to complete and if you will bring this into the (initial capital) Bank we will make all the necessary arrangements. (Paragraph) Yours sincerely (leave space for signature) Manager (Indicate that there is an enclosure. End of question).

(Dictation time: approximately 4 minutes)

(Leaving a margin of 1″/25 mm at the top of the page, centre in closed capitals) Excelsior Assurance Company Limited (turn up 2 line spaces and centre another heading using initial capitals and
50 underscore) Household Goods Policies. (Now type a paragraph in block style) This form must be | returned to the (initial capital) Company within 3 weeks of any change of address, otherwise household goods will cease to be covered by the (initial capital) Company. (Turn up 3 line spaces and type at the
100 left-hand margin, using initial capitals) Name of Insured (now type a line of | dots 2½″/64 mm long, tap along 3 spaces and type using initial capitals) Policy (abbreviation) No (type a line of dots up to the right-hand margin. There now follow 7 questions which should be typed in single-line spacing but using
150 double-line spacing where dotted | lines are typed and treble-line spacing between the questions. The questions should be numbered with arabic numerals.) 1. Address of premises containing the insured goods. (Now type 2 dotted lines across the page.) 2. Is the building of brick or stone and is it roofed
200 (Spelt ROOFED) with slate | or metal. (Question mark, now type one line of dots across the page). 3. (bracket) a (bracket) What is the age of the buildings (question mark, now type dots up to the right-
250 hand margin.) (Bracket) b (bracket) Are the buildings in a good state of repair (question mark, now | type dots up to the right-hand margin.) 4. Are the premises used for any kind of business, manufacture or storage of materials (question mark, sentence) If so, give details. (Now type a line of dots across the
300 page.) 5. Is the residence detached, semi- (hyphen) detached or a flat | (question mark, now type a line of dots across the page.) 6. Is any part of the residence rented to other persons (question mark, type dots up to the right-hand margin.) 7. Does the sum insured represent the full replacement value of the
350 contents (question mark: type a line | of dots across the page. Turn up 5 line spaces and type at the left-hand margin, using initial capital) Signature (type a line of dots 2½″/64 mm long, tap along 3 spaces and
400 type with initial capital) Date. (Type dots up to the right-hand margin. End of | question.)

(SCOTBEC, Audio-typewriting II, June 1984)

THE ROYAL SOCIETY OF ARTS
EXAMINATIONS BOARD
SINGLE-SUBJECT EXAMINATIONS

E 203
AUDIO–TYPEWRITING, STAGE II
WEDNESDAY, 6th MARCH 1985
TWO AND A HALF HOURS ALLOWED

Instructions to Candidates

You have TEN minutes to read through this question paper before the start of the examination, during which time you may make notes on the examination paper.

IMPORTANT: As soon as you receive this paper, read carefully the letter printed on page 4. Notes for a reply to this will be dictated to you as passage 2.

Except where a different instruction is given, all letters should be typed on the headed paper provided, ready for signature as for despatch today. Where no special directions are given regarding display, any method, consistently used within each exercise, will be accepted.

Carbon copies should be taken only where indicated. Dictionaries and calculators may be used.

Candidates must satisfy the examiner in each section of the examination.

PASSAGE 2 (50 marks)

Using the dictated notes, compose and type on plain white paper a reply to the letter given on page 4. Type the appropriate letter-heading for this task.

PASSAGE 4 (20 marks)

A report to be typed in double (or 1½) line-spacing on plain white A4 paper. Heading: DICTIONARIES.

PASSAGE 5 (18 marks)

A memorandum to Company Secretary from Managing Director.   Ref: TWK/NY. Heading: PLATINUM BARS.

12 Market Street
TUNBRIDGE WELLS
Kent
TN7 8BH

1 March 1985

The Manager
Free Advice Centre
Boundary Road
CHICHESTER
West Sussex
CH4 7UN

Dear Sir

Last year I tried very unsuccessfully to grow Freesias in my unheated glass-house. I should appreciate it if you would give me some advice on how to grow these attractive flowers. Please would you also recommend any books or pamphlets that are available as I have been unable to find any information on these flowers in my local library.

Yours faithfully

Margaret Lister

Margaret Lister (Miss)

Passage 2 — Notes for reply to letter printed on page 4

Minutes

Enclose leaflet giving detailed instructions. Wish correspondent good luck. Buy seeds from reputable firm. Soak in warm water for twenty-four hours. Plant seeds in good compost and place in warm position — sixty-five ½ degrees Fahrenheit. Germination takes twenty-eight / days. If flowers wanted January start to germinate seeds July. Contact again if any problems.

(55 words)

Passage 4 — A report of 180 words on dictionaries

Minutes

The first volume of the Oxford English Dictionary was published in eighteen hundred and eighty-four. (full stop) It was then a slim paperback book, which covered most of the letter (initial capital) A. (full stop) It was

½ not until nineteen hundred and twenty-eight that / the whole alphabet was covered. (paragraph)

Today there is a very strong demand for dictionaries - (dash) nearly every household has one - (dash) and rival publishers vie (V-I-E) with each other to be the first to record the latest changes in our language. (full

1 stop) Dictionaries range // from the (initial capitals) Top Pocket Good Dictionary selling under (pound sign) one to the (capitals) O-E-D itself with its thirteen volumes. (paragraph)

The English language is constantly changing, mostly as a result of errors
½ in the ways it is used. (full stop) For example / (open single quotes) 'presently' (close single quotes) originally meant (open single quotes) 'immediately' (close single quotes), but nowadays it means (open single quotes) 'by and by'. (close single quotes) (paragraph)

Dictionaries have changed their functions over the years and instead of helping our language to change slowly they are now helping it to change
2 rapidly. (full stop) The reason for this // is that dictionaries are now stored in computers, and words can be inserted or extracted in a matter of seconds.

Passage 5 — A memo of 160 words to the company secretary

Minutes

I read in my newspaper at the weekend that platinum bars are now available to buy as an investment. (full stop) These bars have a minimum purity of ninety-nine point nine-five per cent. (full stop) I know that the value
½ of platinum, / one of the world's rarest metals, can rise or fall, but at present the price in sterling is about three times as high as it was six years ago. (full stop) The platinum can be bought in different weights
1 from five grams // to ten ounces troy, (T-R-O-Y) each bar being individually numbered. (paragraph)

I attach the newspaper cutting and perhaps you would look further into this matter for me, particularly with regard to how easily the platinum bars
½ could be sold should the need / arise. (full stop) I assume V-A-T would have to be paid. (paragraph)

I think it might well prove to be suitable as a long-(hyphen)term investment for the Company, and I look forward to having your report as
2 soon as possible. //

(RSA, Audio-typewriting II, March 1985)

THE ROYAL SOCIETY OF ARTS
EXAMINATIONS BOARD
SINGLE-SUBJECT EXAMINATIONS

S **238** MEDICAL AUDIO-TYPEWRITING, STAGE II
WEDNESDAY, 27th JUNE 1984
TWO AND A HALF HOURS ALLOWED

Instructions to Candidates

Except where a different instruction is given, all letters should be typed on
the headed paper provided, ready for signature as for despatch today. Where no
special directions are given regarding display, any method, consistently used
within each exercise, will be accepted. Carbon copies should be taken only
where indicated. Dictionaries (general and medical) and calculators may be
used.

Where necessary, the addresses of patients, and the names and designations of
writers are given below, but will not be included in the dictation.

PASSAGE 4 (31 marks)

A medical report on Miss Priscilla Pound, date of birth 22.2.1930, 12 The
Heights, Brighton, to be signed by Dr P M R Masson, Senior Physician,
Department of Rheumatology. Please take one carbon copy on the yellow paper
provided and use today's date. The drug mentioned is Myocrisin.

PASSAGE 5 (23 marks)

A letter to Dr S J Whales, 126 Walsall Road, Small Heath, Birmingham B12 8ED
from B Bewick, MB, ChB, Senior Registrar. Patient: Albert Stone, 11 Mile End
Close, Small Heath, Birmingham.

Passage 4 – Report of 264 words

Minutes

(Heading) Medical Certificate, Miss Priscilla Pound

This is to certify that this patient has been seen here in consultation regularly since January nineteen seventy-three with sero-**(hyphen)**positive erosive rheumatoid arthritis. **(paragraph)**

½   This is now of some ten years' duration and has / left considerable residue in the wrists and feet. **(full stop)** More recently there has been further activity characterised by a rising sedimentation rate, now thirty-one millimetres in one hour and a rising titre of rheumatoid factor –
1   **(dash, initial capital)** Rose test now being one // over sixty-four. **(full stop)** Radiologically she shows extensive erosive changes, particularly in the wrists and feet. **(paragraph)**

The situation has been complicated by a recent fracture of the neck of the right femur in August nineteen eighty. **(full stop)** This fracture has
½   healed well / but the pin is giving some trouble and, of course, there is a risk of an aseptic necrosis of the femoral head developing during the next year. **(full stop)** Should this occur, then she will immediately
2   sustain a severe drop in functional // capacity. **(full stop)** This, combined with the threat of a late relapse in her rheumatoid condition, which has now occurred, added to the fact that she is only just controlled with gold twenty milligrams Myocrisin monthly over long term and cannot
½   tolerate / a larger dose, places her in a situation where she is at quite serious risk of an irretrievable loss of functional capacity. **(paragraph)**

She has been told, therefore, that it is mandatory that she should retire
3   at this stage from her // present appointment. **(full stop)** She has been told that if she continues at work there is a very substantial hazard to her future independence of function.

Passage 5 – Letter of 191 words to Dr S J Whales

Minutes

Dear Dr Whales

Albert Stone, date of birth fifteen nine twenty

I saw Mr Stone here early last week. **(full stop)** He had had quite mild skin reactions following his recent further palliative radiation treatment
½ to the right upper cervical mass, which / I think has regressed slightly. **(paragraph)**

His only complaint at the moment is of cough and sputum which seem to have developed during the previous week. **(full stop)** Apart from a few basal rales I found nothing clinically wrong. **(full stop)** Dr Vicars reports
1 his // chest x-ray as follows: **(colon, inset paragraph, open inverted commas)**

"There is basal emphysema with ill-**(hyphen)**defined consolidations in the left upper zone and apex, and a conspicuous relative increase of aeration of the left lung and actual emphysema in the right upper zone. **(full**
½ **stop)** There is / apparent increase of vascularity around the left hilum and it is quite possible that there may be a peri-**(hyphen)**hilar left bronchial carcinoma, although associated consolidation has not been clearly demonstrated." **(full stop, close inverted commas, end of inset paragraph)**

2 Even if he were found in the future to // have a definite bronchial neoplasm, I would not consider irradiating the mediastinum unless symptoms became distressing. **(full stop)** Natually I am not planning to see him again unless you wish it.

Yours sincerely

————————————

(RSA, Medical Audio-typewriting, June 1984)

Question 8

A letter to an old friend, Richard Wellingborough, of Specialist
Transporters

Dear Richard

Worcester Wild Fowl Centre

You will recall that at the start of our last campaign we retained
your company's services for the local collection of some of the exhibits.
We are very pleased with the care you gave these items some of which were
extremely fragile and would like you to do a similar task for our "adopt
a bird" display scheduled to take place in the winter of 1986. It is
anticipated that the collections will take approximately two days and
the area organiser at Worcester James Osborne and his staff will be on
hand to receive them from you. At the end of the exhibition we shall
of course require your services again to return those items which have
not been sold. Perhaps you would let me have one of your up to date
price lists and I look forward to hearing from you again.

Yours sincerely

Get in touch with David Frobisher the area organiser in the eastern
region. You compose it. Send a memo with a heading Adopt a Bird
Scheme 1986 in closed capitals.

Say that: as he knows, I am trying to get arrangements underway for the
exhibition for our new campaign. Has he kept in touch with that superb
craftsman Lionel Evans who kept visitors from schools and colleges
enthralled at our last exhibition with his demonstrations of woodcarving?
He will remember that Lionel worked on the wood in front of the students
and produced some enchanting figures which were snapped up straight away
by his admiring audience. I think it would be a very good idea if we
could ask him to the Norfolk centre again. I would like him for the
Saturday sessions where I am sure he would captivate both young and old.
Tell him that I did write Lionel a letter of thanks for his contribution
last time, but remember that he was intending to move to the South Wold
area as soon as he possibly cound. If David does have his new address,
will he contact Lionel direct regarding the new campaign and ask if he
will participate again. Ask David to let me know the outcome.

Type the form for enclosure with the circular letter. Should we have it
coloured? Mark it pale green.

Note: Punctuation is not generally dictated. Minimum punctuation shown
here to convey the sense of each passage.

(Extract from LCCI Private Secretary's Certificate, December 1984)

THE MANUSCRIPT BELOW IS REFERRED TO IN THE COURSE OF DICTATION

To: Adopt a Bird
Comlon International Plc
Head Office
etc

ADOPT A BIRD (sp caps & centred)
(Every 'adoption' assists the conservation of our wildfowl)

I wish:

a   To adopt a Bird and enclose £4

b   To adopt .... Birds & enclose £.....

c   To purchase .... Bird Gift Tokens (£4.30)
    in order to send a bird to a friend. I
    enclose £.....

d   To name my Bird ....
              Birds ....

} For each overseas postage please add £1

Delete as necessary.

I prefer, if available (please state any wildbird you would particularly like to adopt)

I am / am not a Member of the Wildfowl Conservation Section

I have / have not adopted birds before

I am, in the interests of conservation, prepared to share my bird with other adopters if no unadopted bird is available.

BLOCK LETTERS PLEASE

Mr/Mrs/Miss _ _ __ _ _ _ _ _ _ _ _ _ _ _

Age (if under 18) _ _ _ _ _ _ _

Address _ __ _ _ _ _ _ _ _ _ _ _ _ _ _

_ _ _ _ _ _ _ _ _ _ _ _ _ _ _ _ _ _ _ _

Post Code _ _ _ _ _ _ _   Date _ _ _ _ _ _ _ _ _ _ _

Signature _ _ _ _ _ _ _ _ _ _ _ _ _ _

Question 9

Une lettre à Monsieur le Président, Chambre de Commerce, 41-45 rue Gallilée 59000 Lille. Objet: Confirmation de location de stand - Vos ref. AS/DF/006.

Monsieur le Président

Nous avons été très sensibles à votre initiative par laquelle vous nous réserviez un stand dans le hall d'exposition dans le cadre de la semaine commerciale lilloise de 1984 (point, a la ligne).

Nous désirons par ce courrier transformer cette option en réservation effective et acceptons vos charges pour les quatre jours de la foire (point). L'expérience a été si fructueuse pour notre entreprise l'année dernière que nous sommes prêts à nous joindre de nouveau au nombre des exposants (point). Nous sommes même flattés que vous nous consentiez un tarif préférentiel (point, a la ligne).

Nous présumons que (virgule), comme par le passé (virgule), vous mettrez à notre disposition une ligne téléphonique et que votre électricien installera les prises de courant selon le schéma que notre service technique lui fournira par un prochain courrier (point, a la ligne).

Recevez (virgule), Monsieur le Président (virgule), l'expression de notre profond respect (point).

Une circulaire adressée aux clients de la région du Nord (avec en pièces jointes un billet d'entrée et un programme de démonstrations). Objet: Exposition.

Monsieur et chers clients

Le bureau du futur est un mélange d'espoir et de crainte que ressentent aujourd'hui les cadres auxquels on présente les perspectives de la formatique (point, a la ligne).

Il est difficile de trouver un personnel compétent (point-virgule); il est important de gagner du temps pour rester compététif (point). Il est souhaitable de se débarasser de nombreuses taches administratives aussi fastidieuses que fatiguantes par le soin et l'attention qu'elles demandent (point). Pour vous qui êtes responsables d'entreprises (virgule), savoir jouer la bonne carte consiste à acheter le bon produit (virgule), parfaitement adapté à sa fonction et utilisé comme in convient (point). Avec nos machines (ouvrez les guillemets) "Bien Fair (fermez les guillemets)" vous éviterez tout gaspillage (point, a la ligne).

Parmi toutes nos machines pour le classement (virgule), le traitement et la présentation des documents (virgule), il faut choisir celle qui remplira exactement le rôle que vous en attendez (point). Dans ce but nous vous proposons de nous retrouver à la foire commerciale (point). Nous serons au stand numéro 42 du 6-9 septembre (virgule), dans le hall d'exposition de Lille (point, a la ligne).

Nous esperons que vous ferez bon usage due billet gratuit que nous insérons ainsi que de notre programme et serons très honorés de votre visite (point, a la ligne).

Notre personnel se fera un plaisir de vous faire partager son expertise (point, a la ligne).

Agréez (virgule), Monsieur et chers clients (virgule), l'expression de nos sentiments les meilleurs (point).

(Extract from RSA Audio-typewriting in French, June 1984)

Question 10

Brief mit einem Durchschlag adressiert Deutscher Innen- und Aussen-
handel, Messgeräte, z. H. Frau Dr. Engles. Anschrift: Ludwigplatz 13,
6291 Freienfels. Inv: 31.05.1984. UZ: RE/fe. Tag: Heutiges Datum.
Betreff: Praxiteles Vertragshotels. Unterzeichner Renate Ebert,
Geschäftsführerin. Anlagen: 1 Tabelle. 1 adressierter Umschlag.

Sehr geehrte Frau Dr Engels

Mit Bezug auf Ihre Anfrage über unsere Vertragshotels können wir Ihnen
folgendes mitteilen (doppelpunkt, absatz)

Unsere Gruppe umfasst 127 Hotels der gehobenen sowie der Luxusklasse
(punkt) Diese Vertragshotels können über das weltweite Computersystem
PRX bei der Flugreservierung gleichzeitig mitgebucht werden (punkt)
In vielen Orten (komma) an denen das Angebot an Hotelzimmern die
Nachfrage nicht befriedigen kann (komma) wird auf diese Weise für
Praxiteles Fluggäste ein Sonderkontingent an Zimmern auch dann zur
Verfügung stehen (komma) wenn das jeweilige Hotel (anführungszeichen)
voll ausgebucht (anführungszeichen) meldet (punkt) Dies ist besonders
in den Staaten des Persischen Golfs sowie anderen Orts vornehmlich zu
Messezeiten von Bedeutung (punkt, absatz)

In der Anlage fügen wir unsere Super Apex Tarife von Berlin nach USA
bei (punkt, absatz)

Mit den besten Empfehlungen   Praxiteles Gruppe

Rundschreiben. Überschrift: AN ALLE KABINENBESATZUNGEN

Von einer internationalen Fluggesellschaft wie der unsrigen erwartet
man mehrsprachiges Personal (punkt) Viele Besatzungen haben gewisse
Sprachkenntnisse aber ihnen fehlt das nötige Zutrauen (komma) um die
Kenntnisse anzuwenden (punkt) Es ist unser Ziel bis zum Jahresende
im neuen Zentrum 20 Prozent der Kabinenbesatzungen in einer Fremd-
sprache ausreichende Kenntnisse zu vermitteln (punkt, absatz)

Wir bieten daher einen sechsmonatigen Fremdsprachenkurs mit 22
zwostündigen Vorlesungen an (komma) der für Gruppen mit mittleren
Kenntnissen gedacht ist (punkt) Die Sprachausbildung ist berufsorien-
tiert und Dialoge mit dem Passagier werden besonders geübt werden
(punkt, absatz)

Grosser Wert wird auf den Flieger- (binderstrich) jargon gelegt (komma)
damit die Vorgänger während des Fluges erklärt werden können (punkt)
Wiederholungs- (binderstrich) Veranstaltungen werden Teilnehmern
(komma) die wegen ihrer beruflichen Pflichten eine Vorlesung versäumen
müssen (komma) die Möglichkeit geben (komma) wieder Anschluss zu finden
(punkt) Obwohl das Training freiwillig ist (komma) empfehlen wir ihnen
an diesem Kurs teilzunehmen (komma) um ihre Kenntnisse aufzufrischen
oder zu verbiefen (punkt, absatz)

Ausserdem möchten wir daraufhinweisen (komma) dass sich nun im Praxi-
haus (komma) in dem sich alle Kabinenbesatzungen vor und nach dem Flug
melden (komma) ein Sprachlabor befindet (punkt) Dort kann Besatzungs-
personal unter sich arbeiten sowie Informationen über Kurse und
Material zur Selbsthilfe erhalten.

(Extract from RSA Audio-typewriting in German, June 1984)

Answers are now presented to the questions given in the previous section. Again, the displays shown are not the only correct versions as any consistent style is generally acceptable, but instructions on layout must, of course, be followed.

1 Notes:

With Pitman audio-typewriting examinations, you are provided with just one sheet of any headed paper you need, so be very careful to use it for the right passage.

During the 4 minute preparation time, you can type the date and address of passage 1 and memo details of passage 2. As memo paper is not provided you will need to be very familiar with the headings to complete them within the time allowed.

In passage 1 take care with consistency of numbers, i.e. 20, 10 etc., and use of capitals. Spellings: receive, sincerely and the alternatives organize (se) and emphasize (se). Remember to note the enclosure.

Display:

```
MEMORANDUM

To   Branch Manager, Stone Heath      Date   2 December 1985

From   Chief Accountant, Head Office


Changes to Clients' Credit Cards

I am sorry that you were unwell and could not attend the
Finance Section's monthly meeting for managers.  It was agreed
at the meeting to start the central credit card scheme at once.

All managers have been asked to send in details of the costs for
starting such a scheme at their branch.  We would like to know
this in 2 weeks' time.  At the same time please could you give
us some idea of a date for the start of the scheme.

As you know, under this scheme a new account card will have to
be send to all clients, and we feel this is a good opportunity
to issue a new type of card.  This work will be put in hand soon.
It has been agreed that the card will bear the name and address
of the main store.  We feel that there may be clients who would
like their account card to show their own branch, and this will
be done.  Clients may pay their accounts at any store listed on
the back of their new cards.  It should be made clear to clients
that receipt of a new type of card means that their old cards
should be cut in half and destroyed.

A draft letter will be sent out soon for your comments.
```

2 Notes:

As with **1**, check that you use the correct sheet of paper for each passage; this time a memo form is provided.

Particular problems in passage 1 are apostrophes, e.g. Company's, everyone's; consistent rendering of sums of money; which words to underline; and spellings: recession, effective and immediately.

In passage 2, pay attention to the rendering of numbers, i.e. ordinals — first, second etc. as words — but follow instructions on 12 point etc. in figures. Spellings: opportunity, definite, decision.

Display: (passage 1)

MEMORANDUM

From Managing Director   *Ref*

To   All Staff   *Date* 1 March 1985

HALF YEARLY REPORT

Some of you may have read in the national press that the Company's half yearly profits are down to £2,000,500. This, as you can imagine, is in large contrast to this time last year when the Company made a profit of £6,000,000.

There are of course many reasons to account for this change of events, not least of which is the general recession in all branches of trade and industry. This Company has been no exception, but we have (perhaps) been slow to take effective measures to try to reduce the deficit. This we now intend to do, and I am afraid that some of the measures we shall be forced to take will not be popular with all Staff. However, for the sake of the Company and the majority of the Staff, certain sacrifices will have to be made.

Your Directors and I have been looking at everyone's Staff Record Card, and we are encouraged to see that many staff are due to retire either this year or next. Those who are due to retire within the next <u>three</u> months may leave immediately on full pay to their normal retirement date and with no loss of pension rights. Those who are due to retire within the next <u>six</u> months may leave within 1 month, on the same terms as above. Those who are due to retire within <u>twelve</u> months may either leave now, with a lump sum redundancy payment or with half pay and all pension rights.

This would leave 500 Staff for whom I regret there will be no jobs after 31 March next. The Accountant has worked out full redundancy payments and these will be made on the basis of "last in first out".

The Company very much regrets having to take this action but has no alternative.

PRATT'S PRESS
Queen Anne's House, Stroud,
Glos 18E 9QQ

Telephone 0226 3945   Telex 59432

27 June 1985

Messrs James & Robert
49 Lovelace Terrace
LEEDS
LS1 3XU

Dear Sirs

Thank you for your letter of 24 June 1985 enclosing the manuscript of a
booklet which you would like us to print for you.

We have now had the opportunity of going through the booklet, and whilst
we are happy to quote you a price for the printing, there are one or two
additional points we need to clear before we can quote anything definite.

In the first place, you have given no indication as to whether you require
the booklet to have a hard or a soft cover. As you can imagine this will
make a considerable difference to the cost.

In the second place, although the cover has a design, you have not indicated whether you wish it to be in black and white or in one or more
colours. Again, this decision will considerably affect the price.

A third point is the type of print you wish us to use and the size. The
type does not affect in any great detail the cost, but the size will. For
instance if you use a 12 point type this would be cheaper than a 10 point,
and in the same way, 8 point would be cheaper than 6 point. I enclose some
sample styles so that you can choose the one you like best. If I may make
a suggestion, the type best suited for this kind of booklet would be
either Diplomat or Elite, but this is entirely your own decision and will
not affect the overall price.

If you will let me have your answers to these points I shall be very
pleased to give you a firm quotation and delivery date.

Yours faithfully
Pratt's Press

J Pratt
DIRECTOR

Pratt's Press Registered in England No 543537
Directors: W Pratt (Managing), R Hill, L Campbell-Jones

3 Notes:

Very detailed instructions are given for the display of this document, so listen carefully, more than once if necessary, and take one point at a time. Do not rush and do not type words of explanation/instructions to you.

Be consistent with numbers and with times, i.e. 7.00 pm, 8.00 pm etc. throughout. Be sure you turn up the number of times indicated and do not confuse this with the number of clear lines resulting. Spellings: equipment, Badminton, professional.

Display:

KINTORE ACADEMY GAMES COMPLEX

List of Activities for Summer Session - 1983

Below you will find details of activities offered to the pbulic during the Summer Session 1983. You must be a member of the Kintore Academy Community Complex and pay a membership fee of £3 before you can take part in any of these activities. The cost of each activity will be £5 for a period of 10 weeks - with reduced charges for children under 16 years of age.

Activity*	Details
Archery	This class will be held on Wednesdays (7.00 pm to 9.00 pm). Members will be required to supply their own equipment.
Badminton	This class will be held on Tuesdays (6.30 pm to 9.30 pm). Where numbers are sufficient 2 classes will operate.
Football	This class will be held on Fridays (8.00 pm to 9.00 pm). Coaching from a professional football player will be available.
Keep Fit	This class will be held on Thursdays (7.15 pm to 8.15 pm). The class is for women only.
Table Tennis	This class will be held on Mondays (.7.30 pm to 8.30 pm). There is a reduced charge of £3 for this activity.

* Classes will operate only if at least 10 people enrol.

Further details available on request at the Complex or write to:

Mr Richard Grant
Games Complex Supervisor
258 Union Street
Kintore
AB5 7SR

4 Notes:

In passage 1, check the size of the postcard before you start and follow instructions carefully.

Extensive instructions are again given in question 4, so take them one at a time and replay them if necessary. You need to know the correct way to present shoulder headings. Spellings: accommodation, programmes.

In passage 3, again take instructions one at a time and remember to insert the leader dots. Note that the 24-hour clock does not need punctuation. Block or align the short column of figures.

Display:

```
                    STRATHCLYDE OFFICE SERVICES
                         213 Bath Street
                            GLASGOW

                                        24 March 1984

        We shall be glad to call and demonstrate
        our latest Photocopying Machine to you at
        any time you care to arrange.

        Perhaps you would be good enough to let
        us know which day would be suitable.
```

NEW SCALE OF CHARGES FOR SERVICE ENGINEER

From 1 June 1984

Prices given are per hour

Basic charge for travelling and labour £13.50

Evening and night call-out during weekdays £21

Call-out from 0900 hrs on Saturday morning to
0900 hrs on Monday morning £29

All Maintenance Contracts will be honoured at the current price, and a new scale of charges will be presented at the time of renewal.

5 Notes:

In passage 1, you must display the letter heading and decide on your layout and punctuation style before you start. Note the length of the letter, set margins accordingly, and be constantly aware of your position on the page to decide whether it will be necessary to use a continuation sheet. Spellings: assurance/insurance, overdraft, instalments, referring, licence, mortgage, overdraw, commitments and hire.

Passage 2 is the display of a form, which is more likely to be presented to you as a manuscript than in dictation. The visual appreciation of layout, length and content is generally very helpful. To achieve a well-displayed form from dictation, many instructions are necessary which must be taken slowly and replayed if necessary. A reasonable length of typing line (minimum 60 spaces) is advisable to allow for later completion. You need to understand the term "arabic numbers". Spellings: detached, signature.

Display:

EXCELSIOR ASSURANCE COMPANY LIMITED

Household Goods Policies

This form must be returned to the Company within 3 weeks of any change of address, otherwise household goods will cease to be covered by the Company.

Name of Insured ....   Policy No ....

1 Address of premises containing the insured goods.

   ....

   ....

2 Is the building of brick of stone and is it roofed with slate or metal?

   ....

3 (a) What is the age of the buildings? ....

   (b) Are the buildings in a good state of repair? ....

4 Are the premises used for any kind of business, manufacture or storage of materials? If so, give details.

   ....

5 Is the residence detached, semi-detached or a flat?

   ....

6 Is any part of the residence rented to other persons? .....

7 Does the sum insured represent the full replacement value of the contents?

   ....

Signature ....   Date ....

Praxiteles Group

PRAXITELES HOUSE ADAM STREET LONDON WC2N 6AJ

Telephone: 01-839 1691

A fictitious organisation: for examination purposes only

Our ref

Your ref

5 March 1985

Miss M Lister
12 Market Street
TUNBRIDGE WELLS
Kent
TN7 8BH

Dear Miss Lister

Thank you for your letter of 1 March, in which you ask for
our help in the growing of Freesias, which we agree are most
attractive flowers.

We enclose a leaflet giving detailed instructions, but would
also like to stress the following points.

Firstly it is essential always to buy seeds from a reputable
firm. The seeds should then be soaked in warm water for 24
hours, planted in good compost and placed in a constant temperature of 65 °F. They will take approximately 28 days to
germinate. If you wish to have blooms in January germination
should be started in July.

We feel sure that if you follow the instructions carefully
you will grow some very beautiful flowers. However, should
you have any further problems, please do not hesitate to
contact us again.

We wish you every success.

Yours sincerely

Manager

Enc

6 Notes:

Passage 2 is the composition part of this examination. Type the dictated notes and read them and the original letter several times. You will find it easier to write or type a rough draft before completing your final letter. This letter requires a friendly, helpful tone, so use the addressee's name and use "Yours sincerely". Use all the information you are given, in a logical order with complete, but not long, sentences. Divide your letter into paragraphs.

For passage 4, decide your margins, bearing in mind the length of the passage – 180 words fit very easily on A4 paper. Note that book titles need initial capitals, a dash needs a space before and after it, and single quotes are specified. Spelling: computers.

For passage 5, A4 memo forms are provided, on to which 160 words will fit comfortably. Note the apostrophe in world's and that per cent must be two words, but you could, in this instance, use the sign. Spellings: platinum, sterling, weights, grams and ounces.

7 Notes:

If you are taking a medical examination, you are presumably familiar with the terms, their meanings and spellings, as well as the rendering of dates on medical documents. These points should not cause you unnecessary problems in these passages, but do listen very carefully to word endings and check figures, dates and names. Use the information on the instruction sheet to help you.

All other problems in passage 4 are the general ones in audio-typing, e.g. apostrophes and general spellings such as occurred.

Passage 5 is a letter which fits easily on A4 paper. The numerous medical terms are the biggest problem with this passage. After the inset paragraph, remember to return to your original margins.

8 Notes:

The audio examination in this group certificate tests your composition and manuscript display as well as basic audio-transcription.

The first letter shown in this extract is dictated. Punctuation is not given, so listen to the inflexion of the voice for full stops etc. and resist the temptation to insert too many commas. Again, Company's could cause difficulty to some students.

The second passage in this extract is the dictation of notes for you to use in composition. Type the notes from the dictation and read them through for content and sense. Using all the information given in the dictation (and sometimes also on the instruction sheet) write it into sentences. It is often necessary to re-arrange the order of the information to improve the style. When complete, divide into paragraphs, check for accuracy, spelling, style and tone and then type your letter. If possible, ask your tutor to check it.

There is always a manuscript in this examination, and on this occasion it was the display of a form. The information given in Chapter 3 regarding form display applies to this document. Any additional instructions given in dictation or on the instruction sheet, i.e. "mark it pale green", must, of course, be completed.

Comlon International plc

Comlon House West Street London SW1Y 2AR
tel: 01 920 0261

telex: Comlond 888941   telegrams: Comlond London SW1

7 December 1984

Mr R Wellingborough
Specialist Transporters Plc
221 Fairfield Road
WORCESTER
HW9 6BR

Dear Richard

WORCESTER WILD FOWL CENTRE

You will recall that at the start of our last campaign we retained
your Company's services for the local collection of some of the exhibits.
We are very pleased with the care you gave these items, some of which
were extremely fragile, and would like you to do a similar task for our
"Adopt a Bird" display, scheduled to take place in the Winter of 1986.

It is anticipated that the collections will take approximately 2 days
and the Area Organiser at Worcester, James Osborne, and his staff will
be on hand to receive them from you.

At the end of the exhibition we shall, of course, require your services
again to return those items which have not been sold.

Perhaps you would let me have one of your up-to-date price lists and
I look forward to hearing from you again.

Yours sincerely

Patricia Williams
Director, Exhibitions and Campaigns
Wildfowl Conservation Section

Display:

form

```
To:  Adopt a Bird                              Pale Green
     Comlon International plc
     Head Office
     Comlon House
     West Street
     LONDON  SW1Y 2AR
```

A D O P T   A   B I R D

(Every 'adoption' assists the conservation of our wildfowl)

```
I wish:

a  To adopt a Bird and enclose £4              )
                                               )
b  To adopt ...... Birds and enclose £......   )
                                               )
c  To purchase ...... Bird Gift Tokens (£4.20) ) For each
                                               ) overseas
   in order to send a bird to a friend.  I     ) postage
                                               ) please
   enclose £......                             ) add £1
                                               )
d  To name my Bird ..........................  )
                                               )
              Birds ..........................  )
```

Delete as necessary.

I prefer, if available (please state any wildbird you would particularly like to adopt)

I am / am not a Member of the Wildfowl Conservation Section

I have / have not adopted birds before

I am, in the interests of conservation, prepared to share my bird with other adopters if no unadopted bird is available.

BLOCK LETTERS PLEASE

Mr/Mrs/Miss ....

Age (if under 18) ....

Address ....

....

Post Code .... Date ....

Signature ....

9 Notes:

If you are entering an audio-typing examination in French, you are presumably familiar with the dictated instructions, layout of documents, style of dates etc. You need to listen very carefully and try to understand the passage to ensure correct spelling, word endings, verb agreements etc. You need to have the accent keys on your machine and check that you use the right one. Each of these passages is presented with the details extracted from the instruction sheet. Check your typing before removing it from the machine.

Display:

GROUPE PRAXITELES MAISON PRAXITELES RUE ADAM 75017 PARIS

Téléphone 839 16.91

Monsieur le Président

Chambre de Commerce

41-45 rue Gallilée

59000 Lille

Vos Références :	AS/DF/006	
Nos Références :	DM/RHM	Paris, le 11 juin 1984
Objet :	Confirmation de location de stand	
Pièces Jointes :		

Monsieur le Président

Nous avons été tres sensibles à votre initiative par laquelle vous nous réserviez un stand dans le hall d'exposition dans le cadre de la semaine commerciale lilloise de 1984.

Nous désirons par ce courrier transformer cette option en réservation effective et acceptons vos charges pour les quatre jours de la foire. L'expérience a été si fructueuse pour notre entreprise l'année dernière que nous sommes prêts a nous joindre de nouveau au nombre des exposants. Nous sommes même flattés que vous nous consentiez un tarif préférentiel.

Nous présumons que, comme par le passé, vous mettrez à notre disposition une ligne téléphonique et que votre électricien installera les prises de courant selon le schéma que notre service technique lui fournira par un prochain courrier.

Recevez, Monsieur le Président, l'expression de notre profond respect.

President-Directeur General

M DUTERTRE (Madame)

Siège Social: Praxiteles Group Praxiteles House Adam Street London WC2N 6AJ

If you are entering an audio-typing examination in German, you are presumably familiar with the dictated instructions, layout of documents etc. Listen for the sense of the passage and pay particular attention to spelling, gender, grammatical agreements etc. Read through and check very carefully before removing your work from the typewriter. Each of these passages is presented with the relevant details extracted from the instruction sheet.

E. COURSE WORK – A STEP FURTHER

Office employment opportunities vary considerably from one region to another, as do the salaries. The wider the variety of office skills you can offer and the greater your competence, the better are your chances of interesting and rewarding employment or promotion.

Audio-typewriting is widely used today alongside, or instead of, shorthand. While the presentation of examination papers here is unrealistic, it can be a guide to their content. You could ask someone to record them for you to practise. Past examination papers and recordings are available from the boards (see p. 00 for addresses); copies of each syllabus and annual reports can also be obtained.

Further Reading

The boards also provide a recommended reading list for each subject included in the group certificates and diplomas, and your teacher may add to these lists. Often it is not necessary to read the whole book, but only the parts relevant to the syllabus. So, be a frequent user of the college and public libraries and read as widely as possible. While this reading is not directly concerned with typewriting, it can improve the integration of your secretarial skills involving composition, transcription and display.

There are several textbooks for audio-typewriting instruction, such as:

Longman Audio Typing, by Marion Prescott. Longman
Audio Transcription, by Archie Drummond. McGraw-Hill
Audio-typing, A Progressive Course, by Edith Whicher. Pitman
Elementary Audio-typing, by Barbara Colley. Pitman

Within this series of guidebooks there are several which should help you with your examinations, especially the *Communications* and the *Office Practice and Secretarial Administration* books.

The need for guidance on group certificates has now been recognised and new books have recently been published, including *Compose and Type* by Margaret Tombs (Pitman). In addition to textbook reading, you are recommended to visit office equipment shops and exhibitions to see the full range of equipment available, especially if you are entering a Secretarial Duties or Office Practice examination or a group certificate.

Chapter 7

Word Processing — Theory

A. GETTING STARTED

The theory of word processing (see Table 7.1) can be examined as a single subject or combined with a practical examination. Even if you are not intending to sit a theory examination, you must still have grasped the basic principles, as an understanding of the theory is essential to anyone hoping to become a proficient word processor operator.

In some examinations, a pass in the theory paper is necessary as well as in the practical; sometimes candidates who do well in the practical examination let themselves down by failing to prepare themselves properly for the theory paper.

A theory examination aims to test your knowledge of terminology and your ability to demonstrate an understanding of the functions of word processors and their application. The make of word processor you are working with will have no bearing on the theory paper, although your practical experience should help you. To be prepared for this examination you must have a thorough knowledge of all the topics in the syllabus and be able to apply this knowledge when answering the written questions.

As we can see in Chapter 2, questions on the theory paper tend to fall into three categories:

1. Multiple-choice
2. Objective questions
3. Case studies

As with any written paper you must read the question carefully to make sure you know exactly what you should be writing about, and then follow the instructions.

Table 7.1 Format of examinations in word processing
Examining board: Pitman Examinations Institute (PEI)

Title and Level	Length of Exam	Format and Regulations		
Practical word processing endorsement (PWP)	½ hour excluding printing	*Practical test* *Part I:* Text creation *Part II:* Text creation	Minimum of six hours tuition in word processing	Pass mark 70% Text typing 50% Text editing 36% Layout and presentation 14%
Word processing theory and practice	1 hour excluding printing	*Part I:* Practical 60% Six tasks. 1 compulsory plus 5 revision tasks from a choice of 10 *Part II:* Theory 40% 10 compulsory questions plus choice of 2 questions out of 3.	Minimum typing speed of 30 wpm. Minimum 30 hours tuition in word processing. Section A. Quiz type questions. Answers written on question sheet. Section B. Objective questions requiring description or comment. Candidates may take either Part I or II first. Both parts must be taken on the same day.	Pass mark 70% Note: 50% must be achieved in both parts.
Word processing: Elementary	1 hour + 5 mins excluding printing	*Practical test* Four tasks. No choice Input task 40% Text revision 20% Insertion 20% Proof-reading 20%	Candidates should have an accurate copying speed of 25 wpm before attempting this examination.	

Table 7.1 continued

Examining board: Royal Society of Arts (RSA)

Title and Level	Length of Exam	Format and Regulations	
Word processing: Stage I	1½ hours	*Part I: Practical paper* 6 compulsory tasks. Input, test revision, insertion, proof-reading.	Board recommends 25–30 hours of word processing operation
	1½ hours	*Part II: Written paper* 30%	
		Section 1 5 compulsory questions 25%	Multiple-choice objective questions
		Section 2 4 or 5 compulsory questions 25%	Objective questions requiring short answers. Proof-reading.
		Part III: Checklist 20% (completed by tutor during course)	16 points relating to use of equipment and safety aspects.

Examining board: London Chamber of Commerce and Industry (LCCI)

Word processing: Intermediate	2 hours	A. *Written paper*	
		B. College certified statement of competence of operation through hands-on experience.	

Multiple-choice

This is a common way of testing one's knowledge on a given topic. Usually a phrase or term is given and you are asked to choose the correct definition from a possible four or more suggestions. It is important that you know the answer as some of the alternatives offered are intentionally ambiguous. If, for example, you are asked to tick or circle only one answer, you should make sure you do this.

Objective

This type of question may require a brief statement, a list of facts, a diagram or a detailed description. The number of marks awarded will indicate the amount of time you should spend and the degree of detail expected. These questions require a factual answer, so make sure you get straight to the point, and don't pad out your answer. Again follow the instructions, so if asked to list or describe in detail, you do just that, otherwise you may lose marks for failing to follow them.

Case studies

This type of question is mainly adopted by the RSA. You are put into the situation of a secretary or word processor operator and given questions to answer.

Topic areas

In the next section we shall consider the five main topics which the majority of examining boards include on their syllabuses.

1. Hardware
2. Types of systems
3. Functions and applications
4. Operators
5. Effects of installing a word processor

B. ESSENTIAL PRINCIPLES

1. HARDWARE

Hardware is the term given to all parts of a word processor that you can see and touch. It is important you understand the components that make up the hardware, as questions on this are very popular. Below is a list describing each component; make sure you fully understand each one.

Keyboard

This is used to type text and to give the word processor instructions for completing special functions. It consists of a Qwerty keyboard identical to those found on a conventional typewriter plus function and control keys.

Visual display unit (VDU)

The piece of equipment that resembles a television screen. They can vary in size, shape and colour, but all have the effect of showing the operator a portion of the prepared text, depending on the size of the VDU.

Central Processing unit (CPU)

This is the nerve centre of the processor which, by means of specialist programming, enables the equipment to carry out automatic functions of editing, storage and retrieval.

Disk drive diskettes (generally referred to as floppy disks)

The disk drive holds the diskettes which contain the software or program which instructs the word processor to perform the various functions and can be used to store text that has been typed in.

(a) exchangeable
(b) fixed
(c) floppy
(d) hard

Printer

The printer provides you with a paper (hard) copy of the documents you type and is not dissimilar to a typewriter without keys.

Printers have certain characteristics with which you should be familiar:

(a) **Separate printer** – the operator can instruct the printer while still using the VDU
(b) **Integral printer** – attached to keyboard
(c) **Remote printer** – common in shared-resource situations where more than one VDU share the printer – therefore forming a print queue.

You should also know the two main types of printers and the various printing elements, and be able to compare them in terms of noise, speed and quality of output, for example:

1. **Impact printers.**
   (a) *Daisy wheel* – able to produce speeds of 15–55 characters per second (cps); quality print but noisy
   (b) *Dot matrix* – prints characters as a set of fine dots within a grid of rows and columns, called a matrix – speed from 30–60 cps, very fast but quality inferior

2. **Non-impact printers.**
   (a) *Ink jet* – ink is sprayed on to the paper at 90 cps, much quieter than the others
   (b) *Laser* – using a laser beam to print the characters – very versatile, capable of printing graphics

Questions frequently come up on the aids for speeding-up paper insertion when printing out, examples of which are:

(a) **Sheet feeder or hopper** – for single sheets
(b) **Tractor feed** – for continuous stationery

2. TYPES OF SYSTEM

Although you will probably know about the word processor you are working with, you should of course be aware of the other systems available. This is not easy with technology progressing so rapidly and with so many different terms used by the manufacturers to describe their equipment.

However, you will need to be familiar with the following.

Stand-alone system

This term refers to a word processor that is dedicated only to the task of word processing. Each word processor has a

(a) Keyboard
(b) Visual display unit
(c) Processing unit
(d) Disk drive
(e) Printer

Shared resources

This is a configuration in which several word processors share a resource, for example a printer. The printer need not be in the same room.

Distributed intelligence system

This is a terminal consisting of a keyboard, VDU and processor which is connected to a large computer so that material can be used from the main

	computer. It means that one word processor can be linked via computer to another terminal miles away.
Microcomputer	This consists of a VDU, keyboard, storage capacity and a printer. It can be used for general computing activities, for example stock control, or payroll procedures and is also capable of carrying out word processing functions by inserting the appropriate program disk.
Integrated office	Rather than have individual pieces of equipment, i.e. electronic typewriters, word processor, telex machine, computers etc., it is becoming increasingly obvious that offices would operate much more efficiently if the machines could all be connected and communicate with each other. This linking together is known as Local Area Networking (LAN) and links office systems together by means of special cable.

3. FUNCTIONS AND APPLICATIONS

Word processors are capable of carrying out a wide range of functions, the number and level of difficulty being dependent on the program that has been written for the particular word processor. Nonetheless, all word processors are capable of performing what is termed basic functions.

In Table 7.2 you will find a list, on the left-hand side, of both the basic and the advanced word processing functions. Cover up the rest of the table and check that you can:

(a) describe each function, and
(b) suggest the possible application of each function

Even if your word processor does not have the capacity to carry out the more advanced functions, you must be aware of them and where possible visit organisations where you will be able to see them in action. Remember, too, that manufacturers' jargon varies, so that a function termed "stop code" on one word processor may be "tab to block" on another. Therefore take care in understanding what the *function* is capable of doing and not what a particular manufacturer calls it.

Table 7.2 Basic and advanced word processing functions

Function	Description	Application
Basic functions		
Text editing – emboldening – justifying – moving text – pagination – headers and footers	altering text which has been keyed in without having to retype	revising draft, reports, minutes
Merging	personalizing standard letters by inserting variable information automatically	circular letters used in "mail shots", routine reminders

Table 7.2 Basic and advanced word processing functions

Function	Description	Application
Updating	naming and renaming files, re-arranging the disk index	directory, inventory, catalogue
Advanced functions		
Document assembly or boilerplating	coded standard paragraphs can be recalled and printed out	legal documents, insurance policies, specifications, customer queries
Spelling check – personal dictionary	incorrectly spelled words can be located	words specific to a particular type of industry or profession, e.g. engineering, medical
Search and replace – global search and replace	a word or "string" of words can be located and replaced automatically	documents
Records processing	rearranging lists into alphabetical order, altering information	personnel, stock clients' records
Calculations	financial and statistical documents can be stored and amended, columns of figures moved around	sales records, accounts
Communicating	integrated office	transmission of data using paper

OPERATORS

Certain skills and qualities are required of word-processor operators so be prepared to comment on them. The most important ones are:

Accurate typing

The operator must not only be accurate but fast as well. Even though it is easy to correct on a word processor, time is still wasted in correcting.

English

A good command of the English language is a necessity, including good spelling, grammar and punctuation. Many word processors now have the function of a spelling check but, even so, they have their limitations and the operator still needs to be able to spell.

Proof-read	The ability to proof-read is important, as no executive wants to be handed work that has errors.
Logical mind	Word processors operate in a logical and methodical way. The operator must therefore adopt the same approach and be able to think out a problem logically.
Interest in machinery	The operator must show an interest in machinery, be enthusiastic, and keen to learn about information technology.
Flexibility	The operator must be able to adapt to new situations, to enjoy a challenge and be flexible in approaching the work.

Health and Safety at Work Act 1974

The operator and employer must be aware of the requirements of this Act and, most importantly, its implications. Questions on this part of the syllabus are very common so be prepared to:

(a) Discuss the *responsibilities* of the employer, employee and the manufacturer with regard to the health and safety in the operation of electronic equipment.
(b) Be able to point out the *hazards* which exist and the *precautions* which could be taken to prevent accidents.

EFFECTS OF INSTALLING A WORD PROCESSOR

If asked a question on this, think in terms of:

1. **Increased productivity**
   (a) text production: e.g. standard letters; insertion of variable information
   (b) amendments carried out more efficiently
   (c) boilerplating
   (d) figure work, using deci tab

2. **Personnel**
   (a) change in job content
   (b) reduction in routine

You must also bear in mind the advantages and disadvantages of installing a word-processing system into the office.

C. RECENT EXAMINATION QUESTIONS

In this section you will find questions from the three examining boards offering a theory of word-processing examination. To gain full benefit, work through each question.

MULTIPLE-CHOICE

There is only one correct answer to this type of question; sometimes an answer book may be provided for you to complete. Make sure you read the question carefully.

1

1a

"Stop Code" refers to

(a) a reminder that the equipment is about to close down
(b) a signal in the text permitting the insertion of variable material
(c) an incorrect attempt to gain access to a file
(d) a warning to indicate a fault in the equipment

(3 marks)
(RSA/WP Stage I, Jan. 1985)

1b

"Pagination" refers to

(a) joining pages together
(b) automatically numbering pages
(c) moving one page to another position
(d) automatically adjusting the page length

(3 marks)
(RSA/WP Stage I, May 1984)

1c

A function key is

(a) a pass key which is used to enter the system
(b) a key on the keyboard which types a specific character
(c) a list of options displayed on the VDU
(d) a key directing the word processor to carry out a specific instruction

(3 marks)
(RSA/WP Stage I, March 1985)

1d

How is the right-margin justification usually achieved on a word processor machine? Tick one

(a) by the insertion of incremental spaces between words
(b) by the insertion of incremental spaces between characters
(c) by the insertion of incremental spaces between words and characters

(1 mark)
(Pitman WPTP-1)

1e

What is the term used to describe the search and replace facility when it is carried out automatically throughout an entire document? Tick one

(a) glossary
(b) global
(c) dictionary

(1 mark)
(Pitman WPTP-1)

1f

After a paragraph of text has been moved on a word processor, the operator should always check that:

(a)   the paragraph does not still remain in its previous position
(b)   the correct line spacing between paragraphs has been maintained
(c)   the margins have not been reformatted

(1 mark)
(Pitman WPTP-4)

1g

Is a Communicating word processor one that can

(a)   be connected to a dictating machine?
(b)   transmit information to another machine?
(c)   provide the operator with messages?

(1 mark)
(Pitman WPTP-4)

1h

If a word processor operator were using a *Foreground* printing facility would he or she be printing

(a)   directly from the contents of the screen memory?
(b)   directly from the contents of a file on the disk?

(1 mark)
(Pitman WPTP-4)

1i

Are "running corrections" undertaken

(a)   when revising text?
(b)   when typing text?
(c)   after text has been stored on disk?

(1 mark)
(Pitman WPTP-4)

1j

"Software" is

(a)   another name for floppy disks used in a computer
(b)   the name given to the instructions that a computer follows
(c)   a term which refers to the pieces of equipment in a system
(d)   the name given to stationery used in the printer

(3 marks)
(RSA/WP Stage I, March 1985)

This type of question usually asks for a word, phrase or sentence as the answer. A guide as to how much to write is shown by the amount of marks allocated or the amount of space allowed on the paper.

Questions 2–7 are all from the PEI Word Processing Theory and Practice examination and require only a very brief explanation. You can assume that you will be awarded one mark per question.

Questions 8–17 require more detail, with the answer in the form of a description, a statement, a list of facts or a diagram.

Questions 10, 11, 12 and 13 are *compulsory* questions. Care must be taken in answering only four out of a possible six options. No extra marks are awarded for answering more than four.

2

What is the name given to the line which appears on a video screen and provides information about the operation of the system?

(Pitman WPTP-1)

3

When centring a heading over continuous text on a word processing machine, between which two points of reference will the line be carried?

(Pitman WPTP-1)

4

What do the initials "VDU" stand for?

(Pitman WPTP-4)

5

An item typed at the top of each of a series of pages of a document is known as a "header". Give an example of a header.

(Pitman WPTP-2(A))

6

What is the name given to the item, which corresponds to a header, but which is typed at the bottom of a series of pages of a document?

(Pitman WPTP-2)

7

What is the term used to describe a disk on which information may be stored on both sides?

(Pitman WPTP-4)

8

A *program* must be loaded into a word processing machine before the operator can begin work.

Define the term "program" and explain

(a)   how a program is loaded and
(b)   the effect of this action

(Pitman WPTP-1)

9

Explain briefly what is meant by *four* of the following terms:

(a) systems disk
(b) tractor feed
(c) page break
(d) shared resources
(e) stand alone
(f) buffer

(7 marks each)
(LCCI SSC/WP, June 1985)

10

(a) Describe the following, to show you understand the difference between them:
  (i) Teletex
  (ii) Teletext (16 marks)
(b) List and briefly describe the consumables necessary to keep a word processor in operation.

(8 marks)
(LCCI SSC/WP, June 1985)

11

Describe the skills and qualities required by a good word processor operator.

(LCCI Intermediate/WP, Summer 1983)

12

You work in an office with two other secretaries. A word processing machine is to be installed shortly which you will all share.

State *6* advantages and *6* disadvantages that might arise from this situation.

(Pitman WPTP-1)

13

Because of the ease with which typographical errors can be corrected on a word processing machine, there is a temptation to regard proof-reading as unnecessary. Comment on this statement and say what steps you would take to ensure that typographical errors are detected.

(Pitman WPTP-2(A))

14

Outline the health and safety factors which have to be borne in mind by both employer and operator when a word processing centre has been set up in a company.

(24 marks)
(LCCI SSC/WP, June 1985)

15

Describe how a word processor would be of particular use in a solicitor's office, mentioning the type of specialised work done and the word processing functions/facilities which would be used.

(16 marks)

Explain what is meant by a "print queue" and describe briefly how the printer would have to be prepared.

(8 marks)

(LCCI SSC/WP, June 1985)

CASE STUDY QUESTIONS

16

On a visit to see your uncle, a solicitor, you tell him about your new job as a word processor operator. You uncle tells you that his staff have recently been asking him to consider purchasing a word processor because they claim it will help in their work. Your uncle decides to "pick your brains" and asks you questions both about software and hardware.

To help your uncle understand what he would need to buy,

(a) draw a labelled diagram detailing the different pieces of equipment which would be needed to comprise a stand-alone system.

(15 marks)

(b) explain briefly the part played by each piece of equipment in producing a word processed document.

(10 marks)

(RSA Stage I WP, Nov. 1984)

17

You are one of a team of three operators using a shared-resource word processing system in the branch office of a publishing company. The Head Office is situated on a different site and has a mainframe computer with which your word processing system can communicate in order to transmit and receive documents.

The Branch Manager has asked you to explain your word processing equipment and its features to a group of visiting authors.

You show the authors a draft document (illustrated below) on which you have indicated, by a circled number, where various word processing functions could be used.

(a) List these numbers in your answer book and against each number name and briefly describe the function which could be used to carry out the author's requirements.

(30 marks)

(b) Briefly explain how the final document could be transmitted to the Head Office computer from your word processor.

(3 marks)

(RSA Stage I WP, Jan. 1985)

INSTRUCTIONS TO OPERATOR:
— — this to be printed at the top of every page

— this to be at the bottom of every page

①

In the framework of a singer's body there are various organs and
muscles which must be strengthened and used correctly. The study of
technique will ensure that these automatically respond correctly whenever
and for whatever they are required. Habits are formed through careful
repetition of the correct actions.

③ Singing requires the use of the body itself as a musical instrument,
so the would-be singer must first make the instrument before learning how
to play it.

Vocal music demands more of a singer than his natural endowments
provide, so he must seek to extend and enhance his natural vocal range
and quality.

④ Having good technique means that all basic processes - such as
breath control and correct tonal placing - have become firmly established
as habits under the control of the subconscious mind.

Young voices should be allowed to develop naturally until the
singer reaches young adulthood - ie approximately 17 years of age. Singers
over this age would commence the study of technique from the beginning of

(continued)

(5) their training.

operator — please include this on the first page

Vocal technique to be studied includes:

Breath Control
Attack and Ending of Notes
Correct Tonal Placing and Intonation
Resonance and Voice Range
Articulation
Expression and Interpretation

display as indicated (6)

(7) **Breath Control** is fundamental to good singing as it is the basis upon which tone production is built.

The voice can be classed as a wind instrument as it relies on air vibrating the larynx to produce a note, each pitch having its own vibration rate. Incorrect pressure of breath will result in pitch variation, and escaping breath not used in the production of a note will give a breathy tone which will be weak in effect/as it will not have the necessary *and the voice will not be heard beyond the immediate vicinity* (8) resonating tone.

Singers need to be able to sustain long phrases so they must learn how to control and budget the outward breath, which requires great muscular control. Muscular control is developed through the ~~extensive~~ study and *ɤ* (9) practice of breathing and breath control and until this is mastered further technical skill and interpretation will be limited.

Preliminary breath control exercises are given on the next page.

NOTE TO OPERATOR: these exercises have already been stored in a separate file — please include them at this point. (10)

(RSA Stage 1 WP, Jan 1985)

D. TUTOR'S NOTES AND ANSWERS

In this section you will find outline notes and answers to the questions presented above, with full answers to questions **14, 15, 16** and **17**.

1

1a(b);   1b(d);   1c(d);   1d(c);   1e(b);   1f(b);
1g(b);   1h(a);   1i(b);   1j(a);

2

Status line

3

Margins

4

Visual display unit

5

November 86

6

Footer

7

Double density

8

Having answered this question make sure you have defined the term "program" and then explained (a) and (b). An outline answer could look like this:

"a 'program' is a piece of software that carries the information to allow the word processor to perform its word processing functions.

(a)   loaded into a disk drive and is either automatically activated or requires a command key, e.g. 'enter', carriage return etc.
(b)   the word processor having 'read' the program is now ready to perform its word processing functions."

9

(a)   special disk which must be inserted into the system before or after switching on − carries software that makes the word processor work.
(b)   attachment to a printer that feeds continuous stationery through.
(c)   code that is inserted during pagination.
(d)   term given to a configuration in which a couple of word processors share a resource, such as a printer.
(e)   name given to a word processor that has a screen, etc. − self-contained unit, not requiring any add-ons or supports.
(f)   name given to the part of the word processor's memory that holds text.

10

(a)

Assume (i) and (ii) will each carry 8 marks

(i) TELETEX — you could mention the following:

- a British Telecom service
- part of an "electronic mail" service
- external mail, i.e. letters, orders etc. can be sent to other terminals automatically, therefore equipment can be used for other work during transmission.
- sender need not contact the recipient before the message is despatched
- quicker and cheaper than telex

(ii) Teletext

- one-way information service provided by TV companies
- examples "Ceefax" and "Oracle"
- service is free
- information provided includes news reports, food prices, weather, stock prices etc.
- text and pictures can be mixed on screen
- nothing to do with Telex or Teletex

(b)

- floppy disks: single/double sided
  single/double density
  hard disks
- daisy wheel
- printer ribbons: single-strike carbon
  multi-strike carbon or fabric
- paper: single sheets, continuous
- cleaning fluids: anti-static cleaner and lint-free cloths

11

Skills required — you could mention the following:

- accurate typing — ideally up to intermediate standard
- good command of English language
- ability to proof-read effectively

Qualities — you could mention the following:

- interest in machinery
- logical mind
- high degree of concentration
- adaptability
- capable of finding out information
- well organised

Remember the question also asks you to *describe* as well as list the skills and qualities.

12

Advantages – make sure you do not overlap advantages; here you will find a few you could have mentioned:

- standard documents can be stored on a word processor for later retrieval
- easier to edit above documents
- secretary can perform other tasks while the machine is printing
- removes need for repetitive typing
- boilerplanting, ie the movement of standard paragraphs
- sharing work load, made possible by pooled data

Disadvantages

- all three secretaries must be trained
- could lead to disagreement as to who uses the word processor
- secretaries could dislike the impersonal, isolated situation
- amending work can be repetitive
- Frequent use of VDU may be disliked by some
- 3 secretaries using some software could lead to interference with an individuals preference for formatting

13

This question is really in two parts:

(a) you should bring out the importance of proof-reading
(b) set out clearly the steps you would take when proof-reading a document – i.e. proof-reading on the screen – you could also mention the facility of spelling checks that some word processors have

14

When setting up a word processing centre, certain health and safety factors have to be borne in mind by both employer and operator, for example:

1. *Work periods.* It is important that an operator has frequent breaks while working on a VDU; this need not be an actual coffee break but a change in job.
2. *Work station.* Each work station must have an adjustable screen, keyboard and chair. Since the operators must sit in a chair for long periods, a well-designed chair is essential.
3. *Noise.* As some printers are noisy, especially where several operate in the same room, acoustic hoods should be used to reduce excessively high noise levels.
4. *Temperature of room.* A comfortable working temperature is important, and ventilation is a consideration to be borne in mind.
5. *Lighting.* Glare from windows and lights are another consideration. The use of fluorescent tubes with diffusers should be adopted. Curtains or blinds should be provided at the windows to cut out any glare.
6. *Trailing flex.* Pocket sockets must be provided in a convenient position; there must never be any trailing flex.

7. *Cleaning.* VDUs must be regularly cleaned by the operators and food and drink must not be allowed into the room.

8. *Eye tests.* Although there is no positive evidence to suggest that VDU operators can suffer permanent damage to the eyes, it is suggested that they have regular eye tests.

9. *Epilepsy – migraine.* People suffering from epilepsy or migraine may find operating a VDU aggravates the condition and are therefore discouraged not to operate one.

Notes

In answering this question take care not to repeat factors, and think in terms of mentioning at least 12 points. The question gives 24 marks so you could assume you will get 2 marks for each point mentioned.

15

Take care with this question to mention work suited to a solicotor's office and not just work in general terms. Also mention the "specialised work" *and* the word processing functions/facilities that would be used.

Specialised work	*Functions/facilities*
Legal documents	these are known as "standard" documents with variables. The secretary may receive this variable information in the name of a vendor, an amount of money, address etc. The appropriate "standard" document is retrieved and the variable information is inserted at stop codes.
Multi-page – inquest reports – need typing, amending	delete, insert, move, repaginate
Trust accounts	automatic decimal tab making up of
Boilerplating	new documents from parts of existing ones

Print queue – if a printer is shared, a print queue may be formed whereby the printer prints out the documents as they are presented to it. The operator is able to get on with other work while waiting for her document to print. Some word processors allow the queue to be jumped so that urgent work can be printed first.

16

Basic stand-alone

The part played by each piece of equipment in producing a word processing document is as follows:

1. Keyboard: document is keyed into word processor using standard Qwerty keyboard.
2. VDU: document is displayed on VDU allowing document to be viewed in large proportions.
3. CPU: allows word processor to perform its automatic functions, i.e. editing, centring.
4. Disk drive: carries program disk and working disk, therefore allowing document to be stored.
5. Printer: prints out a copy of final document.

17

(a)

Name of function	Brief description
1 header	a header is something that is printed at the top of *every* page of a document until the instruction is cancelled
2 footer	a footer is something that is printed at the bottom of *every* page of a document until the instruction is cancelled
3 text movement	the paragraph is to be moved from its original place, and repositioned elsewhere
4 delete	the paragraph has to be deleted from the text and the extra spaces will need closing up
5 paginate	part of a sentence has to be left on the 1st page so a pagination code must come after the word "training"
6 centring	six lines need to be centred over the typing line; automatic function on a word processor.
7 emboldening	a word needs to stand out in a text, therefore the emboldening code is given making sure the printer overstrikes the word, hence making it stand out
8 insertion of words	words have to be inserted − the paragraph will need reformatting after insertion
9 word deletion	a word is to be deleted; paragraph will need reformatting because of the surplus space
10 boilerplating	exercises have been stored on another file and are now needed to be transferred to this text

(b)

To transmit the final document to the Head Office computer from our word processor would require the use of a distributed intelligence system. Each word processing terminal consists of a keyboard, VDU and processor which is connected to a computer. The operator "keys in the code to contact the computer" and the document is automatically sent via a cable to the computer miles away.

As well as suggesting the above in answer to part (b) you could also have suggested LAN/WAN as a means of transmitting the final document.

There is no need to go into too much detail with part (b) as only 3 marks are awarded.

E. A STEP FURTHER

Once the theory of word processing has been established the next logical step is to sit a practical test. While the theory is testing your ability to explain a function in a written form, you now need proof of being able to carry out your knowledge in a practical manner.

During your course you will have probably got used to one particular make of machine, so you must try and see other machines in action. Remember that the theory examination is testing your knowledge of word processing *in general* and not of any one particular system.

Word processing is only the beginning of the "electronic office"; you may now want to go on to learn about information and data processing. Whatever decision you take you should feel satisfied that having completed a theory course you have covered the basics of this so-called "electronic age".

FURTHER READING

Word Processing — A Systems Approach to the Office, by McCabe and Popham. Harcourt Brace Jovanovich
Introducing the Electronic Office by S.G. Price, National Computing Centre.
Useful Magazines:
Which Word Processor, Business and Computer Publishers
Memo and Office Skills, Pitman
Business Systems and Equipment, Business Publications Limited

In addition to the above reading, manufacturers produce a lot of sales literature which provide an ideal way of learning about new technology.

Chapter 8   Word Processing – Practical

A. GETTING STARTED

A practical examination in word processing aims to test your competence in operating the equipment and producing mailable work, so a pass indicates to a prospective employer that you are capable of using a word processor but may require machine-specific training.

EXAMINATION REQUIREMENTS

All the boards which set examinations in word processing stress the importance of "hands on" experience as well as a sound knowledge of typewriting.

Minimum typewriting speed

It is important you are able to touch type and to copy type with the minimum amount of errors and at a reasonable speed. Although no examining board specifies that a particular level of typewriting examination has to be reached, they do recommend a minimum copy typing speed (see Table 7.1 for individual board's requirements).

Familiarity with typewriting theory

This is important, as display can carry a third of the marks, and proof-correction signs are used in all the practical word processing examinations. Marks can be lost for uncorrected typing errors, incorrect margin settings and line spacing, layout errors, and failure to follow the instructions given.

Techniques

There is no need to learn about the technicalities of how a word processor operates, but it is essential that you know *what* word processors are capable of doing and *how* to carry out the various functions, and that you have learnt the correct procedures for operating. Once you have mastered the controls, try to get as much practice as you can on your own. Experience in carrying out the steps involved in, for example, moving a paragraph, and (just as important) in finding out from a manual where you have gone wrong if it won't move, will build up your confidence.

213

Make sure you are fully aware of the syllabus and that you know exactly what functions you might be expected to carry out. You will find a checklist below of all the functions on which you might be questioned. Work your way through this on your own, making sure that you know:

1. the most efficient way of carrying out each function on the word processor you will be using in the examination (without having to refer to your notes); and
2. what remedial action to take in the event that you are unable to carry out the function.

FUNCTION SHEET

EXAMINATION ....

WORD PROCESSOR ....

NAME ....

Tick each box when you are sure you can perform the function.

☐ STARTING UP	☐ REFORMAT
☐ CLOSING DOWN	☐ JUSTIFY
☐ CREATING A DOCUMENT	☐ PAGINATE
☐ SETTING MARGINS	☐ INDENT
☐ CENTRING	☐ SEARCH
☐ INSERTING – Characters	☐ CHANGE PRINT WHEEL
☐ – Sentences	☐ CARE OF DISCS
☐ – Paragraph	☐ BRIGHTNESS CONTROL
☐ DELETING	☐ HOW TO PRINT
☐ MOVING BLOCKS	☐ CANCEL PRINT
☐ AUTOMATIC UNDERLINE	☐ HOW TO STORE
☐ CHANGE LINE SPACING	
☐ CHANGE PITCH	

MACHINE FAULTS

Machine faults can and do occur and, should you think your word processor has a fault, it is very important that you report it **immediately** to the invigilator. It is pointless telling the teacher at the end of the examination as nothing can be done about it after the event.

B. ESSENTIAL PRINCIPLES

All the practical examinations set the following tasks:

1. inputting
2. storing and recalling text
3. revising text
4. proof-reading
5. printing

Some examining boards ask you to create, proof-read and print a document, then to recall it, edit, proof-read and print again, therefore producing two pieces of work. The editing usually consists of five or six functions that have to be performed and marks are lost through misinterpreting them.

1. INPUTTING

This might be called keying in, creating text or creating a file. Whatever the terminology, you will be tested on your ability to type from hard copy, which may be in manuscript with printers' correction signs, or from printed matter. The layout of a document should be *exactly the same* as the one given to you. It would be wrong, for example, to centre a heading because you think it will look better when in fact you were not told to do so. The only difference will be line endings, as you may be using a different pitch than the printed matter. If the exercise you are typing is in manuscript, spend a few seconds reading through the text making sure you understand every word and get a general feel for the document. Previous practice at past papers should have taught you that you can spend a few seconds reading through the document before attempting it.

2. STORING AND RECALLING TEXT

Some word processors automatically store a document on creation but others require a command (make sure you know how to do this). Your teacher may already have stored a document on the word processor for you, in which case you will need to know how to retrieve it.

3. REVISING TEXT

The level of examination you are taking will govern the number of functions you have to perform and the difficulty of the tasks. Check the syllabus you are following to be sure you have covered the right functions. Below is a list of typical functions you might be expected to perform, although it should be treated as a guideline only.

Inserting text

This can be a character, word, sentence or paragraph in any part of the text. Question 1 (part II) below provides a good example of where you are asked to insert a new sentence, i.e. *Mr Parsons has worked for us ...* Care must be taken to leave a sufficient number of spaces after the fullstop, to begin the new sentence with an initial capital letter, and to end the sentence, again leaving sufficient spaces before the beginning of the next sentence. After insertion, the word wraparound function must be adopted, which could be known as "adjust", "line adjust", "merge" etc. The text should look as if the sentence had always been there, i.e. no extra spaces on either side.

Deleting text	Again this can be a character, word, sentence or paragraph in any part of the text, and the word wraparound function is operated. If we turn to the same example as before, i.e. question **1** (part II), it shows a sentence that has to be deleted, i.e. *If these changes are ...* Any remaining sentence must start a sufficient number of spaces after the fullstop and leave no trace that a sentence used to be there.
Centring	A line or group of lines or even the whole exercise may require centring – this only refers to horizontal centring and not vertical.
Moving text	This can be transposing characters, words, a sentence, making two paragraphs out of one, moving complete paragraphs to a different place and transposing columns.
Search	This is where a string of words or just one word may have to be searched for and altered. The search facility can be especially useful for replacing incorrectly spelled words, although many word processors now have the facility of a spelling check.
Justify	The right margin of a portion of text may need to be justified, i.e. a flush right-hand margin.
Line spacing	A portion of text may have to be in double line spacing or a different line spacing from the rest of the text.
Reformatting	After the above tasks have been performed it would be necessary for the text to be reformatted at the right margin, especially if the exercise had many deletions.

Another example of recalling and revising text is the typing in of variables. A skeleton letter is keyed into the word processor with various spaces left blank for perhaps the date, salutation, etc. You will be asked to retrieve this skeleton letter and to complete the various blank spaces with the variables you are given. This is a facility that comes under many headings: stop codes, tab to block, search key, etc. |

4. PROOF-READING

Nobody wants to be handed a document that has errors and it is your proof-reading skill that will prevent you from doing this. Proof-reading your work need only take seconds and it is something that has to be done at the end of every document. Word processing screens vary in size, shape and colour, and it is therefore very important that you have lots of practice at proof-reading on the screen. Place your finger up against the screen and move along character by character, silently saying each word as it is completed. Do not attempt to rush and skip words; it may seem as if you are taking a long time but in actual fact you will probably only be spending seconds. Practice at this will obviously make you quicker, but never allow yourself to skimp your proof-reading. Examiners' reports are always complaining that scripts were not proof-read before being handed in, and therefore silly errors were being printed – do not allow yourself to fall into this category.

As well as looking for typewriting errors, check your display — have you used the margins as instructed? — have you turned up enough to begin with? — when you inserted a new paragraph, did you leave sufficient space before and after it? — when you deleted a paragraph, did you delete the extra space that is not now required? Remember that all this can be altered by the press of a key and so there is no excuse for errors.

While proof-reading the document, check that you have carried out all the functions you were asked to. Start at the top of the exercise and go to each functions as it appears, checking that you have carried it out successfully — it can be easy to miss a small deletion or insertion. Look into the margin — are there any instructions you must obey? If the question asks you to choose a certain number of revisions, make sure you have only completed that amount — you are awarded no extra marks for carrying out more than requested.

5. PRINTING

All tasks will need printing as this is the only proof the examiner will have that you have successfully completed the functions.

By pressing a key, a word processor can be given a command to print. Usually the printer will print at high speed and produce top-quality copies. Make sure you have had ample opportunity to print your documents in your teaching periods; sometimes when a printer is shared, you may not have printed every document yourself and may therefore not really be sure about the printing commands. Take care when inserting the paper — have you allowed for turn ups on the screen or do you have to do it manually? All practical word processing examinations to date allow you to print outside the examination time. Finally, it is important you hand in the correct number of print-outs and that a line is put through any work you want to be ignored.

C. RECENT EXAMINATION QUESTIONS

This section gives a selection of past papers and exercises from each of the examining boards offering a practical word processing examination.

To gain full benefit, systematically work through each exercise regardless of the examination you will be sitting.

1, 2
These exercises are from the PEI Practical Word Processing Endorsement (PWP) paper. The examination lasts for 30 minutes and consists of two parts.
a. Part I — this can be a letter, report, memorandum, or minutes of a meeting. You are asked to key in a copy of the exercise, to proof-read and print before being handed Part II.
b. Part II — shows how to amend Part I and usually consists of performing four or five word processing functions. The exercise must be proof-read again after the revisions, and printed. Parts I and II must be handed in at the end.

To help you with this first word processing paper, each function has been labelled in the order you should attempt them. For future papers I suggest that *you* label and identify each function; it will also help ensure that you do not omit any function. In the next section you will find an answer to this paper, but do not refer to it until you have attempted the exercise first. After completing question **1**, do the same with question **2**.

Question 1   *Part 1*   Type your name in the top right hand corner as shown. Create a document on the storage medium. Proof read, correct and print out your document. Set margins of 1½″ (4 cm) and 1″ (2½ cm).

1 May 1982   PAST PAPER   *(Candidate's name)*

F J Simmons Esq
46 Paxton Close
Fox Hill
FX4 6HL

Dear Mr Simmons

ARTICLES FOR "KNITTING FOR PROFIT" MAGAZINE

Thank you very much for your letter of 25 April 1982 and for coming to see me last week. I was very impressed with the work you presented.

I have read the articles you left with me and, as agreed, have sent them out to one of our readers, Mr Gregory Parsons, for his opinion. He feels that with minor alterations your work would be suitable for publication in our magazine "Knitting For Profit". The suggestions he has made have been written on your typescript and I enclose a copy. I am, therefore, writing to you to ask for your approval of these changes. If these changes are acceptable, we can go ahead with the publication.

If you agree my proposals, we can publish your articles in a series starting in July of this year. There will be six articles in the series and each will contain approximately 2 000 words.

Turning to the illustrations, we feel, however, that we would like our own in-house illustrator to redraw your diagrams so that they will conform to the style adopted - as a matter of policy - in our magazine. As far as possible, our illustrator will retain the ideas you have used. Please be assured that this is not a reflection on any of the illustrations you submitted.

I enclose our formal contract for you to sign if you are in agreement with my proposals. As agreed last week, we will pay you an overall fee of £1 570.00 for your work.

I look forward to hearing from you in due course and receiving your signed contract, so that we may go ahead with publication.

Yours sincerely

Felicity Denton (Miss)
Magazine Editor

Enc

Part II

Recall the document you created in Part I, and make the revisions as indicated. Proof read, correct if necessary, and print out your revised document.

┌─────────────────┐
│ PAST PAPER │
└─────────────────┘

1 May 1982   *(Candidate's name)*

F J Simmons Esq
46 Paxton Close
Fox Hill
FX4 6HL

Dear Mr Simmons

ARTICLES FOR "KNITTING FOR PROFIT" MAGAZINE

Thank you very much for your letter of 25 April 1982 and for coming to see
me last week. I was very impressed with the work you presented.

I have read the articles you left with me and, as agreed, have sent them out
to one of our readers, Mr Gregory Parsons, for his opinion. He feels that
with minor alterations your work would be suitable for publication in our
magazine "Knitting For Profit". The suggestions he has made have been
written on your typescript and I enclose a copy. I am, therefore, writing
to you to ask for your approval of these changes. If these changes are
acceptable, we can go ahead with the publication.

If you agree my proposals, we can publish your articles in a series starting
in July of this year. There will be six articles in the series and each
will contain approximately 2 000 words.

Turning to the illustrations, we feel, however, that we would like our own
in-house illustrator to redraw your diagrams so that they will conform to
the style adopted - as a matter of policy - in our magazine. As far as
possible, our illustrator will retain the ideas you have used. Please be
assured that this is not a reflection on any of the illustrations you
submitted.

I enclose our formal contract for you to sign if you are in agreement with
my proposals. As agreed last week, we will pay you an overall fee of
£1 570.00 for your work.

I look forward to hearing from you in due course and receiving your signed
contract, so that we may go ahead with publication.

Yours sincerely

Felicity Denton (Miss)
Magazine Editor

Enc

(Handwritten annotations:)
- need to insert a sentence ①
- Must have a new paragraph here ②
- line ③ to be deleted
- paragraph to be moved ④
- Mr Parsons has worked for us, in this capacity, for over ten years & he is respected in the profession

219

Notes for guidance

Revisions
1. Make sure you insert the sentence in the correct place having left sufficient space after the fullstop and before beginning the next sentence. Key yrs and & in full. Reformat paragraph.
2. Remember to leave sufficient spaces before and after this new paragraph. Reformat.
3. Easy task of deleting a line – should cause no problem.
4. Paragraph to be moved above: If you agree ..., take care to leave a sufficient number of spaces before and after the paragraph.

You may prefer to reformat the exercise at the end, which is fine as long as you remember to do so.

Question 2   *Part I*
Type your name in the top right-hand corner as shown. Create a document on the storage medium, proof-read, correct and print out your document.
Set margins of 1½" (4 cm) and 1" 2½ cm).

Maxwell, Bramhall & Company Limited   *(Candidate's name)*
14 High Road
Hewington

SALE OF OFFICE EQUIPMENT

The company wish to draw the attention of their clients to a Sale of Office
Equipment which is being held at the end of next month. The Sale will begin
on Monday 26 July 1982 and will last for two weeks.

A complete catalogue of the items in the Sale will be issued nearer the date
but, we can tell you now that the following items will be available:

Desks (executive and secretarial)
Conference tables
Vertical filing cabinets (three-drawer and four-drawer)
Lateral filing cabinets
Rotary indexing systems
Typing stools
Reception desks
Reception chairs (easy chairs and stackable chairs)
Reception tables (desk-level and low level)

The items will be available for inspection by clients on the Thursday and
Friday of the week prior to the Sale, but - in fairness to all our customers
- orders cannot be taken until the Monday.

We would hasten to point out to customers that we are able to offer these
items at exceptionally attractive prices, because our buyers have been
fortunate enough to secure a special purchase. Our sale goods are in no
respect sub-standard and our usual guarantee will, of course, be given with
each item.

Orders for items will be taken on the premises by our salesmen and we expect
to be able to deliver your purchases within two weeks of placing your
order.

Delivery will, as usual, be free of charge to account customers.

Special arrangements will exist for our Mr Henfield to deal with non-sale
business.

We sincerely hope that all customers will take advantage of this opportunity
to purchase items at favourable prices and we look forward very much to
seeing you in July.

Part II

Recall the document you created in Part I, and make the revision as indicated.
Proof-read, correct if necessary, and print out your revised document.

Maxwell, Bramhall & Company Limited   *(Candidate's name)*
14 High Road
Hewington

SALE OF OFFICE EQUIPMENT

The company wish to draw the attention of their clients to a Sale of Office
Equipment which is being held at the end of next month. The Sale will begin
on Monday 26 July 1982 and will last for two weeks.

A complete catalogue of the items in the Sale will be issued nearer the date
but, we can tell you now that the following items will be available:

Desks (executive and secretarial)
Conference tables
Vertical filing cabinets (three-drawer and four-drawer)
Lateral filing cabinets
Rotary indexing systems
Typing stools
Reception desks
Reception chairs (easy chairs and stackable chairs)
Reception tables (desk-level and low level)

The items will be available for inspection by clients on the Thursday and
Friday of the week prior to the Sale, but - in fairness to all our customers
- orders cannot be taken until the Monday.

We would hasten to point out to customers that we are able to offer these
items at exceptionally attractive prices, because our buyers have been
fortunate enough to secure a special purchase. Our sale goods are in no
respect sub-standard and our usual guarantee will, of course, be given with
each item.

Orders for items will be taken on the premises by our salesmen and we expect
to be able to deliver your purchases within two weeks of placing your
order.

Delivery will, as usual, be free of charge to account customers.

Special arrangements will exist for our Mr Henfield to deal with non-sale
business.

We sincerely hope that all customers will take advantage of this opportunity
to purchase items at favourable prices and we look forward very much to
seeing you in July.

Orders for other items (not included in the Sale) may be placed in the usual way.

Question 3 is taken from the PEI Word Processing (Elementary) paper and is a complete paper. The examination itself lasts for 1 hour and consists of four tasks, two of which are presented here. Tasks 1 and 3 would normally have been keyed in and stored by your teacher prior to you sitting the examination. To gain full benefit from this examination try and get somebody else to key in these exercises, so that your job is to recall them and amend as instructed. If this is not possible, **do not cheat**; key in the exercises yourself **before** you begin the paper.

Question 3

3a

This is a copy of the text that should be keyed in by your teacher prior to you sitting the examination. Copy it *exactly* ready for you to recall.

Candidate's Name

PASSPORTS AND VISAS

For a holiday abroad you will need a valid passport, and you should check carefully that it is valid for the entire duration of your holiday and for the country you are visiting.

If you have to apply for a new or renewed passport, this should be done at least four weeks before your departure date. The Passport Office inform us that during April and August applications take longer than at other times of the year, so do think ahead.

For certain countries of the world, a visa or visitor's pass is required. Should this apply to the country which you are visiting, details will be sent to you with your final invoice.

In cases of emergency, or if you need a passport in less than four weeks, you should contact your regional passport office.

May we remind you that it is the responsibility of all passengers to ensure that they comply with the immigration requirements of countries to be visited.

(PEI WP-1 (Elementary))

3b

This is a copy of a skeleton letter referred to on page 00. As with Task 1 this must be keyed into the word processor before commencement of the examination. Copy it *exactly* – even the numbers.

Candidate's Name

Ref: GP/1017/ma

(1)

(2)

Dear (3)

We thank you for your booking form and deposit, and now enclose official confirmation and account for your holiday in (4), departing on (5).

Would you please let us have your remittance for (6) to cover the balance of your account by (7) at the latest.

Yours sincerely
for TRAVELWELL TOURS

Gillian Parsons

Enc

Notes for guidance

The numbers are so that you know where to insert the variable information, for example:
(1)   insertion of date
(2)   insertion of addressee – may need to insert more lines
(3)   insertion of salutation
(4, 5, 6, 7)   for insertion of variable information, remember to leave the correct number of spaces before and after insertion and to reformat page.

(PEI WP-1 (Elementary))

Question **4** is from the PEI Word Processing Theory and Practice paper. The practical examination lasts for 1 hour and consists of two tasks:

a.   Task A is keyed in by yourself, proof-read and printed before Task B is handed to you.

b.   Task B — shows how to amend Task A. Take extra care with this examination as the question asks you to make only *5* revisions out of a possible *9*. You will gain no extra marks for making more revisions.

When attempting this paper, label and identify **every** function and then decide on the five you will carry out.

Both tasks are handed in at the end.

Question 4 *Task A*

Type your name in the top right-hand corner as shown.
Create a document on the correct storage medium. Proof read, correct and print out your document.
Set margins of 1½″ (4 cm) and 1″ (2½ cm).

```
KLM/ty                                          (Candidate's name)
11 October 1982



Mr T Herbrand
Corporate Manager
Financial Services Ltd
Mellax Street
Highborough
HB5 8GH


Dear Mr Herbrand

LOAN AGREEMENT

Thank you for your letter of 8 October 1982 and for sending me a copy of your
report, entitled "Loan Development Plan". I found this document most interesting
and have passed a copy on to my colleague, Mr Champian, whom you met here at
our last meeting.

Here are my answers to a number of your questions:

1    Our taxation affairs have been fully settled for the previous (1981–82) tax year.

2    The following budgets for the current financial year have now been drawn up
and agreed by management:

Capital expenditure          £10 000
Maintenance and services     £7 500
Research                     £7 500
Management expenses          £4 000
Product development          £2 300

Budgets for other areas, and contingency plans have still to be finalised. When
these have been completed I will of course let you have full details.
```

3   Our Sales Director is due to retire at the end of next year - that is, 1983 and not, as mentioned in your letter, 1984.

I think there is a strong possibility that a loan agreement can be reached between our respective organisations to facilitate our new research and development projects. My fellow directors have certainly shown initial interest in your "Loan Development Plan" report and further discussion will take place on these proposals at our next

Board Meeting towards the end of this month. I am sorry that you will, therefore, be kept waiting for a reply from us on this question. A formal reply will, of course, be sent to you as soon as possible after this Board Meeting.

I shall be out of the office for most of next week, and the following week I shall be at our office in Spain. Should you have any reason to contact me this can be done through my secretary. Alternatively, Mr Champian would be able and willing to deputize for me.

Yours sincerely

Keith L Mullins
Finance Director

(PEI WPTP, 4)

Task B
Recall the document you created in Task 1. Make any *five* of the revisions as indicated. Proof read, correct if necessary, and print out your revised document

---

KLM/ty
11 October 1982

Mr T Herbrand
Corporate Manager
Financial Services Ltd
Mellax Street
Highborough
HB5 8GH

Dear Mr Herbrand   *Centre* (1)

LOAN AGREEMENT

Thank you for your letter of 8 October 1982 and for sending me a copy of your report, entitled "Loan Development Plan". I found this document most interesting and have passed a copy on to my colleague, Mr Champian, whom you met here at our last meeting.

Here are my answers to a number of your questions:

1   Our taxation affairs have been fully settled for the previous (1981–82) tax year.

2   The following budgets for the current financial year have now been drawn up and agreed by management:

(2) *Indent 1" from left-hand margin*

Capital expenditure	£10 000
Maintenance and services	£7 500
Research	£7 500
Management expenses	£4 000
Product development	£2 300

(3) *double-line spacing please*

(4)

(5)

Justify this section

Budgets for other areas, and contingency plans have still to be finalised. When these have been completed I will of course let you have full details.

3   Our Sales Director is due to retire at the end of next year – that is, 1983 and not, as mentioned in your letter, 1984.

start new page here (6)

I think there is a strong possibility that a loan agreement can be reached between our respective organisations to facilitate our new research and development projects. My fellow directors have certainly shown initial interest in your "Loan Development Plan" report, and further discussion will take place on these proposals at our next

(7) (*the report was circulated to directors as soon as it was received.*)

(continued overleaf)

227

Board Meeting towards the end of this month. ⑧ ~~I am sorry that you~~ will, therefore, ~~be kept waiting for a reply from us on this question.~~ A formal reply will, of course, be sent to you as soon as possible after this Board Meeting.

I shall be out of the office for most of next week, and the following week I shall be at our office in Spain. Should you have any reason to contact me this can be done through my secretary. Alternatively, Mr Champian would be able and willing to deputize for me.

Yours sincerely

Keith L Mullins
Finance Director

⑨ Please change "Loan Development Plan" to "Loan Agreement Proposals" throughout.

(PEI WPTP, 4)

Questions 5, 6, 7

These questions are from the RSA Stage I Word Processing paper and are exercises from past papers. The examination lasts for 1½ hours and consists of six compulsory tasks. The various tasks would normally have been keyed in by your teacher prior to you sitting the examination. The same principle is adopted as with the PEI Elementary Word Processing examination. Try and get somebody else to key in these exercises, but if this is not possible key them in yourself *before* you begin the paper.

Remember to label and identify every function before attempting the exercise.

Question 5   This is a copy of the text that should be keyed in by your teacher prior to you sitting the examination. Copy it *exactly* ready for you to recall.

```
MATERNITY LEAVE

During the three years 1981, 1982, and 1983, ten staff took
Maternity leave.  Of these, only two returned to full-time
employment, despite the fact that the majority had previously
indicated a wish to return.

We have not experienced difficulties with staff returning to full-
time employment.  Statistics follow:
```

YEAR	TOTAL	RETURNED TO WORK	LEFT	RETURNED TO WORK, THEN LEFT
1981	2	0	2	0
1982	5	1	3	1
1983	3	1	2	0

```
Breakdown:

1982      Mrs G Hayle, Reception, returned to full-time
          employment.


1982      Mrs V Nichols, Administration, returned to full-time
          employment, but then resigned.

1983      Mrs M Stanley, Advertising, returned to full-time
          employment.

It is fair comment that the number of staff returning after
Maternity leave is far lower than was anticipated when this
provision was first muted.
```

Update as indicated and issue as:

Print out one copy.

MATERNITY LEAVE   ⟶   *Centre*   *1984?, total 20?*

During the ~~three~~ *four* years 1981, 1982, ~~and~~ 1983, ~~ten~~ staff took ~~two~~ *twelve*
Maternity leave. Of these, only ~~two~~ returned to full-time *three*
employment, despite the fact that the majority had previously
indicated a wish to return.

NP

We have not experienced difficulties with staff returning to full-
time employment. [Statistics follow:

YEAR	TOTAL	RETURNED TO WORK	LEFT	RETURNED TO WORK, THEN LEFT
1981	2	0	2	0
1982	5	1	3	1
1983	3	1	2	0

delete one line

Breakdown:

1982   Mrs G Hayle, Reception, returned to full-time
         employment.

delete one line

1982   Mrs V Nichols, Administration, returned to full-time
         employment, but then resigned.

1983   Mrs M Stanley, Advertising, returned to full-time
         employment.

It is fair comment that the number of staff returning after
Maternity leave is far lower than was anticipated when this
provision was first muted.

1984   Mrs W Hamilton, Administration, returned to full-time employment to resume her previous position.

1984	*2*	*1*	*1*	*0*

(RSA/WP Stage I (Elementary), March 1985)

Question 6

Print one copy, please. Date today

MEMORANDUM
From: Director of Management Services
To: Divisional Manager, Accounts
Date:

CAPS Maternity Leave – Mrs Amanda Locksway CAPS

Further to our recent telephone conversation regarding the above, I have today written to Mrs Locksway congratulating her on the news of her pregnancy & confirming maternity leave.

In answer to your two queries:

CAPS (Maternity Rights) – a pregnant employee has four particular rights:

- certain protection against dismissal
- maternity pay
- the right to return to work
- time off for ante-natal care.

These rights are service related & strict observance of Company Procedure is required in order to obtain them.

CAPS (Protection Against Dismissal) – dismissal is unfair unless:

- the employee cannot or will not be able to do the job properly because of her pregnancy at the date of dismissal

or

- to go on employing her would violate the law.

If at any time you consider that a pregnant member of your staff is unable to do the job properly because of her pregnancy, please notify me directly when I will obtain medical opinion.

I enclose a handout – Notes for Guidance, Maternity leave – which covers procedure and dates during pregnancy when official steps must be taken. Also, a seven page Company document – Maternity Rights/Benefits, Employment Act 1980 – which sets out in 'layman's terms' the various provisions contained within the Act.

(RSA/WP Stage I (Elementary), March 1985)

231

Question 7 This is a copy of the text that should be keyed in by your teacher prior to you sitting the examination. Copy it *exactly* ready for you to recall.

```
                    NORTH-WEST COASTLINE
                    THE WIRRAL "WRECKERS"




          To understand this dedication one must first look back to the
          days when this coastline was notorious for shipwrecks.  Boats
          entering/leaving Liverpool were often caught in severe gales
          and blown on to the sea-facing coast.

          Passengers had to choose between being half-drowned on deck or
          half-suffocated below.  Life aboard was very difficult as
          there was not only the threat from the weather, but also from
          local "wreckers".

          Along the road to Poulton on the Mersey Tunnel approach road
          (formerly the Seacombe-Bidston railway) stands the Boode
          Memorial.  Margaret Boode, "the kind old lady of Leasowe
          Castle", was killed in 1926 when she was thrown from her horse
          in a carriage accident.

          Not all wrecks were due to natural elements.  Professional
          wreckers would lure unsuspecting boats onto the treacherous
          sands.

          The survivors would be mercilessly robbed and left on the
          sands, often dead or badly wounded.  In 1839 the Royal
          Commission reported:

          Margaret Boode helped the shipwrecked and turned Leasowe
          Castle into a shelter for survivors.  Seamen from all parts of
          the world came to know and respect her name.  The notorious
          "Mother Redcap" harboured the wreckers, and now the tunnels
          exist which led underground from the Black Rock to her abode,
          to St Hilary's, and Bidston Hill.

          From this position, high on the hills, the ships were sighted
          before entering the "passage", and the wreckers could then
          display the flag of the ship's line to their accomplices.  The
          wrecking procedures could then be set in motion.
```

                                             (RSA/WP Stage I (Elementary), 1985)

Recall this article stored under amend where shown, save under amend and print one copy please.

~~NORTH-WEST COASTLINE~~
THE WIRRAL "WRECKERS" → *Centre*

Leave 3 clear line spaces only

To understand this dedication one must first look back to the days when this coastline was notorious for shipwrecks. Boats entering/leaving Liverpool were often caught in severe gales and blown on to the sea-facing coast.

Passengers had to choose between being half-drowned on deck or half-suffocated below. Life aboard was very difficult as there was not only the threat from the weather, but also from local "wreckers".

more para

Along the road to Poulton on the Mersey Tunnel approach road ~~(formerly the Seacombe-Bidston railway)~~ stands the Boode Memorial. Margaret Boode, "the kind old lady of Leasowe Castle", was killed in 1926 when she was thrown from her horse in a carriage accident.

Not all wrecks were due to natural elements. Professional wreckers would lure unsuspecting boats onto the treacherous ~~sands.~~ *rocks* *erect false beacons and*

The survivors would be mercilessly robbed and left on the sands, often dead or badly wounded. In 1839 the Royal Commission reported: *Her fame as the sailor's friend spread far & wide.*

Margaret Boode helped the shipwrecked and turned Leasowe Castle into a shelter for survivors. Seamen from all parts of the world came to know and respect her name. The notorious "Mother Redcap" harboured the wreckers, and ~~and~~ the tunnels *to this day* exist which led underground from the Black Rock to her abode, to St Hilary's, and Bidston Hill.

Leave at least 6 clear line spaces

From this ~~position, high on the hills,~~ *vantage point* the ships were sighted before entering the "passage", and the wreckers could then display the flag of the ship's line to their accomplices. ~~The wrecking procedures could then be set in motion.~~

Inset this para from both margins by 1" (2.5 cms)

"On the Cheshire coast not far from Liverpool, wreckers will rob those who have escaped the perils of the sea and come safe on-shore and will mutilate dead bodies for the sake of rings and personal ornaments."

(RSA/WP Stage I (Elementary), 1985)

233

Question 8 This is a copy of the text that should be keyed in by your teacher prior to you sitting the examination. Copy it *exactly* ready for you to recall.

INSTRUCTIONS FOR COMPLETION OF SICKNESS BENEFIT CLAIM FORM

SICKNESS ABSENCE

WHAT TO DO ON RETURN TO WORK

IMPORTANT

THE PROCEDURE IS MANDATORY FOR ALL EMPLOYEES IN ACCORDANCE WITH THE SELF-CERTIFICATION SCHEME GOVERNING ABSENTEEISM.

1. If you are absent on any day through illness or accident, you must ask your SUPERVISOR for a form SELF-CERTIFICATION of SICKNESS ABSENCE as soon as you return to work.

2. In your Supervisor's presence, you must write on the form your name, the time and dates of your absence, the reason why you were not at work, and the remedial action you took.

3. Finally, you are required to sign the form as a true record of your absence. Your Supervisor will also sign as witness to completion of the form and your signature.

If, in the opinion of management, unfair advantage is taken of this scheme, we reserve the right to terminate employment.

(RSA/WP Stage I (Elementary), Nov. 1984)

INSTRUCTIONS FOR COMPLETION OF SICKNESS BENEFIT CLAIM FORM

SICKNESS ABSENCE ← Delete this heading

Leave at least 1½" (38 mms) here

Centre → WHAT TO DO ON RETURN TO WORK

move para

IMPORTANT

THE / PROCEDURE IS MANDATORY FOR ALL EMPLOYEES IN ACCORDANCE WITH THE SELF-CERTIFICATION SCHEME GOVERNING ABSENTEEISM.

ABOVE

1. If you are absent on any day through illness or accident, you must ask your SUPERVISOR for a form (SELF-CERTIFICATION of SICKNESS ABSENCE) as soon as you return to work.

2. In your Supervisor's presence, you must write on the form your name, the time and dates of your absence, the reason why you were not at work, and the remedial action you took.

began and ended

3. Finally, you are required to sign the form as a true record of your absence. Your Supervisor will also sign as witness to completion of the form and your signature.

If, in the opinion of management, unfair advantage is taken of this scheme, we reserve the right to terminate employment.

Change this para to CAPS

FAILURE TO COMPLETE OR SIGN A SELF-CERTIFICATION FORM OR SIGNING A FALSE STATEMENT COULD LEAD TO SERIOUS DISCIPLINARY ACTION.

(RSA/WP Stage I (Elementary), Nov. 1984)

D. TUTOR'S NOTES AND ANSWERS

In this section you will find full answers to the questions in the previous section. You will notice that for the first few answers each function has been labelled and identified. Go straight to answer **1**, and systematically work through the functions checking them against your copy. Do the same with all the answers.

As well as checking whether the functions are correct, look also for typing display and especially for any uncorrected typing errors. Remember, however, your line endings may be different because of the different pitch sizes.

1 May 1982

F J Simmons Esq
46 Paxton Close
Fox Hill
FX4 6HL

Dear Mr Simmons

ARTICLES FOR "KNITTING FOR PROFIT" MAGAZINE

Thank you very much for your letter of 25 April 1982 and for
coming to see me last week. I was very impressed with the
work you presented.

Sentence inserted

I have read the articles you left with me and, as agreed,
have sent them out to one of our readers, Mr Gregory Parsons,
for his opinion. ① Mr Parsons has worked for us, in this
capacity for over ten years and he is respected in the
profession. He feels that with minor alterations your work
would be suitable for publication in our magazine "Knitting
For Profit".

new paragraph ②
The suggestions he has made have been written on your
typescript and I enclose a copy. I am, therefore, writing to
you to ask for your approval of these changes. ③ *line deleted*

④ *paragraph moved*
Turning to the illustrations, we feel, however, that we would
like our own in-house illustrator to redraw your diagrams so
that they will conform to the style adopted - as a matter of
policy - in our magazine. As far as possible, our
illustrator will retain the ideas you have used. Please be
assured that this is not a reflection on any of the
illustrations you submitted.

If you agree my proposals, we can publish your articles in a
series starting in July of this year. There will be six
articles in the series and each will contain approximately
2 000 words.

I enclose our formal contract for you to sign if you are in
agreement with my proposals. As agreed last week, we will
pay you an overall fee of £1 570.00 for your work.

I look forward to hearing from you in due course and
receiving your signed contract, so that we may go ahead with
publication.

Yours sincerely

Felicity Denton (Miss)
Magazine Editor

Enc

2 Display:

Maxwell, Bramhall & Company Limited
14 High Road
Hewington

SALE OF OFFICE EQUIPMENT

The company wish to draw the attention of their clients to a
Sale of Office Equipment which is being held at the end of
next month. The sale will begin on Monday 26 July 1982 and
will last for two weeks.

A complete catalogue of the items in the Sale will be issued
nearer the date but we can tell you now that the following
items will be available.

Desks (executive and secretarial)
Typing stools
Reception desks
Reception chairs (easy chairs and stackable chairs)
Reception tables (desk-level and low level)
Conference tables
Vertical filing cabinets (three drawer and four drawer)
Lateral filing cabinets
Rotary indexing systems

The items will be available for inspection by clients on the
Thursday and Friday of the week prior to the Sale, but - in
fairness to all our customers - orders cannot be taken until
the Monday.

We would hasten to point out to customers that we are unable
to offer these items at exceptionally attractive prices,
because our buyers have been fortunate enough to secure a
special purchase. Our usual guarantee will, of course, be
given with each item. Orders for items will be taken on the
premises by our salesmen and we expect to be able to deliver
your purchases within two weeks of placing your order.

Delivery will, as usual, be free of charge to account
customers.

Order for other items (not included in the Sale) may be
placed in the usual way.

Special arrangements will exist for our Mr Henfield to deal
with non-sale business.

We sincerely hope that all customers will take advantage of
this opportunity to purchase items at favourable prices and
we look forward very much to seeing you in July.

3a Display: TASK 1

① Heading Centred

PASSPORTS AND VISAS

② word deleted (valid)

For a holiday abroad you will need a/passport, and you should
check carefully that it is valid for the entire duration of
your holiday and for the country you are visiting.

③ words deleted (or renewed)

If you have to apply for a new/passport, (or for a renewal of ✓ ④
your existing one, this should be done at least four weeks   sentence
before your departure date. The Passport Office inform us   inserted
that during April and August applications take longer than at
other times of the year, so do think ahead.

⑥ In cases of emergency, or if you need a passport in less than

paragraph
moved

four weeks, you should contact your regional Passport Office.

⑤ words deleted (of the world)

For certain countries, /a visa or visitor's pass is required.
Should this apply to the country which you are visiting,
details will be sent to you with your final invoice.

May we remind you that it is the responsibility of all
passengers to ensure that they comply with the immigration
requirements of countries to be visited.

3b Display: TASK 3

Ref: GP/1017/ma

(1) 6 March 1986

(2) Mrs L M Johnson
    49 High Cedars
    UCKFIELD
    East Sussex

(3) Dear Mrs Johnson

We thank you for your booking form and deposit, and now
enclose official confirmation and account for your holiday
in Bellagio, departing on Thursday 5 July.

④   ⑤   ⑥
Would you please let us have your remittance for £492.47 to
cover the balance of your account by 24 May at the latest.

⑦

Yours sincerely
for TRAVELWELL TOURS

Gillian Parsons

Enc

4 Display:

KLM/ty
11 October 1982

Mr T Herbrand
Corporate Manager
Financial Services Ltd
Mellax Street
Highborough
HB5 8GH

Dear Mr Herbrand   ① Centre

LOAN AGREEMENT

Thank you for your letter of 8 October 1982 and for
sending me a copy of your report, entitled "Loan
Development Plan". I found this document most interesting
and have passed a copy on to my colleague, Mr Champian,
whom you met here at our last meeting.

Here are my answers to a number of your questions;

1   Our taxation affairs have been fully settled for the
previous (1981-82) tax year.

2   The following budgets for the current financial year
have now been drawn up and agreed by management:

Indent 1"

                Capital expenditure   £10 000

②   Maintenance and services   £7 500   ③ double
                                                       line spacing
                Management expenses   £4 000

                Product development   £2 300

                Research ④ moved line   £7 500   ⑤
                                                          Justify

Budgets for other areas, and continguency plans have still
to be finalised. When these have been completed I will of
course let you have full details.

3   Our Sales Director is due to retire at the end of next
year - that is, 1983 and not, as mentioned in your letter,
1984.

I think there is a strong possibility that a loan agreement can be reached between our respective organisations
to facilitate our new research and development projects.
My fellow directors have certainly shown initial interest
in your "Loan Development Plan" report and further
discussion will take place on these proposals at our next
Board Meeting towards the end of this month. I am sorry
that you will, therefore be kept waiting for a reply from
us on this question. A formal reply will, of course, be
sent of you as soon as possible after this Board Meeting.

I shall be out of the office for most of next week, and
the following week I shall be at our office in Spain.
Should you have any reason to contact me this can be done
through my secretary. Alternatively, Mr Champian would be
able and willing to deputize for me.

Yours sincerely

Keith L Mullins
Finance Director

---

5   Display:

MATERNITY LEAVE

During the four years 1981, 1982, 1983, and 1984, a total of
twelve staff took Maternity leave. Of these, only three
returned to full-time employment, despite the fact that the
majority had previously indicated a wish to return. We have
not experienced difficulties with staff returning to
full-time employment.

Statistics follow:

YEAR	TOTAL	RETURNED TO WORK	LEFT	RETURNED TO WORK, THEN LEFT
1981	2	0	2	0
1982	5	1	3	1
1983	3	1	2	0
1984	2	1	1	0

Breakdown:

1982   Mrs G Hayle, Reception, returned to full-time
       employment.

1982   Mrs V Nichols, Administration, returned to full-time
       employment, but then resigned.

1983   Mrs M Stanley, Advertising, returned to full-time
       employment.

1984   Mrs W Hamilton, Administration, returned to full-time
       employment to resume her previous position.

It is fair comment that the number of staff returning after
Maternity leave is far lower than was anticipated when this
provision was first muted.

6 Display:

M E M O R A N D U M

From: Director of Management Services

To: Divisional Manager, Accounts

Date: 6 March 1986

MATERNITY LEAVE - MRS AMANDA LOCKSWAY

Further to our recent telephone conversation regarding the above, I have today written to Mrs Locksway congratulating her on the news of her pregnancy and confirming maternity leave.

In answer to your two queries:

MATERNITY RIGHTS - a pregnant employee has four particular rights:

- certain protection against dismissal
- maternity pay
- the right to return to work
- time off for ante-natal care.

These rights are service related and strict observance of Company Procedure is required in order to obtain them.

PROTECTION AGAINST DISMISSAL - dismissal is unfair unless:

- the employee cannot or will not be able to do the job
  properly because of her pregnancy at the date of dismissal

  or

- to go on employing her would violate the law.

If at any time you consider that a pregnant member of your staff is unable to do the job properly because of her pregnancy, please notify me directly when I will obtain medical opinion.

I enclose a handout - Notes for Guidance, Maternity Leave - which covers procedure and dates during pregnancy when official steps must be taken. Also, a seven page Company document - Maternity Rights/Benefits, Employment Act 1980 - which sets out in 'layman's terms' the various provisions contained within the Act.

Enc

Along the road to Poulton on the Mersey Tunnel approach road
stands the Boode Memorial. Margaret Boode, "the kind old
lady of Leasowe Castle", was killed in 1926 when she was
thrown from her horse in a carriage accident.

To understand this dedication one must first look back to the
days when this coastline was notorious for shipwrecks. Boats
entering/leaving Liverpool were often caught in severe gales
and blown onto the sea-facing coast.

Not all wrecks were due to natural elements. Professional
wreckers would erect false beacons and lure unsuspecting
boats onto the treacherous rocks. The survivors would be
mercilessly robbed and left on the sands, often dead or badly
wounded. In 1839 the Royal Commission reported:

> "On the Cheshire coast not far from
> Liverpool, wreckers will rob those who
> have escaped the perils of the sea and
> come safe on-shore and will mutilate dead
> bodies for the sake of rings and personal
> ornaments."

Margaret Boode helped the shipwrecked and turned Leasowe Castle
into a shelter for survivors. Her fame as the sailor's friend
spread far and wide. Seamen from all parts of the world came
to know and respect her name.

The notorious "Mother Redcap" harboured the wreckers, and to
this day the tunnels exist which lead underground from the
Black Rock to her abode, to St Hilary's and Bidston Hill.

From this vantage point the ships were sighted before entering
the "passage", and the wreckers could then display the flag of
the ship's line to their accomplices.

WHAT TO DO ON RETURN TO WORK

IMPORTANT

1. If you are absent on any day through illness or accident, you must ask your SUPERVISOR for a form (SELF CERTIFICATION of SICKNESS ABSENCE) as soon as you return to work.

2. In your Supervisor's presence, you must write on the form your name, the time and dates your absence began and ended, the reason why you were not at work, and the remedial action you took.

3. Finally, you are required to sign the form as a true record of your absence. Your Supervisor will also sign as witness to completion of the form and your signature.

THE ABOVE PROCEDURE IS MANDATORY FOR ALL EMPLOYEES IN ACCORDANCE WITH THE SELF-CERTIFICATION SCHEME GOVERNING ABSENTEEISM.

FAILURE TO COMPLETE OR SIGN A SELF-CERTIFICATION FORM OR SIGNING A FALSE STATEMENT COULD LEAD TO SERIOUS DISCIPLINARY ACTION.

IF, IN THE OPINION OF MANAGEMENT, UNFAIR ADVANTAGE IS TAKEN OF THIS SCHEME, WE RESERVE THE RIGHT TO TERMINATE EMPLOYMENT.

E. A STEP FURTHER

The more "hands on" experience you can get, the more familiar you will be with your word processor. In a classroom situation it is better to work alone rather than with a colleague as you may be carried along without realising it. Visiting exhibitions is an excellent way of familiarising yourself with the various types of word processors available. If you have an opportunity to visit offices, do so, paying special attention to the type of work that is done and the type of machine in use. No employer will expect you to know every type of word processor, but he will expect you to be able to adapt and know how to read a manual and above all to be interested. Taking an examination in word processing means that you need lots of practice at doing past papers and the majority of these should be timed and under examination conditions.

Have you ever thought about working as a word processor operator in your holidays? This need only be for one week, but the experience gained will be invaluable. Obviously the length of your course will govern whether this is possible. Secretarial agencies deal with word processor operators and would be only too pleased to give help and advice.

Have you ever thought about teaching word processing? The Joint Examining Board now offer a Teachers' Diploma in word processing and this could be a very worthwhile path to follow if you enjoy instructing. There are teaching opportunities not only in a school or college but also in companies which employ staff specifically to train their secretaries.

Whichever path you take, having completed a word processing course and taken the examination at the end, you can only go forward in learning new technology and operations.

FURTHER READING

There is a vast range of textbooks available concerning word processing and the following list is a guide to interesting reading.

Word Processing, by M. E. Bradshaw and B. M. Garstang. Edward Arnold. An elementary workbook for students
Word Processing, by M. E. Bradshaw and B. M. Garstang. Edward Arnold. An intermediate/advanced workbook for students
Word Processing in the Modern Office, by Paula B. Cecil. Benjamin/Cummings Publishing
Making the Most of Word Processing, by T. H. Chambers. Business Books

Useful magazines include:
Which Word Processor, Business and Computer Publishers.
Memo and Office Skills, Pitman.
Business Systems and Equipment, Business Publications Limited.

Index

A Step Further
  Audio-typewriting 190
  Shorthand 119
  Shorthand-typewriting 149
  Typewriting 65
  Word Processing Practical 244
  Word Processing Theory 212
Abbreviations 22, 80
Accuracy 19, 74, 83, 154
Advanced Word Processing Functions
  198
Agendas 25, 45, 61
Apostrophe 80, 154
Association of Medical Secretaries,
  Practice Administrators &
  Receptionists: 1, 2
  Certificate for Medical Secretaries 2
  Diploma for Medical Secretaries 2,
  83

Basic Word Processing Functions 197
Boilerplating 198, 210, 211
Buffer 203, 207
Business and Technician Education
  Council 1, 2, 6
  National Award 2
Business Terminology 76

Cards 23, 168, 184
Case Studies (WP) 195, 204–6
Central Processing Unit 195
Centring (WP) 211, 214, 216
Charts 24, 41, 434, 58, 60
Communication 16, 84, 198
Composition 157, 171, 186–7
Consistency 20, 155–6
Continuation Sheets 23
Correcting 20, 78, 121, 155
Creating text/file (WP) 5, 215

Data writers 66
Deleting Text 211, 214, 216
Dictation 76, 77
Disk Drive 195
Distributed Intelligence System 196
Document Assembly 198

Editing Text 197
Emboldening 197, 211
English Grammar 4, 5, 16, 32–3, 50,
  76, 80, 119
Equipment
  Audio-typewriting 151
  Typewriting 17
Essential Principles
  Audio-typewriting 153
  Shorthand 74
  Shorthand-typewriting 123
  Typewriting 18
  Word Processing Practical 215
  Word Processing Theory 195

Figures 24
Financial Statements 24, 36, 53
Footnotes 23
Forms 23
Foreign Language
  Audio-typewriting 157, 190–1
  Shorthand 1, 5, 72, 74, 81–2, 94
  Typewriting 26
French Shorthand 1, 68, 69, 72, 81, 94,
  112
Function Sheet 214
Functions and Applications (WP)
  197–8
Further Reading
  Audio-typewriting 190
  Shorthand 119
  Shorthand-typewriting 149

Typewriting 65
Word Processing Practical 211
Word Processing Theory 212

Getting Started
  Audio-typewriting 150
  Shorthand 66
  Shorthand-typewriting 121
  Typewriting 17
  Word Processing Practical 213
  Word Processing Theory 192
Gregg Shorthand 66, 119, 109–11, 137,
  139, 142, 144, 146

Hardware 195
Headers and Footers 197, 202, 207, 211
Headings 22
Health and Safety at Work Act 1974
  199
Homophones 78
Hopper Feed 196
Hyphenated words 80

Impact Printers 196
Inputting Data 215
Inserting Data 211, 214, 215
Instructions 19, 21, 22, 154, 158
Instruction Sheet (Audio-typewriting)
  154
Integrated Office 197

Journalists' Shorthand 4, 5, 70, 74, 82,
  83, 97, 115
Justifying 17, 21, 197, 216

Keyboard (WP) 195
Keying in 215

Legal
  Typewriting 25, 47, 48, 63, 64,
  Shorthand 5, 69, 74, 82–3, 99, 116,
  120
Letters 22, 31–33, 49, 50
Line Spacing 21, 216
Local Area Networking (LAN) 197
London Chamber of Commerce &
  Industry 1, 2, 6–9
  Advanced Secretarial Language
    Certificate 2, 7
  Audio-Typist Certificate 6
  Audio-Typewriting Examinations
    151
  Information Processing Group
    Certificate 6
  Private & Executive Secretary's
    Diploma 2, 7
  Private Secretary's Certificate 2, 6
  Secretarial Language Certificate 2, 7

Secretarial Language Diploma 2, 8
Secretarial Studies Certificate 2, 6
Shorthand Examinations 68, 92
Shorthand-Typist Certificate 6, 7
Typewriting Examinations 28
Word Processing Examinations 194

Margins 21
Memoranda 22, 33, 51
Medical
  Audio-typewriting 158, 187
  Shorthand 5, 70, 71, 74, 82, 83–4,
    95–6, 113–4, 120
  Shorthand-typewriting 5, 121, 123,
    124–6
Merging Text 197
Microcomputing 197
Methods of Testing 4
Minutes 25, 46, 62
Moving Text 197, 211, 214, 216
Multiple Choice Questions (WP) 194,
  199–201

Non-impact Printers 196

Objective questions 194, 202–4

Page Break 203, 207
Pagination 197, 211
Paragraphing 77, 78
Pitman Examinations Institute: 1, 2,
  8–9
  Audio-typewriting Examinations 151
  Basic Secretarial Group Certificate
    2, 8
  Higher Secretarial Group Certificate
    2, 9
  Secretarial Group Certificate 2, 8
  Shorthand Examinations 68–9,
    97–9
  Shorthand Theory Examinations 69,
    74, 86–90, 105–8
  Shorthand-typewriting Examinations
    122
  Typewriting Examinations 28
  Word Processing Examinations 193
Pitman Shorthand 66, 75
  2000 74, 88–90, 109–18, 119, 120,
    137, 139, 142, 144, 146
  New Era 74, 86, 109–18, 119, 120,
    137, 139, 142, 144, 146
  Pitmanscript 109–10, 116–8, 119
Practice 15, 17–18, 75, 150
Printers – separate, integral, remote
  195–6
Printing 217
Program 202, 207
Programmes 24, 42, 59
Proof Reading 16, 19, 80, 155, 216,

Punctuation 20, 22, 77, 78, 121, 154, 156, 157

Records Processing 198
Reforming Text 216
Recent Examinations Questions:
  Audio-typewriting 160–179
  Shorthand 85–101
  Shorthand-typewriting 74, 127–36
  Typewriting 31–48
  Word Processing Practical 217–235
  Word Processing Theory 199–206
Regional Boards 73
Revising Text 215
Royal Society of Arts 2, 3, 9–11
  Audio-typewriting Examinations 152
  Certificate for Secretarial Linguists 3, 11
  Certificate in Language for the Office 3
  Diploma for Bi-lingual Secretaries 3, 11
  Diploma for Personal Assistants 3, 11
  Diploma in Business Studies 3, 10
  Diploma in Distribution 3, 11
  Diploma in General Reception 3, 10
  Diploma in Office Studies 3, 9
  Diploma in Secretarial Studies 3, 10
  Shorthand Speed Examinations 71, 91
  Shorthand Transcription Examinations 71, 76–7, 78, 80
  Typewriting Examinations 29
  Word Processing Examinations 194

Scottish Business Education Council 2, 3, 11–14
  Audio-typewriting Examinations 153
  Certificate in Office Skills 3, 11
  Diploma for Graduate Secretaries 3, 15
  Diploma for Medical Secretaries 3, 13
  Higher National Certificate in Secretarial Studies 3, 13
  Higher National Diploma in Secretarial Studies 3, 14
  Higher National Diploma in Secretarial Studies (with languages) 3, 14
  National Certificate in Secretarial Studies 12
  National Diploma for Agricultural Secretaries 3, 13
  Secretarial Certificate 3, 12
  Shorthand Examinations 72
  Typewriting Examinations 29

Scottish Examination Board 2
  Shorthand Examinations 72–3, 93
Secretarial Skills 4
Search 198, 216
Shared Resources 196, 203, 207
Sheet Feeder 196, 203, 207
Single Subject Examinations 1, 5, 28–30, 68–73, 122–3, 151–3
Spanish Shorthand 1, 68, 82
Speed
  Audio-typewriting 155
  Typewriting 21, 27
Speedwriting 4, 5, 66
Spelling 4, 5, 16, 20, 78–9, 121, 154–5, 198
Stand Alone System 196, 210
Stenotyping 66
Storing and Recalling Text 215
Syllabus 4, 81, 125–6
Systematic Notetaking 70, 73, 74, 84
Systems Disk 203

Tab to Block 216
Tabulation 24, 37–40, 54–7
Tear-off Slip 23, 35, 52
Technique
  Audio-typewriting 150
  Typewriting 18
Teeline Education Limited 2, 66, 73, 109–12, 114, 120, 137, 139, 142, 144, 146
Teletex 203, 208
Teletext 203, 208
Tractor Feed 196, 203, 207
Transcription
  Audio-typewriting 156
  Shorthand 4, 16, 74, 78, 81, 121
  Typewritten (shorthand based) 70, 74, 84, 100–4, 117–8, 122
Trap Words 78
Tutor's Notes and Answers
  Audio-typewriting 180–190
  Shorthand 105–19
  Shorthand-typewriting 74, 127–36
  Typewriting 49–64
  Word Processing Practical 235–243
  Word Processing Theory 207–212

Updating 198

Visual Display Unit 16, 195

Welsh Joint Education Committee 2
  Shorthand Examinations 73, 82
  Typewriting Examinations
Word Processor Operators 198